The
Estate Planning
Companion

A Practical Guide To Your Estate Plan

Mark T. Coulter
Attorney at Law

Borders Personal Publishing

This publication is intended to provide information and guidance of a general nature, and is not sold with the expectation that it will be applied to any particular situation. You should consult with your own professional service provider for information applicable to your own situation and circumstances.

ISBN : 978-1-60552-063-6

All inquiries should be directed to Mark T. Coulter, Esquire, via email to MCoulter@EstatePlanningCenters.com.

For Barbie and our children,
Thanks for your patience.

TABLE OF CONTENTS

WHAT DO YOU HAVE? 45

UNDERSTANDING PROPERTY THAT IS SELF-PLANNED 55

SHOULD I GIVE SOME AWAY? 69

HOW AND WHY TO USE THIS BOOK

PURPOSE

This book is intended to help bridge the knowledge gap between your estate planning attorney and you. Frequently, estate planning clients don't truly understand the elements of a plan created for them, or why those elements were selected. Uncomfortable with their lack of understanding and perhaps worried that a long explanation means a big attorney's bill, the client may be left with a plan with which they aren't comfortable. Several disastrous results can occur from this. First, a client may blindly move forward with the plan proposed, but their lack of understanding results in the plan being thrown off balance by the changes in their life and assets down the road. Second, a client who doesn't understand the plan isn't empowered to ask the right questions to their attorney about other planning options, resulting in missed opportunities or gaps in their plan. Finally, and perhaps most dangerously, a client who is uncomfortable about their plan is far too likely to simply put the draft documents in a drawer where they feel the documents can do no harm, awaiting the fanciful day in the future when they will magically understand the documents, execute them properly, and take the necessary steps to put them to work. Or not.

The goal of this book is to provide you, as a person interested in the state of your estate plan, with a working knowledge of estate planning issues which will permit you to

1. Identify what your own planning goals and needs may be,
2. Actively participate with the attorney in selecting and designing estate plan elements which reach the desired results,
3. Feel comfortable asking questions which you won't worry are 'stupid',
4. Understand what your plan does, and why, and
5. Take the steps necessary to implement the plan created by your attorney, both now and in the future, since life moves on.

What this book is not intended to do is replace hiring an estate planning attorney. As I discuss in a later chapter, most people should not undergo estate planning on their own. While the estate planning websites which you only contact over the internet, and the book/form/kit sellers, would like you to believe that you can do it yourself, such advice is almost always simply a sales pitch, not competent counseling for your needs. As for my own interests, you've already paid for this book, and far too few of you will be my clients, so this advice is not an effort to feather my own nest. It's just the advice of an attorney who has seen things work well, and has seen things work badly.

In the following chapters, you will read about why estate planning is important for everyone, why an estate planning professional is far superior to using a generic form, taking the time to consider what you want your estate plan to do, the perils of various death-related taxes, learning about what your 'estate' really contains, ways which property is transferred outside of probate, the benefits of gifts to family and charity, how to plan in advance for estate problems encountered while you are still alive, the use of life insurance in your estate, and an examination of the ins and outs of wills, trusts, and probate. I hope you find it useful. The end result is not intended to be for you to go out and make your own estate planning documents, so you'll notice that I don't provide a bunch of fill-in-the-blank forms. Instead, the information in here is intended to help enhance your relationship with your estate planning attorney, and give you enough confidence about your understanding of your plan to be able to ask probing questions, make suggestions, and take the action necessary to implement and maintain your estate plan. The best legal documents in the world don't do any good if they sit unsigned in a drawer because a client wasn't quite sure yet what the documents really do.

PLEASE NOTE:

Speaking of advice, I'm certain that you already realize that nothing in this book should be construed to represent the advice of YOUR attorney. We don't have an attorney-client relationship merely because you happened to read this book. In fact, I don't have an attorney-client relationship with anyone unless we have signed a contract wherein you hired me to be your attorney. If you did, then you know who you are. As for this book, I have to let you know that nothing in here is legal advice for any individual case or situation, but instead it is only general in nature. Further, the law varies from state to state, and even within states, and a book of this nature can't cover all of those bases. Instead, it is a general review of the issues involved. You shouldn't rely upon the information in this book for your legal advice, but instead you should be consulting with a qualified attorney. My goal in this book is to enhance that relationship with your attorney by adding to your general fund of background knowledge, not to replace your attorney.

MOVING ON...

Congratulations on being one of the minority of people who have the foresight, drive and confidence to take control of the security and wellbeing of their family and other loved ones by planning ahead. I hope you find this assists you in your quest.

CHAPTER 1

INTRODUCTION TO ESTATE PLANNING

CONQUERING YOUR TOP REASONS NOT TO PLAN

Mention the phrase "Estate Planning" to a group of friends, and you'll see a variety of different understandings, and expressions. To some, estate planning is just having a will. To others, it's handling affairs for the children if the parents die. For some, it's college and houses and financial planning. Some may consider it their own inheritances. The fear of incompetence from Alzheimer's disease concerns others. And on and on. Truth is, they are all correct. Estate planning boils down to making decisions in advance of life's unfortunate events, and then taking the necessary steps required to implement those decisions in order to manage the important financial items in your life. Sound simple? Good.

Seriously, though, if it was easy, everyone would do it, and do it for themselves. The fact is, however, that too many people don't get around to doing estate planning. No one likes to think about their death, but like it or not, it's coming. Death, to perish, to cease to exist, to enter the great unknown, to pass to heaven or nirvana or whatever you believe. You can't shy away from the thought that it is out there someday, hopefully far away, though maybe not. Instead, confront it head on. Timeless wisdom says that the two certain things are death and taxes. We can't stop death, but we can beat the devil out of taxes with proper planning, minimize the hardship of death on surviving loved ones, and achieve a lot of other important ends too. Nevertheless, too many people don't. Perhaps a list of good reasons people claim to have for putting off their estate plan would look something like this:

"TOP 10 REASONS WHY I DON'T NEED TO DO ESTATE PLANNING YET"

1) I think the government should take as many of my dollars as they can in estate tax, and I'd hate to save most of my estate from huge taxes. I'm a patriot who thinks government is doing a great job with the money.

2) My family would just waste the money they get anyway, so I might as well spend it on unnecessary nursing home costs, estate taxes, and things like that.

3) The politicians in my state can make better decisions than me about who should get my estate, so I want to let the government decide.

4) A judge I've never met can probably pick a better person to look after my children and their affairs than I ever could.

5) It would be fun to 'watch from above' as my family members fight about who gets what, why and when.

6) I'd rather see the government get my estate through taxes than send it to a charity which might just give it away to the needy or sick or something silly like that.

7) My grieving spouse and family, after I'm gone, will be able to make decisions about all this money and property easier than they could while I'm still alive.

8) My family is better off letting a judge pick a friend of his to be the representative handling my estate, rather than me selecting someone I know and trust now.

9) I don't want to spend any money now just to save a bunch more for myself and/or my family. That sounds too much like something my parents or grandparents would do.

10) I know I'm going to be around a long time. Accidents, strokes, Alzheimer's disease and those scary things only happen to other people.

The fact that you are reading this book, or talking to a planning professional, means that you may indeed be ready to conquer your own 'Ten Reasons', and make the responsible decision to begin to plan.

A PLAN REQUIRES ACTION

The phrase "estate planning" is a bit deceptive. Okay, a lot deceptive. First, you aren't planning just your "estate", or what is left when you die. Instead, you need to consider steps you may need to take while you are alive to manage your affairs (perhaps a trust, or retitling property jointly), steps to take to protect yourself from incapacitating illness or disability (a power of attorney, health care proxy and living will), in addition to handling your "estate" at death. Second, the phrase "planning" makes it seem deceptively easy. A plan isn't enough: You have to take the necessary action. "Planning" is something you can do in your head. What you need is ACTION. You can't just decide how you want your property to be distributed at your death. Instead, you need to have a will drawn up, sign it, and let people know where it is. Get the documents executed to place property into a trust you've 'planned' for. Give a living will to your doctor in the event you develop a terminal or incurable condition and can't make known whether you want them to pull the plug. Planning without action is about as useful as buying a car but no gas. Let's discuss what kinds of Planning for Action you may need to look at.

QUESTIONS THIS BOOK CAN HELP ANSWER

Let's start with a list of the categories of things you should be considering. You may not know if you need all of this planning at your current stage in life, but at least you will have considered it.

1. Identify your estate goals.
   a. What is your estate?
   b. What is your general goal for your estate when you die?

    c. Who do you want your estate to go to?
    d. How much flexibility do you want or need?
    e. How might you minimize onerous taxes on your estate?

2. Identify what you own.
   a. What are your assets?
   b. Where are your assets?
   c. Who owns your assets, i.e. how are they titled?
   d. What property might you receive, or lose, before you die?

3. Consider what property is already part of a plan if you die, even if is an incomplete plan.
   a. What real estate will pass to others automatically?
   b. What does your life insurance contract(s) say about your benefits?
   c. How do your retirement accounts, pensions and Social Security change?
   d. Do your financial accounts include beneficiaries?
   e. What does your state do with property if you don't have it in a plan?

4. Decide if you should give some assets away now.
   a. What tax savings can you get by making gifts to family while you're alive?
   b. What risks do you incur by gifting some of your assets?
   c. Do you want to benefit any charities?
   d. Do you want to protect or control the use of assets you give?

5. Consider if you need to worry about nursing home costs.
   a. Are long term care needs anywhere on the horizon for you?
   b. Are you poor enough to get directly onto Medicaid for nursing care?
   c. Are you wealthy enough to pay for your own nursing care?

     d. How would nursing care expenses of $500,000 affect your family?

6. Execute a will.
     a. What happens if you don't have a will?
     b. Who will handle your affairs to implement the will?
     c. Who gets what, when, and how?
     d. How to minimize taxes?
     e. How do you make a will?
     f. Where will the will be kept, and who will know?
     g. What will happen if your spouse dies before, or after, you?

7. Provide for your children
     a. Will your family have quick access to money and important information if you die?
     b. Who will care for your children if both parents aren't around?
     c. How do you want any money for a minor child to be managed and controlled until they are old enough to do it themselves?

8. Decide if a trust is appropriate, before or after your death.
     a. What does a trust do?
     b. What are the pros and cons for a trust for your family?
     c. Are trusts just for the ultra-rich?
     d. What types of trusts should be considered, and why?

9. Consider how your family's affairs will be handled if you are not dead, but you can't look after them yourself
     a. What happens if you are incapacitated, either temporarily or permanently?
     b. What powers of attorney should you consider giving to someone?
     c. When should those powers of attorney take effect?
     d. Who do you want to direct decisions about your health care if you are incapacitated?

e. What medical measures should be taken if you are unconscious with a terminal disease or in a permanent coma?

10. Consider how you would like to see your family deal with the probate of your estate?
    a. How difficult would probate be for your estate?
    b. Who would handle the probate duties for your family?
    c. Do you want to spend the time and money now to reduce the expense and delay of probate later?
    d. How can you simplify the process for your family?

MOVING ON...

These questions, and others which you have in your mind already, help to form the basic outlines of a comprehensive estate plan. In the pages ahead, I hope you can find information which helps you reach towards answers.

CHAPTER 2

LIFE DOESN'T FIT IN A FORM

Why You Don't Want To Purchase Forms For Estate Planning

IF LEGAL FORM SELLERS RAN OTHER BUSINESSES

Imagine this ad for a grocery store:

> Why pay more for your food?
> Our food is less expensive than other stores
>   and
> We can send it to you right now! It's easy. Just click and off you go!!!

Sounds pretty appealing doesn't it? Would you be less interested if they said this too?

> We are not grocers, so we can't guarantee the usefulness of this food. You should ask your grocer if our food is safe and/or tasty,

and ask them any other questions you may have. You have to decide if this is food which will work for you. We have no liability to you for anything wrong with this food. If the food gets you sick, hey, we told you we aren't grocers...

Now, how would you feel if that stuff above about what they don't do for you wasn't in the ad, but was buried somewhere in small print? Would that inspire confidence? You wouldn't hire someone to advise you how to handle your family's future and life's savings with this kind of garbage, would you?

Nevertheless, I routinely get questions from people asking why they shouldn't just download a form off of the internet. Even before I give my ardent opinion about the importance of customized estate planning advice, based on your own personal situation, explained to you and implemented along side of you, I just show them the language on the sites maintained by these form-mongers. That should usually finish the discussion.

FORM SELLERS ADMIT THEY CAN'T BE RELIED UPON

Many people are aware of a site maintained, or at least advertised, by a famous criminal defense attorney who used to represent a football player who may or may not have brutally murdered his wife and another man. This nationally advertised site airs commercials which encourages you to go on the internet and download their legal forms for just about everything, including estate planning. The Big, Bold Print letters talk about how good and useful they believe their product is. WOW! Just answer a few questions, and they take care of the rest, fast and easy.

Then, buried on their site in a hyperlink, small type, down at the bottom of the page, is something you can click on called "terms and conditions". Tiniest print on the page. Click on it, and you get to see how they feel about their own service. In order to avoid a complaint that I infringed on any copyright protection they might have to their rather lengthy disclaimer, I have provided a similar, tamer version of what you would see there:

We don't check the legal sufficiency of your answers, determine if they are legally correct, or see how the law affects the answers you supply. We are not your attorney, and this isn't legal advice we are giving you. We don't guarantee that the information we give you is correct. If you need legal advice, you should hire an attorney. What we are selling to you is strictly "As Is", as far as the law will let us. We give no warranty of any kind for our products, and particularly we don't give you any warranty that they are merchantable, or fit for any particular purpose. We don't even warrant that our documents aren't infringing on someone else's rights. We can't say if the information we give you can be relied upon or will meet your expectations. Use us at your own risk. We aren't liable for any damage you suffer because you bought our products. We aren't a law firm, and again, we aren't your attorney. We don't provide legal advice. Instead, we just let you help yourself. We don't do legal services that an attorney does.

I'm not kidding. And this is from a major player in the document-mill industry. Can you imagine how confident you could feel using some generic form from a less prominent company?

ATTORNEYS HAVE CLIENTS, NOT CUSTOMERS

Now, I invite you to instead ask any attorney you might consider consulting for your estate planning if you can have a look at their standard client agreement. I would bet you my kid's college money that you aren't going to find anything even remotely close to the above kind of nonsense. Why? Because your attorney is there to provide advice and counseling in the protective envelope of the attorney-client relationship, not just trying to make a buck selling the same form to anyone willing to pay for it. It's your choice, but the smart money hires an attorney.

Even if you managed to get a competent form off of some website, then what? Who do you call with questions about how to make it work for you? Who does your family work with if you die and they need to know what to do next? In a nutshell, when life happens, who do you think is going to be there for you? Your personal attorney, or some nameless customer service salesperson located in an unknown location working for a website. Edward Topsell summed it up well in 1607; "Penny wise, and pound foolish"...

MOVING ON...

I hope that you now have some perspective to decide that your life, your family, and your estate are entitled to a plan for the future which reflects your individual and unique features. A form document which you purchase is simply never going to provide that for you. Armed with that confidence, lets now examine the beginning of the estate planning process, taking a look at what you want your plan to do for you.

CHAPTER 3

WHAT DO YOU WANT?

Identifying Your Goals For Your Affairs In This Life And Beyond...

THINKING ABOUT YOUR GOALS

You sit now at step one of the estate planning process. The blank page. Ahead of you in this book are a variety of topics about what you can do with your money, affairs and life. The possible paths you can take are many, and often more than one path will lead to the same end. Too often, people get caught up in the details right at the start, and come into a lawyer saying "I need a living trust", or "I need a will that says XYZ". If one jumps straight to making decisions about what estate planning tools to use, you may miss the forest while you are looking at the trees.

Instead, take a moment now to consider the big picture. What is it that you want to see happen with regard to your money, your family, and your property? Relevant to this chapter, let's ask the following questions.

WHO IS YOUR PLAN FOR

Who are the 'objects of my bounty'? This colloquialism is unique to English law, and refers to those people who would inherit your property if you died without a will (discussed later herein). In this discussion, though, I mean to ask you to consider who you would like to benefit from your estate when you pass on. Your spouse? Ex-spouse? Children? Brothers, sisters, parents, friends? Charities? Business partners, or life partners? Who else?

I'm going to assume that we can leave "Big Government" off of the list. If, however, your goal is to leave a bunch of money to the government, then stop reading now, and let nature take its course. Just as nature abhors a vacuum, government abhors an untaxed body of money, and will reach into yours and suck out as much as it can, if only you are kind enough to take no steps to prevent them. Then, the government will give your remaining assets to whoever it has chosen to name in statutes under your state's rules for intestacy, with no consideration of the unique aspects of your life and situation. This book, however, is written with the underlying assumption that the government does not sit in a comfy chair within the circle you would like to consider the 'objects of your bounty'. I agree. Government may still get a piece, but we will work to keep it as small as possible. Now actually take out that blank page I mentioned, and write them all down.

WHAT DO YOU WANT TO ACHIEVE

Congratulations! You are closer to finishing an estate plan than most people you'll pass on the street. You actually have a piece of paper with something on it. Now let us flesh it out a bit. What is it that you would like to do for these people? Here, the world is your oyster. The United States recognizes the "freedom of testacy", which means you can do what you want with your will. There are, quite predictably, some limitations (can't completely disinherit a current spouse, must pay your creditors before a bequest to a beneficiary of the will gets their share, taxes due must be paid, etc), however most reasonably sane goals for your estate plan can be accommodated. Truth be told, some questionably sane ones have worked as well. One man in 1910 left money to a nurse who helped remove "a pink monkey that was in my bed". A few years later, a man left is estate to whoever had the most babies in the decade after his death. (Reportedly 6 women shared the inheritance, with 6 babies each over those 10 years). One man left his estate to his wife, conditioned on her smoking five cigars a day until she died. Legendary director Bob Fosse left over 60 people money to go and "have dinner on me". A centerfold model requested to be buried in her mink bikini a few years back. Compared to these, your plan is likely rather normal, so don't be afraid to write down your thoughts.

Some examples may be useful to move you forwards here, but don't feel constrained by what is here. There should be no 'typical' or 'normal' plan for a will. The question is how do YOU want to exercise YOUR 'freedom of testacy'? Among the millions of possibilities:

> ➢ A single man, no kids, might leave half his property to his siblings, and half to charity.
> ➢ A married woman, two young kids, might leave it all to the husband, or she might leave 60 percent to the husband, and 20 percent to each of her children, but want her grandmother's pearls to go to her sister.
> ➢ An older widow or widower might want to give 65 percent to her children, and 25% sprinkled, evenly or unevenly, among her grandchildren, leaving 10 percent to give to the church she belonged to.
> ➢ A middle aged woman with a same-sex life partner who is employed, and with an adopted child, may leave 75% for the child, and 25% for the life partner.

I could do this all day long. The list of who you can give to, and how and what you want to give them, is limitless. For now, just try to think about what your general outline would be. Who gets the most, who gets less, about how much would you see them getting, and any specific items or categories of assets you would want to treat separately.

Apart from basic question of how you see your early estate plan, you should also consider what your underlying goals are. Some common examples include:

1. Minimizing probate expense
2. Eliminating estate taxes
3. Reducing family stress and confusion upon your death
4. Protecting beneficiaries from mishandling their inheritance
5. Protecting your assets from creditors
6. Relieve surviving spouse of estate management duties
7. Paying for nursing home or other long term care
8. Shielding inheritances from beneficiaries' creditors or spousal claims
9. Avoiding chaos if you are incapacitated by physical or mental disease
10. Providing for a special needs child
11. Supporting charities without impoverishing yourself
12. Transfer specific assets to specific individuals
13. Pre-planning for end-of-life decisions
14. Emergency planning due to terminal illness or incapacity
15. Maintaining funds for a comfortable retirement
16. Provide funds for education of family members
17. Plan which assets go to beneficiaries, creditors or taxes
18. Provide equitably for family members

There are no right or wrong answers here. The question is simply what are you hoping to achieve in the estate planning process? If you know that answer, then you have equipped yourself to consult with an attorney and responsibly address your needs, instead of simply buying some document which someone wants to sell you.

WHO GETS WHAT

The next issue may be to determine what you want these 'objects of your bounty' to receive. Your estate won't all be in cash, unless you've lost all faith in the financial systems of the world. (The 2008-

2009 recession is not the way things usually work). You likely may have a home, other property in your state, property in other states, stocks, bonds, antiques, jewelry, automobiles, and a world of other things you've built up in life. With the exception of those items truly of only 'sentimental' value, the rest can be sold and converted to cash for your estate, but do you really want that? Do you want to give your daughter your wedding ring, or the 'value' of your wedding ring? Does the hunting cabin go to your son, or just the value of the cabin after your executor sells it? Take the time now to think, and note on this page you've been scribbling on, what physical items you would want someone to have. These can later become either gifts from you (items given away during your life) or legacies (property given away by your will).

CONSIDER GIFTS TO FAMILY, FRIENDS, CHARITIES...

You may want to give away some of your property, whether real estate, money, personal items or otherwise, before you die. Many people like the idea of seeing others enjoy the gifts which they have made. A parent may help a child make a down payment on a home, or pay for a grandson's semester at college, or just give away Great Aunt Martha's antique dining room set (assuming, that is, that you now own Aunt Martha's dining room set. You can't give away other people's stuff!). There are tax considerations which are relevant to making gifts, but those aren't important right now. This is your list of goals; we'll figure out how to address them later.

One other area you might consider is charitable contributions. Some people make them, some don't. If you have an affiliation with a religious or philanthropic organization, they certainly welcome your support. You can give them portions of your estate before or after you pass on (gifts vs. legacies again). There are beneficial tax considerations which arise from making charitable deductions, but it is something which you should do because you want to do it. The tax considerations alone are unlikely to warrant a donation all by themselves.

BALANCING ASSET CONTROL AGAINST TAX SAVINGS

Maintaining adequate flexibility in your estate plan to address the future needs for you and your beneficiaries is an issue which will have to be addressed too. Often, there is a trade-off between saving on taxes, and maintaining control of your estate while you are alive or even later. Viewed most simply, if you could give away everything today, all at once, then you'd have no 'estate', and thus owe no estate taxes. You'd also have no control over what used to be your property and assets. At the other extreme, you can keep everything you own in your name until you die, and keep total control over it, while maximizing your estate subject to the dreaded Federal Estate Tax. In between, various options present themselves, which will be a focus of your estate plan; finding that balance between maintaining control of your assets, and maximizing the benefit to your ultimate beneficiaries.

A common planning goal is to reduce estate taxes in order to maximize the assets passed to your intended beneficiaries. Taxes on your estate can be minimize or eliminated through a variety of tools. The chart below summarizes some of these tools, but the explanation of these will have to wait until the appropriate part of this book. For now, it is simply to acquaint you with the concept.

Common Estate and Gift Tax Saving Methods			
Method	**What it is**	**Advantage Summary**	**Disadvantage Summary**
Gifts	Giving assets to someone while you are still alive.	Reduces your taxable estate, and provides present enjoyment of the gift by the recipient.	Loss of control and/or use of the asset by you, and subject to gift tax on amounts over $13,000.
Life Insurance	You pay premiums, and Insurer pays benefits to whoever you	Creates a substantial pot of money from the premiums, which is income tax free,	Confusing array of insurance types, expensive at times, and can increase the

Common Estate and Gift Tax Saving Methods			
Method	**What it is**	**Advantage Summary**	**Disadvantage Summary**
	direct when you die.	and can be made estate tax free.	federal estate tax if not handled carefully.
Credit Shelter Trusts	Putting some or all of the amount exempt from estate taxes into a trust, paying income to a spouse, with the trust balance going to someone else upon the spouse's death.	Provides substantial use of the money in the trust to the spouse, without making the money a part of spouse's estate to be taxed at their death, thereby letting two people or groups benefit without taxing the money. You may choose to decide who ultimately gets the money when your spouse passes on.	Expense and inconvenience to create and maintain the trust. Surviving spouse may not be able to use the money as they see fit, but only receive 'income' from the money. Surviving spouse may not be able to give the remaining money away in his/her own will.
Marital Exemption	Anything going to your spouse is tax exempt.	Lets the spouse take as much as your plan provides, completely free of taxes or restrictions on control.	Spouse can do whatever she desires with money (include cut off your children, give it to a new spouse, waste it away, etc.), unless you adhere to strict statutory guidelines regarding limiting spousal

Common Estate and Gift Tax Saving Methods			
Method	What it is	Advantage Summary	Disadvantage Summary
			access to marital exemption property.
Charitable Donation	Giving to an IRS approved charity.	100% deduction in estate for amount given, and 100% benefit to the charity.	Only the charity and its beneficiaries benefit. No direct pecuniary benefit to you or your survivors
Trusts	A trustee holds and manages money or property for the benefit of identified beneficiaries	Many types of trusts decrease taxes on your estate by getting the money out of your control while you are alive, and/or decrease taxes on someone else's estate later by keeping it out of their 'control', while still permitting you and them to enjoy some of the benefits/income from the money.	Many confusing types, which may be 'sold' to a confused consumer, with varying costs, effects and risks. Many don't reduce taxes at all, and some severely limit your use/control of the assets in the trust.

MOVING ON...

So, where are we now? Hopefully you have a piece of paper with the names of who you would like your property to go to, and a very rough idea of what property or what portion of your property they would receive. You have also heard some of the terms which will arise in the estate planning discussions which follow, so you won't be alarmed. Finally, you hopefully have developed a scorn for paying unnecessary estate taxes, to motivate you to march forward into the discussions ahead. If you haven't developed a sufficient distaste for taxes yet, then the chapter on Estate and Gift Taxes is right for you.

CHAPTER 4

ESTATE AND GIFT TAXES

Are They As Bad As Everyone Says?

ESTATE TAXES ARE BAD.

I'll state as an initial premise the following. "Estate Taxes are bad." You may choose to agree or disagree. Some people like paying taxes: It makes them feel patriotic or generous or whatever. While I agree that part of living in our society involves paying our fair share, I disagree with the implied conclusion that the government has done an adequate job of making sure that what we pay is truly fair. The tax code is riddled with loopholes and exceptions, exceedingly complex and incomprehensible to most, expensive to have 'translated' by experts in taxation, and poorly enforced, let alone subject to political manipulation to benefit this group over that group, and moreover constantly in a state of flux so that no one can count on what they knew last year to be true this year. And that is just off of the top of my head. It is therefore often fair game under our system to adjust your financial affairs in a manner so as to take advantage of the tax system as it exists. If, using the laws in place, your tax liability goes down, then as far as I'm concerned, you score. If you fail to use the available methods to reduce or eliminate tax liabilities, then the government scores. Just so you know, the score is kept with your money!

What is the Estate Tax? In a nutshell, the government taxes your Gross Estate, which is all the property you own or in which you hold an interest. There are certain exemptions, deductions and the like to decrease the size of your estate, planning tools to get assets out of your estate, and rules by which things you thought weren't yours anymore are still yours for the purpose of calculating this tax. Put it all together, and then cut it into two roughly equal parts: The government gets the half that's a little bit smaller, and your family, friends and other beneficiaries get the half that's a little bit bigger. That, my friend, is why "Estate Taxes Are Bad."

As an oversimplified example, let's suppose Mr. Smith has passed away in 2008. He lived in a nice house worth $1,500,000. His 401K swelled to $1,750,000, and he had separate invested savings of $750,000. His parents died 15 years ago, leaving him $500,000, which has since grown to $1,500,000 in the meantime. He has other assets (stray investments, cars, vacation condo, jewelry and whatnot), totaling $500,000. Total assets: $6,000,000. Mr. Smith did pretty well for himself.

How'd he do for the government and the beneficiaries under his Will? Here's the math, in simplified format. $6,000,000 estate, minus $2,000,000 unified credit equals $4,000,000 taxable Gross Estate at 45% = $1,800,000 in estate taxes, leaving $4,200,000 for the heirs. Ouch.

Would Mr. Smith and his family agree that Estate Taxes Are Bad? You decide.

A LITTLE HISTORY, IF YOU PLEASE

Taxes on your estate will, to be sure, be a primary part of making estate planning decisions. Estate taxes as we know them are a relatively new phenomenon. (If you hate history and background, skip the rest of this paragraph and the next, but I find it interesting!). According to the National Center for Policy Analysis, the first estate tax in the U.S. was passed in 1797 to raise money for naval rearmament after the Revolutionary War. Four years later, it was repealed. In 1862, during the Civil War, an inheritance tax was imposed, with rates from 0.75 percent up to 6.0 percent, and then this tax was again abolished in 1870 when the need for this revenue passes. From 1898 to 1902, an estate tax was imposed to help pay for the Spanish-American War, with a maximum rate of 15% on estates in excess of $1,000,000 (that would be about $25,000,000 in current dollars). Only in 1916 did the estate tax return to stay. At first, the maximum rate was 10 percent for estates over $5,000,000 (in 1916 dollars! That's about $15,000,000 today). The maximum rate increased to 25% the following year, but only on estates exceeding 10,000,000. Then entered F.D.R. and the New Deal era. President Roosevelt felt that the estate tax should be used to redistribute money from the wealthy to the less fortunate, stating "Great accumulations of wealth cannot be justified on the basis of personal and family security...In the last analysis such accumulations amount to the perpetuation of great and undesirable concentration of control in a relatively few individuals over the employment and welfare of many, many others." Restated: Take from the rich, and give to the poor. Great if you're poor, but not so much so for the rich. Fortunately for FDR, there were more poor than rich, and his plan took root.

Under FDR, the top rate for inheritance taxes went as high as 70 percent in 1935. In very recent years, the maximum tax rate has been dropping, and it is now down to 45%. In the years to come, more changes await us. Under the Economic Growth and Tax Relief Reconciliation Act of 2001, estates up $3,500,000 are essentially tax free in 2009, and the estate tax is scheduled to disappear for one year in 2010, after which in 2011 the terms of the 2001 relief disappear, and the estate exemption drops back to $1,000,000. Between now and then, Congress will have the opportunity to change the laws yet again, and likely will. If this tax was anything other than a money grab, it wouldn't have to move around like this every time the grabber-in-office changes. Right now, the estate tax only raises about $20 billion for the federal government, compared to the Federal Income Tax, which raised $2.5 trillion dollars, and payroll taxes, which raised approximately $2 trillion dollars. The income for the government from this estate tax is relatively minimal, which leads to arguments to abolish it again altogether. Currently, however, that doesn't appear likely, and thus our tax-saving efforts must continue.

CURRENT ESTATE TAX RATES

What are the tax rates currently? As of 2008, the marginal rate was 45% after a $2,000,000 exemption amount. In 2009, the exemption equivalent raises to 3,500,000 before the 45% marginal tax rate applies. In 2011, the exemption equivalent is scheduled to drop down to $1,000,000, which will ensnare far more people in an estate tax trap then we have seen in the last few years.

Can you reduce your estate taxes otherwise due, using proper planning tools? Definitely so. Will it happen without planning? Definitely no. We need to examine the estate tax a bit more closely in the following discussion, so you have a better understanding of why some of the planning tools discussed later may have a place in your estate plan.

OVERVIEW OF THE FEDERAL ESTATE TAX AND FEDERAL GIFT TAX

The Estate Tax is described by the IRS as a "tax on your right to transfer property at your death." Stated otherwise, the government is making you pay for the privilege of letting you give someone your property when you die, instead of the government seizing it. The toll for this privilege currently runs as high as 45% under the applicable tax codes. In reality, however, the Estate Tax is nothing more than an effort to take money from the modestly wealthy and up, and give it to the U.S. Treasury to do with as the government sees fit. The Estate and Gift tax frameworks are designed to assure that those who manage to amass substantial wealth don't keep it in their families for generation after generation to enjoy, but instead makes them either spend it or give a giant piece of it to the Treasury. The concept of amassing substantial wealth, however, has been watered down over the years, so that is not just the Rockefeller's and Carnegie's of the world who see their estates taxed, but also the owner of a successful small to medium sized business, professionals like doctors and lawyers who have spent a career working and saving, and many others.

The basic calculation framework for estate tax is not complex. All of the things you own or have certain ownership-type rights in are called your "gross estate". Deductions (debts, probate expenses, charitable gifts, spousal transfers and others) permitted from your gross estate leaves a balance called the taxable estate. Gifts made during your lifetime which exceeded the annual gift tax exclusion are added back to your estate, and the tax due computed based on the tax tables. This tax is then reduced by the Unified Credit, and the balance is the amount due. Tax-focused estate planning works to reduce the size of your gross estate, increase your deductions, and make the most efficient use of the Unified Credit in order to decrease your ultimate tax liability.

WHAT IS THE UNIFIED CREDIT?

The first years of the 21st century have brought some awkward language into estate planning. First, remember that a tax "deduction" will decrease the sum from which a tax is calculated, while a "credit" actually reduces the tax itself. In 1976, Congress created a Unified Credit, which provided for the tax credit for Gift Tax and Estate Tax purposes to be unified, i.e. the same. For example, in 2003, the Unified credit was $345,000, and whether you used it against Gift Tax or Estate Tax liabilities or a combination of both didn't matter much in the end. Since they shared the same tax rates, it all worked out evenly, regardless of whether asset transfers were made by lifetime gifts or testamentary disposition. This uniformity, however, was lost beginning in 2004 as the 'Unified' credit for Estate Tax purposes went up (sheltering more of your estate from taxes), while the Unified credit for Gift Tax purposes stayed frozen. The following table demonstrates the progression of the credits:

Year	Gift Tax Unified Credit	Gift Tax Applicable Exclusion Amount	Estate Tax Unified Credit	Estate Tax Applicable Exclusion Amount
2003	345,800	1,000,000	345,800	1,000,000
2004/2005	345,800	1,000,000	555,800	1,500,000
2006-2008	345,800	1,000,000	780,800	2,000,000
2009	345,800	1,000,000	1,455,800	3,500,000
2010	345,800	1,000,000	Estate tax repealed 2010 only	Estate tax repealed 2010 only
2011 - ??	345,800	1,000,000	345,800	1,000,000

The phrase "applicable exclusion amount" has been created to demonstrate how much of a gross estate can be sheltered through the Unified Credit. On the IRS Estate and Gift Tax forms, you apply the credit to the tax. Many people, however, find it more comfortable to work to understand their table situation by looking from the view of the overall estate value, such that the formal Unified Credit was calculated to correspond with desired applicable exclusion amounts which Congress was targeting. Thus, in 2009 for example, the actual credit for Gift Tax purposes is $345,800, which has the same effect as excluding, or sheltering, $1,000,000 of value from your estate.

The Economic Growth and Tax Relief Reconciliation Act of 2001, signed into law by President Bush, made substantial but temporary changes to the transfer tax system, including the un-linking of the formerly 'unified' estate and gift tax credit. The goal seems to have been to establish a trend of increased estate tax exemptions, in the hope that public support for this less onerous tax system would force Congress to extend it past 2009/2010. As you will note, in 2009, the estate tax applicable exclusion amount jumps up to $3,500,000 which can be passed by your estate to your heirs free of estate tax, and in 2010, the estate tax disappears entirely. Unfortunately, that same law, in order to get support for its passage, has a provision that it expires after 2010. If Congress does not act before the end of 2010, then the provisions of the 2001 Act will lapse, and the law will revert to a state of affairs where the credit is down to $345,800, or $1,000,000 of Applicable Exclusion Amount for both Estate Tax and Gift Tax purposes.

GIFT TAX BASICS

In order to avoid having you deplete your estate, and escape taxes, by giving away your fortune, the IRS separately imposes a Gift Tax. The goal of the Estate Tax and Gift Tax statutes together is for your substantial assets to pay the same tax, whether given away during your lifetime or after. The Gift Tax attaches to any property which you give or transfer to someone else for less than its fair market value. So if you give your $100,000 house to your child, you gave a $100,000 gift. If you sell your child the same house for $30,000, then you still have given a gift of the remaining value, or $70,000.

There are certainly some exclusions to the gift tax, or else everyone would be filing Gift Tax returns every year. The two biggest exclusions are the unlimited spousal exclusion, and the annual gift tax exclusion. Between spouses, almost no taxable events occur, either in Gift Tax or in Estate Tax. Separately, the annual exclusion for Gift Tax provides a set amount ($13,000 in 2009) which can be gifted to any individual per year. You can give up to $13,000 in value to as many people as you want, free of any gift tax. If you give more than the annual gift tax exclusion, then you will have to complete a gift tax return. In most cases, no tax will be due on amounts over the $13,000, but you will consume some of your tax credit in the process. For example, if you give a gift to your son of $113,000 in 2009, then 100,000 of that gift is subject to gift tax. Using the IRS table, the tax calculated on that will be $23,800. You don't have to pay that tax so long as you have sufficient credit left in your Unified Credit, which is then decreased by the amount of the tax calculated. Other gift tax exclusions include political contributions, charitable donations, and certain medical or educational expenses which you pay directly to the institution on behalf of someone else. The following table shows the gift tax rates for 2008:

2008 IRS Gift Tax Table			
Column A	Column B	Column C	Column D
Taxable amount over	Taxable Amount Not over	Tax on amount In column A	Rate of tax on excess Over amount in Column A
-0-	$10,000	-0-	18%
$10,000	20,000	$1,800	20%
20,000	40,000	3,800	22%
40,000	60,000	8,200	24%
60,000	80,000	13,000	26%
80,000	100,000	18,200	28%
100,000	150,000	23,800	30%
150,000	250,000	38,800	32%
250,000	500,000	70,800	34%
500,000	750,000	155,800	37%
750,000	1.000,000	248,300	39%
1,000,000	1,250,000	345,800	41%
1250,000	1,500,000	448,300	43%
1,500,000	2,000,000	555,800	45%
2,000,000	-unlimited-	780,800	45%

For any year in which gifts in excess of the annual exclusion for gift tax ($13,000 in 2009) are made, a gift tax return must be filed, and the gift tax paid or accounted for on any net taxable transfers. To determine taxable transfers, you must add together your non-charitable, non-spousal gifts for the year in excess of 13,000 per individual, applying the gift tax rate (45% in 2009), and then reducing that tax by however much credit from the Unified Credit for gift tax ($345,800) has not yet been consumed by gifts in prior years.

GENERATION SKIPPING TRANSFER TAX

For those people who expect to see their estate be subject to substantial estate taxes, one enticing work-around has been to leave some property in their will to their grandchildren, skipping over their own children, based on their own calculation that the children will just end up leaving portions of their inheritance to the grandchildren. The goal is to avoid one layer of taxation by skipping over the tax which would be paid if the money was left first to the children, and then passed through the children's estate to the grandchildren. This 'generation skipping' can be worked to some advantage, but is by no means invisible to the IRS. There is a Generation Skipping Transfer Tax imposed on such transfers, which is assessed in addition to the Estate or Gift tax otherwise applicable, and is designed to make up for the potential lost revenue from such skips. The GST is a second round of taxation, imposed at the maximum estate tax rate, on transfers to a person who is two or more generations removed from the transferor. The most common example is grandparent to grandchild.

Three essential variations of the skip are addressed under current GST law. In the first, a 'direct skip', a person transfers property, by gift or will, directly to a skip generation person, or to a trust in which a skip person has a financial interest. The second, a 'termination skip', applies when a skip generation person benefits from the termination of an interest previously given to a non-skip person (such as the Grantor's own child). Finally, a 'distribution skip' occurs when a trust distributes income or principal to a skip generation person. The GST framework essentially borrows its exclusion from the Estate Tax exclusion amount. It does not add to the amount which you can convey tax free. So if, for example, in 2009 the estate tax exclusion amount is $3,500,000, and the GST exclusion amount is $3,500,000, then a grandparent could leave up to $3,500,000 free of estate and generation skipping tax to a grandchild. Any amount in excess of that sum would be subject to a whopping tax bill, including both the estate tax rate and the GST rate. Together, these taxes would almost completely consume the gift or inheritance, so most generation skipping planning is conducted within the confines of the applicable exclusion amount.

WHY BOTHER WITH SKIPPING A GENERATION?

A GST transfer can be worked to have multiple advantages for a donor making a gift to a skip generation person, or a testator leaving property to a skip generation person. Most simply, suppose that Grandmother and Grandfather combine their Gift Tax exclusion amount ($1,000,000 each) to gift property to a trust to benefit their grandchildren after the grandchildren turn 35. $2,000,000 is now in the trust, free of gift or GST tax. During the grandchildren's early lifetime, this money then has the opportunity to grow and appreciate, creating a larger trust corpus than could have been transferred tax-free if the grandparents delayed funding the trust. At the death of the grandparents, they could then leave more money for the trust in their will, up to the amount of the then-existing applicable exclusion amount. If the grandparents both died in 2009, when the applicable exclusion amount is $3,500,000, then each of their wills could conceivably leave $2,500,000 ($3,500,000 applicable exclusion amount, minus $1,000,000 consumed by lifetime gift), or a total of $5,000,000 additional inheritance. This is added to the initial 2,000,000 which has since been growing during the grandparent's lifetime in the grandchildren's trust. As such, a sizable sum of money can be left to skip generations.

In practice, most people do not use the maximum exclusion amount to favor the grandchildren, but instead their estate only provides for consuming some of the GST exclusion, with the majority of their assets passing to their own children. Nevertheless, there are substantial non-tax benefits which can be realized with a generation skipping trust, as with many trusts, including:
1. Protection of the grandchildren from their own folly through the use of spendthrift provisions in the trust, keeping it free of the hands of their current or future creditors;
2. Trust provisions which clarify and limit the Trustee's ability to distribute trust proceeds and principal, protecting the family assets from claims by a future ex-spouse of a grandchild;

3. Incorporation of terms giving the grandchildren a 'limited power of appointment' in their will, which provides that the grandchild can leave any balance in the trust at their own death to a limited list of people which the grandparent who created the trust pre-approves, such as a requirement that the money be left to other descendants of the grandparents to assure that the family money stays in the family;

4. Insulating the trust assets against lawsuits and judgments which a grandchild might experience, such as a malpractice claim or an automobile accident caused by a grandchild; and

5. Distribution provisions calculated to temper the temptation of a trust fund, providing for modest distributions in early years when grandchildren should be making their own way in the world, but greater distributions later when they are more mature.

A generation skipping transfer can be a part of many people's estate plan, and can usually accomplish most, if not all, of a grandparent's goals within the limits of the GST exclusion.

CALCULATING THE ESTATE TAX

To oversimplify the calculation of the Estate Tax, it can be said that after the applicable exclusion amount has been consumed, the remaining taxable estate must be compared against the graduated tax rate schedule. As an example, here is the 2008 Estate Tax schedule:

2008 IRS Estate Tax Schedule			
Column A **Taxable** **amount over**	Column B Taxable amount not over	Column C Tax on amount in column A	Column D Tax on excess over amount in column A
0	$10,000	0	18
$10,000	20,000	$1,800	20
20,000	40,000	3,800	22
40,000	60.000	8,200	24
60,000	80,000	13,000	26
80,000	100,000	18,200	28
100,000	150,000	23,800	30

150,000	250,000	38,800	32
250,000	500,000	70,800	34
500,000	750,000	155,800	37
750,000	1,000,000	248,300	39
1,000,000	1,250,000	345,800	41
1,250,000	1,500,000	448,300	43
1,500,000	2,000,000	555,800	45
2,000,000	-unlimited-	780,800	45

In 2008, the applicable exclusion amount was $2,000,000. This means that up to $2,000,000 could be left by will free of Estate Taxes. Thereafter, the maximum tax rate of 45% applies to the balance of the taxable estate. Many people are confused by these graduated rates for sums less than the applicable exclusion amount, as the lower tax rates between $0 and the applicable exclusion amount for a given year don't seem relevant. It must be remembered, however, that lifetime gifts which exceed the annual exclusion amount for gift tax can consume some of the Unified Credit. In such circumstances, your estate, though under $2,000,000, might still be taxable, since your credit, and therefore your applicable exclusion amount, would be less than the maximum. In such cases, the tax rate assessed is based on the Estate Tax rate table.

A basic diagram of the Federal Estate Tax computation process would look something like this.
1. Determine the amount of the gross estate
2. Subtract specified deductions to get the adjusted gross estate
   a. Deduct Funeral and Administration expenses
   b. Deduct Debts of the Estate
   c. Deduct Tax liabilities paid by the estate
   d. Deduct state death related taxes
   e. Deduct Losses incurred by the estate
3. Subtract broad deductions to get the taxable estate
   a. Deduct property passed to surviving spouse
   b. Deduct property passed to charity
4. Add adjusted taxable gifts to get tentative tax base
   a. Add value of lifetime gifts not to spouse/charity
   b. Amount of annual gift tax exclusion reduces each gift

5. Compute tentative tax on tentative tax base from estate tax table
6. Subtract any Gift Tax previously paid from tentative tax
7. Subtract tax credits:
   a. Unified Credit
   b. Other credits if applicable
8. Federal Estate Tax is the result.

This outline intentionally oversimplifies the process, but does give a rough idea of how the Estate Tax computation is conducted. It can also provide a useful exercise for an executor who is planning the eventual distribution of the estate. By doing an early outline of these steps using what is known about the composition of the estate, the executor can get a good handle on what type of cash or liquid assets will be needed to administer the estate. The executor is going to have to be able to pay, or reimburse, for items 2a-d, and 8. In addition, cash will need to be on hand or available via liquid assets to accommodate any cash bequests made in the will. Thus, this exercise can help the executor to plan the management and distribution of assets which will be required to accommodate the cash flow needs of the estate.

DETERMINING THE GROSS ESTATE

Taking a closer look at these steps, the first critical information is to determine what the estate assets are for tax purposes. The most obvious part of this is simply the property owned at death. This includes the value of financial and investment accounts, bonds, real estate, personal possessions, and financial payments whose benefits continue or accrue at death. Such death accruals include annuities and retirement benefits payable after death, and life insurance which the decedent owned, controlled or benefited from in certain ways. In addition, some property given away during the decedent's lifetime is still considered a part of the estate, such as gifts where the decedent still kept an interest in the property, perhaps the right to use the property until they died, or get the income from it, or gifts which required the decedent to die before the gift permanently vested. Other less common items exist as well.

In addition to determining what property is in the estate, you have to know what its value is. The general rule is that the taxable estate is based upon the fair market value of the assets at the date of death of the decedent, or 6 months after the date of death. The purpose of this 6 month option is to mitigate the damage when estate asset values plummet during administration (i.e. the recession in 2008). The executor must select one method or the other to apply to all of the assets, and cannot pick and choose at which date assets are valued individually. It is fair, however, to pick the method which provides the lowest taxable estate value. For some assets, the value is easily ascertainable by reference to publicly available standards (stocks, bonds, motor vehicles). For others, you may need to hire an appraiser to reasonably ascertain the fair market value, both for the purpose of taxes and for distribution.

HOW DOES THE ESTATE VALUE JOINT TITLED PROPERTY?

When a decedent's property was jointly held with another, the presumption is that all of the joint property is included in the estate of the decedent. To the extent that other joint owners can reasonably demonstrate that they contributed to the equity or cost of the asset, then that portion of the asset value can be excluded from the estate. If the surviving owner paid 25% of the purchase price, and the decedent paid 75%, then 75% of the jointly owned asset value would be taxable for federal Estate Tax purposes, even though title automatically went to the surviving owner upon the decedent's death. The calculations become more complicated when only one of the owners used or enjoyed the property, or capital expenditures for the property were not shouldered in the same proportion as the initial purchase.

The primary exception to the rule that the value of jointly owned property is presumed to be included entirely in the taxable estate of a decedent is for property jointly owned by spouses. Married people often own their property jointly, either with rights of survivorship, or by the entireties. For such property, the modified presumption is that 50% of the value of the property is included in the decedent's estate for tax purposes. This is true regardless of whether the survivor contributed more or less than 50% of the cost of the property. The disadvantage of this rule is that upon the death of the surviving spouse, 100% of the property is taxable to their estate, such that the half of the property from the first spouse to die is seemingly taxed twice. Remember, however, that the transfer between spouses was, in fact, tax free. The only taxable transfer of the property occurs when it exits the estate of the second spouse to die. Moreover, an advantage can inure to the surviving spouse, because the taxable basis of one-half of the property is 'stepped up' to the time-of-death value when the first spouse dies, such that the surviving spouse, if they choose to sell the asset, will incur less of a capital gain.

ESTATE EXPENSES CAN REDUCE THE TAXABLE ESTATE

Once the gross estate value is determined, the executor can deduct certain specified expenses to calculate the adjusted gross estate. These are mainly funeral expenses, expenses from administration of the estate, debts and taxes owed, and certain losses an estate may incur. The funeral expenses include all the costs related to burial, site care, services and transportation. Administrative expenses include the costs incurred by the executor on behalf of the estate during probate, including professional fees, incidental costs, and the executor's compensation. The debts of the estate which it stands to reason should be deducted from the gross estate value include items like mortgage debts, credit obligations, loans, and the like. Further deduction is permitted for death related taxes imposed at the state level. These are variously titled as estate taxes, inheritance taxes or similar titles, imposed by states wherein the decedent resided and/or maintained assets. Other taxes due are likewise deductible, including pre-death income tax obligations and property taxes. Finally, a deduction against the gross estate is permitted for losses incurred by the estate in the nature of fire, water, casualty or theft losses occurring during the estate settlement, if not paid by insurance or used to reduce the value of the property involved

On a cautionary note, some of these items may be deductible on either the estate tax return or on the estate income tax return. The executor may choose on which return to include these deductions. Where the executor elects to deduct these expenses could affect the composition of final dispositions to the beneficiaries, so an executor may wish to obtain the approval of the beneficiaries in such circumstances, though such consent is not required.

DEDUCTIONS PERMITTED TO REDUCE THE ADJUSTED GROSS ESTATE

The taxable estate is then obtained by reducing the adjusted gross estate by any value embodied in a marital deduction, charitable deduction or, in some instances, a family-owned business deduction. The marital deduction is the most commonly used, and includes the value of any estate property which passes to a surviving spouse, either for their full enjoyment, or under terms of a trust which pays the income to the surviving spouse for life, and either gives the surviving spouse an unlimited power of appointment over the trust, or satisfied the requirement for a Qualified Terminable Interest in Property. The value of this deduction is essentially unlimited.

QTIP interests must give the surviving spouse at least annual income from the estate asset in question in order to qualify as property passing to a spouse under the marital deduction. The executor must make an election on the estate tax return to qualify QTIP assets, and this election cannot be revoked. For example, if Husband's will leaves assets in a trust which pays income to Wife for life, and at her death the remaining assets pass to their children, the husband's executor can make the QTIP election to deduct the value of the assets from his estate, obligating the surviving wife to include all of the assets in her estate, even though she only had access to the income. Notably, her estate can recover the tax burden of the balance passing to her children from them at her death, but most wills are drafted to reject this option in order to increase the amount passing to the children.

The family owned business deduction has been repealed for 2004 through 2010. Its future will no doubt be addressed in legislation Congress will put forth in 2009 or 2010, so the best purpose served here is just to be alert to its possible existence depending upon when you do your planning.

ADJUSTING FOR PRIOR TAXABLE GIFTS

Now that the full current taxable estate assets are accounted for, a final correction must be made to account for gifts made during the decedent's lifetime. Due to the efforts of Congress to unify the estate and gift tax schemes, taxable gifts previously made must be added to the taxable estate assets before the unified credit for estate taxes can be applied. While at first glance this may seem to negate the tax benefits of lifetime gifts and the unified gift tax credit, it must be remembered that the purpose of the unified credit system is to permit a person to transfer a certain amount of property, in life or at death, free of tax. The credits are not meant to be cumulative. By adding the taxable gifts back to the remaining estate assets, a final Unified Credit for estate tax purposes can be applied to the collected body of lifetime gifts and assets remaining at death. Under the 2001 Tax Act provisions applicable now until 2010, the Unified Credit for estate tax purposes greatly exceeds the amount of the credit permitted for lifetime gifts anyway, so it is truly not a losing proposition to have to add the gifts back to the taxable estate for this calculation. The portion of lifetime gifts which get added to the estate is only the taxable portion, i.e. not gifts to a spouse, not gifts to charity, and other gifts only to the extent they were not within the annual gift tax exclusion amount ($13,000 in 2009). This aggregate figure, the taxable estate plus the adjusted gifts, is known as the taxable base.

Calculating The Estate Tax Due

With the taxable base determined, the executor consults the IRS Estate Tax rate schedule, as demonstrated above, to determine the initial tentative tax. From this tentative tax, the executor can deduct any Gift Tax paid already. The balance of tax remaining is then subject to one final set of revisions for specified tax credits. The most important of these is the Unified Credit for estate tax purposes, which is $1,445,800 in 2009. This has the effect of sheltering $3,500,000 from estate tax liability from the taxable estate. Additional credits are available for taxes paid in foreign jurisdictions, and for certain assets inherited by the decedent upon which Estate Taxes were recently paid.

The tax due must be paid within 9 months of the date of death, though an extension can be requested for the Estate Tax return if reasonable cause exists. The tax is considered due after 9 months though, even when an extension is granted. Interest will be due on any unpaid amount, and penalty situations arise as well. You should have the advice of your attorney or accountant before blindly requesting an extension.

DOES AN ESTATE TAX RETURN EVEN NEED TO BE FILED?

Not every estate has to file an estate tax return. In fact, most do not. If the gross estate described above is less than the applicable exclusion (3,500,000 in 2009) minus adjusted taxable gifts, then a return is not ordinarily required. A quick and easy method for approximating estate tax liability for planning purposes is simply to estimate the taxable estate, reduce it by the size of the applicable exclusion amount, and multiply the balance by the maximum marginal estate tax rate. This gives a workable number to get your arms around the size of your estate tax issues, if any.

WHAT HAPPENS TO ESTATE TAXES IN 2010, 2011, AND AFTER?

Under the terms of the 2001 Tax Act, the Estate tax is repealed in 2010. In addition, the 'step up basis' which property gains through inheritance, whereby the taxable 'cost' of property increases to its fair market value at the time of the inheritance, effectively reducing capital gains taxes on later sales, is eliminated, and the system reverts to a 'pass through' basis, where the inheritor/beneficiary takes the property along with the basis of the decedent. An executor may be able to elect to increase the basis of specified property, with a limit of $1,300,000 (in addition to a $3,000,000 step up permitted for a surviving spouse). The Generation Skipping Tax is also repealed for

2010 only. The gift tax on cumulative gifts over $500,000 is subject to a maximum tax rate of 35%.

In 2011, the 2001 Tax Act disappears, along with its decreased tax rates, generous credit and exemption amounts, and the 2010 elimination of estate tax altogether. If Congress doesn't act to pass a new law, or repeal the 'sunset' provisions of the 2001 Tax Act which call for it to expire after 2010, then estate taxation principles will be governed by pre-2001 law. In a nutshell, a $1,000,000 estate tax and gift tax unified applicable exclusion amount, and the former tax rates with a maximum level of 55% will apply. In addition, a 5% surtax on very large estates (over 10,000,000 dollars) will be reinstated in 2011 under current law. The tax rates on amounts over the applicable exemption for 2011 look like this currently:

2011 Estate Tax Rates			
Taxable estate Low range	**Taxable estate Top range**	**Tax on Low Range**	**Plus marginal tax Within range**
$1,000,000	$1,250,000	$0	41% over 1,000,000
1,250,000	1,500,000	102,500	43% over 1,250,000
1,500,000	2,000,000	210,000	45% over 1,500,000
2,000,000	2,500,000	445,000	49% over 2,000,000
2,500,000	3,000,000	680,000	53% over 2,500,000
3,000,000	unlimited	945,000	55% over 3,000,000
10,000,000	17,184,500	5% surtax added	Large estate Surtax

Hopefully, Congress will act in the meantime to avert the reversion to pre-2001 law. I don't think anyone can accurately gauge what Congress will do, but my belief is that with an Obama presidency, the prospect of wealthy citizens avoiding estate tax by having the audacity to die in 2010 during the repeal of the estate tax will be enough incentive for them to push reform through Congress before that can happen. At the very least, I expect Congress will extend 2009 law into 2010 to avoid the total repeal, and buy time to work out a comprehensive solution. The estate tax is not a giant revenue producer for the government, and I'm guessing that an applicable exclusion amount around $3,500,000 will be put in permanently, with some type of inflationary indexing to keep it current with the economy. Still, that is just a guess.

MOVING ON...

Before you can get a clear picture of your estate tax issues, you need to know the size of your estate. I say we move on with the planning, and start getting down to brass tacks. The next chapter will let you look at what you own, and how you own it, so that you can understand how your estate looks right now.

CHAPTER 5

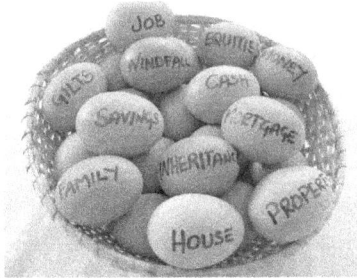

WHAT DO YOU HAVE?

Taking Inventory Of The Assets In Your Personal Estate

DISCOVERING WHAT YOU HAVE

Now you are an investigative reporter, assigned to do an article about what assets you have, and what your estate looks like today. Journalists are all told to ask the 5 W's: Who, What, Where, When, Why, and How? (Somehow calling it the '5 W's and an H' wasn't as catchy, I suppose, but that was the list we were given.) We need to uncover those answers for your estate in order to properly plan for it. For this assignment, we'll ask:

1. What do you own?
2. Who owns each item?
3. Where is it?
4. When did you get it?
5. How much did you get it for?

Each of these questions is important to your planning.

- What are all of the things which you own? A home? Retirement account? Joint savings account? 1965 Corvette Stingray convertible? You need a list of you assets in order to decide what to do with them, and also to guide any executor which may later need to account for each of your assets by filing an inventory.

- We need to know who owns each item. Some things are owned just by you. Some may be held jointly with a spouse, sibling, and business partner or otherwise.

- Where is it? Property held in the state in which you reside may be handled differently than property out of state, or out of the country. Further, someday an executor is going to have to find all your stuff, accounts, policies, etc. A list will help.

- When did you get it, and how much did you pay? While the current tax code doesn't concern itself with how much profit or capital gain you made on an item (everything is taxed at current value, and your heir inherit property with a 'step up' basis in value to the fair market value used for estate tax calculation), the current tax code is scheduled to undergo enormous change in 2010, at which time your 'basis', or cost and expenses, in an asset may become critical to the tax calculation.

If you're reading closely, you've noticed that I didn't spend time on the 'why' question. For the purpose of estate planning, why you have certain assets isn't particularly important to us. It may, however, be important to you, or those to whom your property passes. Maybe it is a good idea to explain to your son, to whom you intend to pass some Berkshire Hathaway stock, that you consider Warren Buffet a guru. If you purchased index funds because you believe that low-cost index funds offer the best odds at decent returns over time, and then explain this wisdom to the recipient. Frequently, those who receive your assets are at a bit of a loss regarding what to do with them, because they lack the background about why you acquired them in the first place. Armed with your knowledge about what the assets represent, they may then make a more informed decision about what they want to do with them; about how the assets fit into their own planning outline. Thus, you may want to add the "Why" question to your list.

As a final planning step, you should include an estimate of the current fair market value of each of your assets. When estate planning is undertaken, the size of your gross estate for tax purposes is based on the fair market value of the property included, so it will be important to know approximately how valuable each of your assets is. You don't need to be precise on these values, and instead a rough estimate will suffice for these purposes.

Now let's take a closer look at each of these other items.

WHAT DO YOU OWN? COMPILING YOUR ASSET INVENTORY

If your estate planning is to be effective, you need a comprehensive list of what it is that you own. Armed with this information, then intelligent decisions can be made about the numerous planning decisions, including legacy gifts of specific items of property, lifetime gifts, trusts, estate taxation minimization plans, etc. This list can also be crucial to any executor or trustee ultimately required to take action with respect to the property. Armed with a good listing, it is relatively easy and inexpensive to effect the transfers of title, prepare tax returns, locate information, and take the many other steps such representatives are required to take on your behalf. Absent such an inventory, however, your executor or trustee may have to spend many fruitless and/or expensive hours attempting to review your records, account statements, files, and other places to attempt to create the comprehensive list required. Make their life, and your family's, far easier by just preparing a list ahead of time. This may be one of the most useful steps you can take, and yet one which is far too often overlooked.

The list doesn't need to be anything fancy. Just write it down. Over half the battle is just committing the time and attention to make a list. Examples of things to include would be:

➤ Real estate
➤ Bank accounts
➤ Investment accounts
➤ Retirement accounts
➤ Bonds
➤ Annuities
➤ Valuable collections or heirlooms
➤ Life Insurance policies
➤ Loans you have made to others
➤ Vehicles
➤ Business Investments
➤ Safety deposit box contents
➤ Significant jewelry
➤ Guns
➤ Boats and other recreational vehicles
➤ Other items of value

One sub-part of listing what you do own is to acknowledge what you don't 'own', or don't own outright. Do you have a mortgage? Is there still a loan (and lien) on your car? Are there unpaid tax debts you know of which could impair title to your property? Is there a lawsuit against you pending? These types of liabilities are relevant to the property you own, and should be a part of the same list, along with enough indentifying information for someone to get to the information they might need if you are unavailable. I'll show you a valuable form at the end of this discussion.

A final category of assets you might consider to 'own' for estate planning purposes may be described as expectancies. An expectancy is property which you don't have now, but you expect to in the future. Some common examples include inheritances, trust fund distributions, social security survivor benefits, or any other property.

WHO OWNS YOUR PROPERTY? DETERMINING ASSET TITLE

The owners of any piece of property, and the relation between them and their property, are reflected in what is called the 'title' to the property. You might own a piece of property yourself, jointly with someone else, in the role of a trustee for someone else, or in other manners. Depending on how you own a piece of property, some or all of it may be a part of your estate which needs to be addressed. Some common examples of ownership, or title, include:

Sole Owner. If your checking account is just "Bill Smith" in the title, then you are the sole owner. You own it all, and no one else gets it unless they get it from you.

Tenant in Common (TIC). If you and someone else own property together, and each of you consider yourself to own a part of it, then you are thinking of being a Tenant in Common. Each of you owns an equal, or perhaps unequal, share of the property, and can dispose of that share without consent of the others. An example would be a vacation condo purchased by several friends. They each own a share of the condo, and can sell it or give it away as they see fit.

Joint Tenant (JT). If you and someone else own property together, and don't want either to be able to dispose of it without the others consent, then you are thinking of being Joint Tenants. This is also described as Joint Tenants With Rights of Survivorship (JTWROS). By mentioning the WROS language, the title recognizes that if any of the owners/joint tenants should die, the property automatically belongs to the remaining joint tenants. No will or trust is required to pass on joint tenancy property to the remaining tenants, and usually no will or contract can give away your share.

Comparing JTWROS and TIC: People often are cloudy on the distinction between these two similar concepts. If you imagine a cake on a plate, ownership by TIC involves each owner holding title to a piece of the cake. JTWROS is more akin to each owner holding title to the entire cake. While everyone is alive, they share the whole cake. When one dies, the others already had title to the entire cake, so they simply still own it. Nevertheless, a person holding title as a joint tenant can often turn title into a TIC ownership (so as to permit them to dispose of their share somehow) by either filing a court action, or sometimes merely by taking steps inconsistent with JT ownership (such as by putting a mortgage on the property which isn't signed by all of the owners).

Tenants by the Entirety (TBE): Married people in over half of the states receive special protections as to their joint tenancies, typically referred to as Tenancy by the Entirety. Your house deed may say "Mr. and Mrs. X, as Tenants by the Entirety". Even if it doesn't, these states usually recognize this form of ownership automatically for any property acquired jointly during the marriage. The difference is that property owned as joint tenants by the entirety receives great protection against attack on the title, in order to protect a weaker spouse from a predatory one. Thus, a husband cannot unilaterally mortgage the house if it is held as TBE, nor will his doing so sever the TBE. Moreover, most creditors can't attack a TBE account seeking payment for the debt of only one spouse. So if a wife racks up gambling debts in Vegas, a casino can't force the husband to make payment from any joint tenant by the entirety assets, but instead the collection is limited to assets she may hold as a sole owner, or perhaps a TIC or JT with someone else. This is one reason why a bank will require both spouses to sign any mortgage papers relating to jointly held property.

This ownership information will all become relevant later during the estate plan. By way of example, all of the TBE property must go to the spouse, even if a will tries to state otherwise. Instead it transfers automatically via its title. The same with JTWROS, as it goes to its remaining joint tenant(s). TIC property will need to be disposed in some fashion. Moreover, there are separate considerations which enter into how these are taxed for federal purposes.

A summary of the estate taxation would be:
  ➢ **Sole Owner**: Value of the property, minus the mortgage to be paid by the executor, is part of your estate.
  ➢ **Joint Tenant (non-spouse)**: It is presumed that the first JT to die owned the entire property, so the government can get its tax

money all from the first owner. The burden is on the estate and remaining owners to demonstrate that the deceased only owned a 'part' of the property relative to the financial contributions of the other owners, and thus only a part of the property should be included in the estate. Interestingly and unfortunately, if they do not do this, then when the next joint owner dies, the government will again tax the entire value of the property as it passes through the second estate. It's good to be the government.

> **Tenants by the Entirety:** The government assumes that the spouses each owned 1/2 the value of TBE property, and thus half the value of the property is included in the estate.

Without attempting to confuse the matter further, a later issue to be addressed concerns how the property is to be treated for estate, or capital gain, purposes by the inheriting spouse. Absent estate issues, if you buy a house for $100,000 and sell it for $400,000, you've made a $300,000 capital gain, with income taxes calculable thereon. If, however, one spouse dies when the house is worth $350,000, then the surviving spouse has a portion of her 'basis', or tax cost, in the home, increased, or "stepped up". In this example, when the first spouse dies, 175,000 of value in the home is in his estate and goes to the surviving spouse. Her taxable basis in the house is 'stepped up' to 175,000 for the half she received at his death, and remains at 50,000 for the other half (1/2 of the 100,000 initial basis), such that if she sells the home for 400,000, her basis now is 225,000, reducing her capital gain to 175,000. Other income tax deductions can apply here, but the purpose of the exercise is just to demonstrate the 'step up' in the tax basis of the property.

WHERE IS WHAT YOU OWN LOCATED?

Many a widowed spouse, grieving child, or even their attorney has been reduced to tears by the effort which may be required simply to locate bank accounts, bonds, investment accounts and other assets when the person who handled the financial affairs is no longer available. In many couples, one person does most of the banking and/or investing, and the other may be innocently ignorant about the details of these financial affairs. Most fundamentally, those who survive you might not even be fully aware of all of the places where your financial transactions are conducted. It is not uncommon today to have different institutions for checking, savings, lines of credit, taxable investment accounts, retirement accounts, insurance, annuities, etc. What a nice planning gift it is for the responsible person to prepare a simple list saying where these are located. Moreover, for estate planning purposes, the location of items may be relevant. If property is located outside the state where you reside, then different steps may be required to properly consider the trust or estate administration of the property. If property or documents are in your safety deposit box, then it may not be accessible if you are incapacitated or deceased. If it is held at an internet-based financial institution, then no-one may even know it exists. Put them on the list, and all is made easier, as shown below.

WHEN DID YOU ACQUIRE THE PROPERTY AND HOW? ASSESSING BASIS

Under the current tax law, your taxable 'basis' in property isn't particularly important in planning inheritances, since the property all 'steps up' in value to the value at the time of your estate, such that no capital gains are per-se due. Instead of the government taxing the unrealized capital gains which you may have built during your lifetime (i.e. the paper gains from increased value of property during your ownership which you didn't sell before dying), the tax instead comes through the Estate Tax described further on herein. Your heirs inherit your property with a new 'stepped up' basis, valued around the time of your passing, so that the 'basis' you had in the property becomes irrelevant for that purpose.

It may become very important, however, as the nature of the tax law from 2010 onwards is very unclear right now, and post-2010 tax law could start to tax the 'gain' on property. Moreover, if your estate planning includes the use of lifetime gifts from you to some of the 'objects of your bounty', then the basis is very relevant, as those gifts have their basis 'carry over' to the donee/recipient. For example, if you purchased IBM stock years ago for $5,000, and you give it to your son today with a value of $12,000, then several things happen. First, you have decreased your potentially taxable estate by $12,000, the value of the gift. Your son has now received a gift worth $12,000 upon which he owes no taxes, but his basis is $5,000. If he sells it tomorrow, his 'gain' is calculated from your basis ($5,000) which 'carries over' to him, yielding a gain of $7,000. Further, the date when you acquired the assets may determine whether your son has a long-term or short-term gain when he sells, which are taxed at different rates. Finally, post-2009 tax law may revert to a 'carry over' basis for inherited property too. As such, you can see why it is important to try to record WHEN you obtained each property item, and for HOW much.

MOVING ON BONUS – MY PERSONAL INVENTORY INFORMATION FORM

I've included a Personal Information Inventory form at the end of this book, which includes space to include this information, if you'd like to use it. This comprehensive form is a good tool for helping you to identify the information you may need to locate, organize it, record it, and make it available for your family, executor or trustee if the need should arise. I encourage all of my clients to permit me to help them to prepare a customized one for them. My computerized version is easily updated, and can be password-secured. Its form in this book, however, is sufficient to permit you to make your own list, or you can copy and enlarge the book pages if you prefer. My contact information is included on the form if you have further questions about the form or how to get one for yourself.

CHAPTER 6

UNDERSTANDING PROPERTY THAT IS SELF-PLANNED

How Title And Beneficiary Designations Affect Your Estate Plan

Not all steps in an estate planning program require complicated legal or financial devices. Instead, many common forms of asset ownership already have built-in provisions to transfer title upon one owner's death, which effects at least one component of your overall estate plan. For example, when a spouse dies, and owned a home with the surviving spouse as joint tenants, the house will automatically go to the surviving spouse. If that is the intended result, then positive estate planning has occurred. If, however, a mother has placed one child on her deed as a joint tenant, but not others, then the resulting transfer of title upon the mother's death may or may not comport with the rest of the overall estate plan. Tools such as this are often referred to as 'Will Substitutes', since they operate to pass title upon your death, as a will would, but are not controlled by your will at all. Before we examine in a later chapter what all you can do with a will, it might be good to understand what property is already provided for, though sometimes unintentionally. We will discuss these issues further in this chapter.

TRADITIONAL PROPERTY TITLE AND ITS EFFECT ON YOUR ESTATE

As we discussed in an earlier chapter, the different ways in which a piece of property is 'titled' can have a large impact on what happens to it within your estate plan. The joint tenants in the introduction above not only take title automatically upon the death of the other Joint tenant, but further enjoy the protection in many states that this result cannot be altered by a will or other contract. The Mother above cannot say in her will "I want my children to sell my home and share the proceeds", since the home already will belong, immediately upon her death, to the one child on the deed with her. Any suggestion to the contrary in the will should be of no effect. Let's look at what some of these methods of holding title will do to property rights when the owner dies.

> ➤ **Joint tenancy (with rights of survivorship)**

The most common form for one person to be holding title to property with another person is as joint tenants. This form, as described earlier, means that each owner is entitled to the entire property upon passage of the other tenant. More than two people can be joint tenants, and they all have title to the entire property, subject to the ownership of the other surviving joint tenants, until only one remains, at which time he or she becomes the sole owner. This passage of title to a surviving tenant is automatic; technically, no document is required to 'transfer' the title, since the survivors already had title. Instead, when a joint tenant dies, the paperwork for the title is merely to keep the 'chain of title', or the series of documents which overtime show who owns property, relatively clean. Usually, just submitting the deceased person's will for probate, along with a death certificate, will establish a record of the death which is sufficient to show the vesting of title in the remaining owners.

As such, joint tenancy can be an effective tool in your estate plan. If you own property jointly with the person to whom you would like it to pass upon your death, then this result will be achieved automatically, without expense or delay upon your passing. The price for this convenience, however, may be a loss of control, along with potential tax liabilities being inadvertently created. Suppose, for example, that a widowed mother wants her property to pass to her adult son upon her death. Mother adds Son to the deed as a joint tenant. Later, Mother gets remarried to a wonderful man with a young daughter whom Mother comes to cherish as her own. Everyone lives in Mother's house. Can New Husband or Beloved Step Daughter get the Mother's home in her will? Do they even have a right to keep living there if she dies? No, because the property will automatically go to Son. Moreover, Mother has given up a lot of flexibility over what she does with the house while she is alive, because she now needs Son's signature on any attempt to alter their joint title. If Mom wants to drop the Son, or add the New Husband along with him, or even get a loan secured by the equity in the house, the Son must consent. You can see that in a stable, well established estate plan, joint tenancy can be useful, but it is not without its risks, and in particular it brings a limitation on flexibility as life changes around us.

There are also potentially significant tax ramifications. When Mom places Son on the deed, she has effectively given him a gift of one half of the value of the house. Annual gifts in excess of $13,000 per person (2009) are considered taxable gifts. Thus, Mother either has to pay the applicable tax (approximately 45%), or use up a part of her Unified Credit discussed in the tax chapters in this book. Taken together, the control and tax problems arising from the use of joint tenancy for estate planning make it a method which is to be carefully, not haphazardly, implemented. Far too many people cavalierly put intended heirs on their deeds and accounts, based only upon the advice of a neighbor or friend who in turn heard that it was the 'right thing to do." There is a reason that attorneys and accountants spend all of that time in school; you should let them help you.

> ## Tenants by the entirety (joint tenancy with a spouse)

Recognizing the unique way property is accumulated and shared between married people, the law recognizes a unique title scenario applicable to married people in most states: Joint Tenants by the Entirety (TBE). In some states, the deed must state that title is taken in this manner. In others, it is presumed whenever spouses have joint title to property. TBE property automatically passes to the surviving spouse upon the death of one, and thus this operates as a valid will substitute. Unique to this method, however, is the relative unassailability of the ownership. Typically one spouse cannot sell, gift, mortgage, or otherwise dispose of the property, or any portion thereof, without the consent of the spouse. A bank loaning money on TBE property without both spouses signature has no claim against the property. Further, creditors of one of the spouses cannot seek repayment of the spouse's debts from TBE property, though joint creditors (i.e. a creditor to whom a debt is owed by both spouses) may. Divorce will sever the TBE title and protection, leaving the title typically to be as tenants in common (see below) unless it directed otherwise in the divorce proceedings.

If you and your spouse wish to own property as TBE, it is best to specify it as such on the deed. Further, state law changes over time, and what was once a valid titling tool in your state may not continue to be so (though even if TBE is abolished in a state, it will usually maintain its effect for those who took title while it was valid, so as to not prejudice the position of current property owners). Some states only permit TBE for real estate (Illinois, Indiana, Kentucky, Michigan, New York, North Caroline and Oregon), while many others permit it for real estate and other property, for example investment and bank accounts (Alaska, Arkansas, Delaware, District of Columbia, Florida, Hawaii, Maryland, Massachusetts, Mississippi, Missouri, New Jersey, Oklahoma, Pennsylvania, Rhode Island, Tennessee, Vermont, Virginia, Tennessee, and Wyoming). Notably, Hawaii may be the only state which recognizes TBE between same-sex partners in a registered "Reciprocal Beneficiary Relationship". Whether this emerges as a trend remains to be seen.

> ## Tenants in common

Owning property as tenants in common is akin to buying a pizza with friends: You each own a share of the entire pizza, with the size of your ownership interest being proportionate to your contribution unless you agree otherwise. Tenants in common are similar to joint tenants owning property, but without the right of survivorship or limits on transfer. Each tenant's piece of the ownership value is their own, and they can sell or will or gift it as they see fit (absent agreement to the contrary). If one of the TIC owners dies, then that share is handled as part of his or her estate, and does not automatically transfer to the remaining owners. As such, tenancy in common is not a method of passing property outside of your will in most circumstances. Nevertheless, this TIC title is often used between unmarried persons, or persons who have contributed different amounts to the purchase, where it is expected that each owner will provide for the disposition of their own share of the ownership. Another feature of TIC ownership is that the owners, or even one owner, can readily break the common ownership by asking for a 'partition'. In a partition action, the court effectively splits the property into pieces, giving each of the owners their respective share. Unlike TIC, where you own a title share to the entire property, a partition action actually gives each owner a separate share of the property, like handing them their piece of pizza. They no longer own a portion of the entire pizza; they now own entirely the smaller piece they are holding.

> ## Sole owner

Plenty of property is owned by a sole individual. This classic title is simple. You own it, you own all of it, and no one else owns any of it. As such, straight sole ownership will not pass title outside of your estate nor work as a will substitute. One notable exception is a minority of states which recognize Transfer on Death deeds. In these jurisdictions, a deed can provide that on the death of the owner, title is transferred to someone else. For real estate, such deeds are only recognized currently in Arkansas, Arizona, Colorado, Kansas, Missouri, Montana, Nevada, New Mexico, Ohio and Wisconsin, as near as I can tell. Most states, however, do permit this type of title for non-real-estate properties, as is discussed further below.

ADDITIONAL TITLING METHODS FOR FINANCIAL ACCOUNTS

In addition to the above descriptions of title ownership, most states have statutes which permit other methods of joint ownership for various types of assets which can also operate as will substitutes. Since most people hold a great portion of their assets outside of real estate, it is important to understand the operation of these in order to consider whether they hold or deserve a place in your estate plan. While you may not be familiar with these, they see frequent use in financial planning as will substitutes, though often without consideration of whether they are truly appropriate. You can go into a bank and have an account titled to operate as a will substitute. The bank, however, is not going to be in a position to fully consider the tax and planning impact of this decision in the context of your overall estate plan. You must therefore be careful to understand what these mean, and consider them as available tools, not exclusive solutions. It has been said that "If your only tool is a hammer, then every problem looks like a nail". In this vein, banks see all planning issues as ones which can be solved by the bank's tools, life insurance salesmen can find an insurance purchase to answer any problem, and your lawyer certainly can offer a number of legal solutions of varying complexity. The secret, in my opinion, it to be informed and educated about what is being offered, the alternatives, and the potential risks and benefits of each. Depending upon your level of comfort with this, you then may have to accept a level of trust or confidence in the advisor with whom you are speaking (owing to their education and experience in the field), but blind trust may lead to unexpectedly disappointing results.

Let's now examine some of the most useful alternate financial titling methods.

➤ Pay on death (POD) accounts

A "Pay on Death", (or POD) account is one which is owned by one person, but will pass to another (the beneficiary of the POD) upon the death of the owner. While you are alive, your POD accounts remain in your exclusive control, and the future beneficiary has no right to limit your control over the account, to access the money, or to expose it to claims of creditors. A POD account which you create remains your account. You can change the beneficiary anytime you see fit, so long as you are alive and legally competent to handle your affairs. Even if you are incompetent, an effective power of attorney for financial matters can keep a measure of control over these accounts and their beneficiary designations. If you spend all the money and empty the account, then the POD beneficiary simply is entitled to nothing. When, however, you do pass on, the money in the account will automatically go to the POD beneficiary named on the account. An example of this would be a savings account titled "Mary Jones, POD to Rebecca Jones". The balance in the account at the death of Mary would pass to Rebecca outside of probate, free of any dispositions made in Mary's will. Note that if Rebecca predeceases Mary, then the POD payment at Mary's death is simply void, and the account proceeds would go into Mary's estate. Most states permit this type of account for savings and checking accounts or even Certificates of Deposit. The United States Treasury also permits this for savings bonds which they issue.

You can usually use this type of account to transfer the remaining balance to a trust, if you do not intend it to go directly to a beneficiary. For example, if you have a minor child, the account may be "Rebecca Jones, POD to Living Trust of Rebecca Jones", and it thereafter will be handled under the trust terms wherein you have arranged for your trust assets to be used for your child after your death.

One frequent purpose for a POD account is to make funds available for current family or estate needs immediately following the owners death, such as living and funeral expenses. Because this money automatically is transferred to the beneficiary (usually upon presentation of an original death certificate for the owner), it is not delayed by probate or extensive paperwork requirements. Sometimes this arrangement is called a Totten Trust, after a 1904 case in New York which affirmed the legality of this practice despite it being neither a trust nor a will. While there may be a delay or a day or two until a death certificate is available, many people find the comfort of retaining absolute control over the account to be worth the minor delay, rather than placing the money in a joint account, where it would be instantly available to the joint owner, both before and after death.

> ### ➤ Transfer on death (TOD) accounts

Close kin to the POD account is the TOD (Transfer on Death) account. Truth be told, they are identical, for all practical intents and purposes. The main distinction seems to be only the particular state statute which authorizes their existence. Banking POD accounts have been around a while, and thus most bank accounts are labeled as POD's when this method is used. Stock brokerages and other types of financial institutions often were not covered under these early statutes, and thus a Uniform Transfer of Securities on Death Act has been passed in almost every state in this country. As such, brokerage accounts are typically labeled "Transfer on Death" accounts. One further distinction is that the money in a bank can be 'paid' to the beneficiary, while titled instruments like a stock certificate are 'transferred'.

For either TOD or POD accounts, you do not want to list a minor child as a direct beneficiary. In these circumstances, the Courts will require that the money be held in a trust until the child reaches the age of majority. This may restrict the funds from being used for the purpose you intended. For example, most courts will not permit the money to be used for expenses for the care and support of the child, whereas you may have anticipated that the funds would be used for that purpose. As such, any money to a minor child should probably go into some type of trust arrangement where it can be managed under your terms, not the bank or court's.

Both TOD and POD accounts provide will substitutes to transfer assets at your death to another, without some of the burdens of joint ownership. For instance, a joint owner may sell or lien a portion of the asset, or interfere with your disposition of the asset. These methods are thus another tool to put in the estate planning toolbox for use in the right situations.

LIFE INSURANCE POLICIES

It would be fun to record a thousand people's faces when they hear that a life insurance sales agent is on the phone. The resulting montage of rolled eyes, crinkled noses and visible sighs would be a hoot to see. Nevertheless, life insurance is a part of many of our lives, and can serve a valuable role in estate planning. For the purpose of the current discussion, we are focused on its use as a will substitute. By design, life insurance does not need to be a part of your probate estate. In fact, it should not be, ideally. Instead, life insurance benefits are paid to the beneficiary named in your policy. Only if you fail to name a beneficiary, or fail to name one or more beneficiaries which survive you, will the policy default to paying the benefits to your estate. Life insurance benefits are received by the beneficiary free of any income taxes, and are paid relatively promptly following submission of a death certificate for the insured person. Since the payment of benefits is controlled by the policy, and not by the terms of your will unless the policy reverts to paying your estate, it can be considered a will substitute. The tax ramifications of who owns the policy (distinguished from who the beneficiary of the policy is) are discussed separately in the chapter on life insurance in this book.

INVESTMENT ACCOUNTS, RETIREMENT ACCOUNTS AND PENSIONS

Millions of Americans have saved trillions of dollars in various investment accounts, retirement savings accounts and retirement plans, all of which may be considered will substitutes if the proper steps are taken. Whenever you open an account, or begin to participate in a plan, you are offered the ability to name a beneficiary, who will receive any benefits to which you may be entitled upon your death. For example, a vested pension may provide for post-death benefits to your spouse or another. More modern savings vehicles (for example, the IRA and 401k families) all permit you to name a beneficiary to receive any balance left in your account when you pass. If you fail to name a beneficiary, then any amounts remaining due will go straight into your estate. Merely by naming a beneficiary, however, your funds skip probate, and are paid directly to the survivor. Some paperwork may be required to effect this new ownership, due to the tax and legislative tangle which surrounds retirement account legislation, but the process is still relatively streamlined as compared to formal probate of these assets. You can name a single beneficiary ("Jane"), a class of beneficiaries (equally among my children living at my death), a trust, or other options. If you fail to include these assets in your overall estate plan, then it may be off balance and inconsistent with your wishes.

A note of caution for married people is required. If you intend to name someone other than a living spouse as a beneficiary, then you should get your spouse's consent to this arrangement in writing. Otherwise, the spouse may have a legal entitlement to some or all of your remaining accounts despite what your written beneficiary designation form may state. Further, if you get divorced, you should change your beneficiary to remove your ex-spouse. This is easily forgotten, and can lead to the unexpected result of the ex-spouse taking your retirement funds, rather than your family. Ambiguity is created if you don't take care of these items. For example, if you list as a beneficiary "My wife Jane", and then you get divorced and remarried, do the benefits go to your wife (i.e. current wife), or to Jane? You have created an ambiguity which a court may need to resolve, with both expense and delay. In some states, such beneficiary designations naming a divorced spouse are automatically void when a divorce occurs, but you do not want to have to rely upon that, especially where making the change is usually as simple as submitting a form to the institution holding the account, or even by performing an account update online at some institutions.

GIVING GIFTS WHILE YOU ARE ALIVE

One more way to dispose of your assets without a will is to give them to others during your life. The law refers to these as 'inter vivos' gifts ('during life'). If you give an asset to someone, then that asset is no longer a part of your estate subject to probate. (Hurray!) It also isn't yours anymore however. (Boo!). Inter vivos gifts are just that, gifts. You no longer have the control over the asset which you did when you owned it. Still, they can be a valuable estate disposition tool. You can give gifts to anyone, solely or jointly. You can give gifts to minors, including not only Uniform Gifts to Minors Act (UGMA) gifts and Uniform Transfers to Minors (UTMA) custodial accounts for minors, but also in trusts, by insurance, and otherwise.

The subject of Lifetime Gifts comes with many twists and turns, mostly with regard to the effect of Estate Taxes and Gift Taxes. We'll discuss taxes separately in the tax sections of this book, but for now, you need to consider two key points. First, you can gift up to $13,000 (2009) to an individual with no tax due whatsoever. The recipient accepts your gift, you don't own it anymore, and that is about it. The recipient owes no income tax on a gift either. Instead, the recipient takes over your 'basis', or taxable cost, in the asset. This basis is used to calculate if any capital gains are due on the gift when the recipient later disposes of it. For example, if you purchased a rare vase for $3,000, and gave it to your son when it was worth $10,000, then no tax is due by anyone. If he later sells if for $14,000, then he has a capital gain of $11,000 ($14,000 proceeds minus $3,000 basis from you) which may be subject to taxation. If, on the other hand, you give your son $10,000 in cash, then the basis/cost for the cash will simply be $10,000. Any profit he can make on it through his own investment will be treated the same as if it were his own money from that point forwards (which it is!). Note that you can give this $13,000 to as many different people as you want. If 10 people get $13,000 from you, then you've decreased your potentially taxable estate by $130,000. This is an annual exclusion, so you can do this as often as you like, so long as no person gets more than $13,000 (2009) in value from you in any given year.

If you exceed $13,000 in gifts to an individual, then gift tax may be due on the excess, subject to the gift tax applicable exclusion amount, which is discussed further in the tax chapter.

VEHICLE TITLES

A motor vehicle may be titled with a Transfer on Death designation in many states. The new owner must apply for a new title after the death of the transferor, but each state permitting this process has a form to handle this quickly. If there is a lien or lease on the vehicle, such titling will not likely be permitted, since the bank or leasing company has a security interest in the car in exchange for a loan or lease with you, not a beneficiary. Still, in exchange for mailing an appropriate form to change the current title to include a TOD beneficiary, and perhaps paying a small fee, then one more asset will pass free of probate.

SMALL ESTATE PROCEDURES

If some of the above tools are used, you may find that what seems like a relatively wealthy person can die, and still have very little left in the way of formal 'probate' assets. Suppose a husband and wife own a home worth $800,000, an IRA for the husband worth $500,000, investment accounts worth $500,000, bonds worth $50,000, two cars and a modest checking/savings account. If the home is owned as tenants by the entirety, the IRA's, investment account and bonds name beneficiaries, and the cars, checking and savings accounts have Transfer on Death provisions in their title, then all that is left to probate are the personal effects, which are of nominal value for probate purposes. As such, a surviving spouse from a relatively comfortable couple could engage in a simplified probate process typically called 'Small Estate Procedures'. These streamlined procedures for small probate estates provide several forms which must be submitted to the probate clerk in the county in which they live, and the executor can finish the probate process with very little time and expense involved. Almost everyone has some probate to be done, even with the most advanced estate planning. Minimizing its time and expense, however, can be a valuable benefit if some of these tools discussed herein are properly analyzed and applied.

It is important for you to remember that the goal of this book is not to give you all of the tools you need to 'go it alone' with your estate planning. In my opinion, that is a bad idea. There are numerous state and federal statutes and regulations to consider, different types of property, multiple planning tools, and myriad possible planning goals which must be brought together to craft a plan that works well for you. Instead, it is my hope that by having a resource to help explain what these tools are and how they may work, you will be better able to participate with your planning attorney by providing useful information, asking probing questions, and understanding what you are given as it is prepared, modified and executed. If so, I submit that you will be in a far more confident position about the condition of your estate plan than most of the other people you'll ever meet, or even see. You will have an understanding of the current state of your financial affairs, an understanding of what will happen following your death, and the peace of mind that you have taken steps to decrease the confusion, expense, strife and delay which your loved ones will experience after your death. A nice gift indeed.

MOVING ON...

Speaking of nice gifts, many estate plans are crafted to take advantage of the numerous benefits of making gifts during your lifetime. In the next chapter, we'll look at the tax, control, and charitable benefits which a gifting strategy may bring to your estate planning efforts.

CHAPTER 7

SHOULD I GIVE SOME AWAY?

The Power Of Gifts And Charitable Contributions In Managing Your Estate

---

Gifts are like puppies; everyone loves them. It's fun to give a gift, and its fun to get a gift. Leave it to the government to rain on the parade. What other heartless Grinch could possibly come up with something called a Gift Tax? The Gift Tax is like poop from the puppy, ruining an otherwise perfectly good time for all.

Still, giving gifts of your assets is a very useful planning tool, which can be used to reach multiple goals, including not only showing your generous side, but also decreasing your taxable estate. Most gifts can be structured so as to escape paying taxes. Moreover, appropriately planned gifting strategies can actually decrease your tax liabilities, if careful attention is paid to staying inside the various boundaries Congress has created. Gifts have the ability to not only decrease the size of your taxable estate, and also to keep the appreciation in value and/or income which an asset may accumulate out of your estate as well. For our estate planning purposes, it can thus be a powerful tool, and is in fact one which is frequently used.

WHAT ARE 'GIFTS' IN ESTATE PLANNING?

For our purposes, a "gift" occurs anytime you transfer anything of value to another person or entity in exchange for less than the full value of the property. Obviously, handing someone a gift wrapped shirt is a 'gift', and most people have come to understand that giving money to your children or others is legally a 'gift', but what about less obvious examples. Paying your wife's credit cards from your own checking account is a 'gift'. Paying a portion of a grandson's college tuition is a gift. Loaning money to your son and daughter-in-law to make a down payment, but not really making them pay it all back, is a gift to the extent that the loan isn't repaid (known as 'forgiveness of debt'). Even adding someone to the title of property, such as placing your child's name on your home's deed, is a substantial gift since you have in effect given them partial ownership of your home. The issue isn't whether you meant something as a gift at all, but rather whether you transferred property in exchange for less than fair market value.

In gift terminology, the person who makes the gift is called the Donor, and the recipient of the gift is the Donee. When a gift is made, the donee does not have to report the gift itself as income, nor pay income tax thereon. Instead, any tax implications of the gift itself are the responsibility of the donor, through completion of a Gift Tax Return (IRS Form 709) if necessary, and payment of any tax found to be due (discussed below). The donee is responsible, however, for any income the gift creates or accumulates after the transfer of the gift, as well as for any capital gains received if the donee sells the gift.

HOW ARE GIFTS TAXED?

The purpose of the Gift Tax in the United States is to prevent people from escaping the Estate Tax altogether by giving away their assets before they die. The government has spun a web of laws and regulations intended to make sure that if you accumulate property, the government has an opportunity to tax it when you get rid of the property, whether you dispose of it during your lifetime (income and gift taxes), or at your death by will or otherwise (Estate Tax). Because of the government's intent to weave these different taxes into a comprehensive tax-catching net, it is important to watch and understand the interplay between these taxes: In particular, the interaction of the Gift and Estate Taxes is relevant to us now.

In order to achieve this comprehensive coverage, the Estate Tax and the Gift Tax were revised to make their rates uniform. The maximum rate for both taxes is now 45%. The tax laws, attempting to be somewhat reasonable, permit you to die without taxing some of your estate assets, and thus do not start to tax your estate until its assets exceed $2,000,000 (2008) to $3,500,000 (2009). Recognizing that people might give away their assets to get under these limits, the law taxes all gifts made during your lifetime, as the gifts will have the effect of reducing your taxable estate. Fortunately, however, there are important exclusions to paying the gift tax which make it a viable strategy. By using these gifting rules, you can decrease the size of your taxable estate, and decrease your estate's tax liabilities, and thus instead put the money directly into the hands of your beneficiaries right now. You escape taxes, and you get to see the recipients of your generosity enjoy the use of these gifts right now (in most cases).

CAN YOU ESCAPE GIFT TAXES?

Fortunately, there are valuable exclusions to the gift tax which can be used to avoid gift tax liabilities in many situations.

Annual Exclusion: Perhaps the most commonly used exception is the Annual Exclusion. As of 2009, the annual exclusion is $13,000 (2009). This lets you give up to $13,000 in value to any person, or to as many people as you want, without having to pay any gift tax or file any report or return with the IRS. You can thus give up to $13,000 to each of your three children and effectively reduce your taxable estate by $39,000. Do this for a period of 10 years, and $390,000 is now out of your estate, and in the hands of your children, completely tax free.

You can do this to anyone; children, grandchildren, or even complete strangers. Moreover, married couples can give 'split gifts', and effectively double this amount, such that Mom and Dad can together give $26,000 to each of their children. (Note: the amount of this exclusion is pegged to the inflation rate, but only increases when inflation requires that it increase a full $1,000.

Spousal Gift Exclusion: Another valuable exclusion is the Spousal Gift Exclusion. You may make unlimited gifts to your spouse, free of any tax consequences. Why is this useful? Suppose in a marriage that one spouse starts with, or acquires, substantially greater assets held in their own name. If Husband has $8,000,000 in property, and Wife has $1,000,000 in property, then an estate tax disaster is in the cards. If Wife dies, say in 2009, then her estate will pass entirely tax free, since it is below the $3,500,000 estate tax exclusion for 2009. Unfortunately, if Husband later dies, say in the following year, then of his $8,000,000, more than half of it will be taxed ($8,000,000 minus $3,500,000 applicable exclusion leaves $4,500,000 taxable). At the 45% estate tax rate, $2,025,000 in tax is due, leaving his beneficiaries $5,975,000, plus $1,000,000 from his wife. Total to beneficiaries: $6,975,000. The tax situation is even worse if Wife's will left her property to Husband, as too many do. Wife has only added to the value of Husband's taxable estate, increasing the Estate Tax by another $450,000.

If, however, Husband gave a gift to Wife of $2,500,000 before her death, then the math changes. At Wife's death, her $3,500,000 passes tax free to their children, as it is equal to the exclusion. Husband's estate would now have $5,500,000, minus the $3,500,000 applicable exclusion, leaving a $2,000,000 taxable estate. At 45%, taxes are now $900,000. Net tax savings, and net increase in assets to beneficiaries: $1,125,000. A huge savings can thus be effected with this tool, in the right circumstances. Note: Spouses must be U.S. Citizens. Non U.S. Citizens, even if U.S. residents, can only be given up to $125,000 (under current law) free of gift taxes. The government still believes in 'Made in America', I suppose.).

Tuition Exclusion: Other useful exceptions exist as well. You may pay college tuition for a child or grandchild, or really for anyone, without using any of your Unified Credit or affecting other exclusions. Such payments must be made directly to the college or university, and not to the child. You may still, however, use your $13,000 annual exclusion to give further funds to that student for housing, expenses, etc. Remember that a married couple can double that amount too. While we are discussing education gifts, one shouldn't fail to consider Prepaid Tuition plans and 529 College Savings plans. The details of these programs are outside the intent of this book, but suffice it to say that both permit you to put money away for future college expenses. Parents, and grandparents, can front-load their contributions to such accounts by combining up to 5 years of gift tax exclusions (or $65,000 each, up to $130,000 with a split gift) into one year, making a potentially huge dent in future college expenses. You have now used up your gift tax exclusion for that individual for the next five years, but what a wonderful gift!

Medical Expense Exclusion: Similarly, if you pay medical expenses directly to a medical institution on someone's behalf, such payments are not considered to be taxable gifts by the IRS.

CHARITABLE EXCLUSIONS TO REDUCE YOUR ESTATE

After a lifetime of working to make money, and then making your money work for you, many people consider whether they want to share their good fortune with one or more charitable organizations. Gifts to IRS approved charities reduce the size of your taxable estate, and thus your estate taxes. If the gift to charity is effected during your lifetime, then no gift tax is due on the donation. Moreover, you can use charitable donations to offset substantial income taxes on your other income, and/or avoid income itself, such as capital gains, by donating assets which have appreciated while you held them.

This relatively simple concept is complicated, however, by the various goals and tools which people have come up with in an effort to obtain the greatest possible benefit from their charitable intent. In the "old days", whenever they were, you just donated to a charity. Now you might consider a charitable remainder trust, a charitable lead trust, perhaps a charitable annuity, a life insurance policy in favor of a charity, or other options. You might even form your own private foundation to hold your charitable contributions and effect your goals. A brief discussion of these should be adequate for now; if you need further details, your attorney advisor may be best suited to answer your specific questions.

Charitable Remainder Trust: Sometimes people want to make a charitable donation, for tax and/or personal reasons, but do not want the entire asset to go to the charity at the expense of their own lifestyle, or perhaps that of their remaining family. One tool for giving a partial gift to charity, and getting a partial tax break, is the Charitable Remainder Trust, created by Congress in 1969. This trust can let you benefit charity, avoid capital gains, reduce your estate tax burden, and get a current income tax deduction too. In this trust, you place property into an irrevocable trust (i.e. you can't get it back if you change your mind). During your lifetime, you can have the 'income' from the trust (such as interests, dividends, a portion of capital gains, etc) paid to you or your family. When you die, the 'remainder' of the trust, or what is left, will pass to the charity. You, as the donor, receive a current tax income tax deduction when the gift is made, based upon the value today of the amount which will pass to the charity in the future (called its 'present value'). The IRS requires that you receive at least 5% of the fair market value of the assets in the trust per year to qualify, though you can defer that in some years and make it up in others. You can set your payout, or income rate, higher too, however the more you take as income now, the less will be left to grow for charity at the end, and thus the lower your current income tax deduction will be calculated to be. Between 5 and 10 percent annual income paid to the charitable donor is fairly typical.

Because the trust will ultimately go to a charity, its capital gains are not taxed. Thus, if you donate highly appreciated, or highly appreciating, property to the trust, you can get some of the benefits of the gains, without having to carry the tax burden. For example, if you purchased Berkshire Hathaway stock around 1990, it was worth $7,000 per share, more or less. In December of 2007, it was trading around $150,000 per share. Obviously, if you sell the stock, then you will pay a substantial capital gains tax. If, on the other hand, you donate it to a Charitable Remainder Trust, then you get the lifetime benefit of the income on the $150,000 (say at 5%, that's $7,500 per year for life), plus you get a deduction for the present value of the charitable remainder (which will itself be substantial). In addition, you have made a charity more powerful than before. Everybody wins!

The amount in your Charitable Remainder Trust is not considered to be part of your estate for Estate Tax purposes, so you have also saved estate taxes. Despite the fact that this trust is not part of your estate, you can still maintain control over the trust. While you can't 'back out' of the trust and take the underlying assets, you can serve as the trustee, and direct the investment activity of the trust. You do still, as trustee, have some obligation to your remainder beneficiary to act prudently in your investment management, but you retain substantial flexibility. You can even alter the charity which will benefit from the charity at your death.

If you set a certain amount to be paid as income yearly when the trust is established, it is referred to as a Charitable Remainder Annuity Trust. If instead the trust provides for flexible payments calculated as a set percentage of the investment assets in the trust, then it is referred to as a Charitable Remainder Uni-Trust.

Charitable Lead Trust: If you made it through the trust discussion above, then you are interested enough to read about the Charitable Lead Trust. (If you didn't read the last one, then this won't interest you either). The essential opposite of the Charitable Remainder Trust is the Charitable Lead Trust. In this form of trust, the charity gets its money from the beginning of the trust (thus, the "lead"), drawing income from the trust assets until such time as the trust balance then passes to your beneficiaries (whether at your death, or after a certain number of years you specify). The main advantage of this type of trust is its ability to get assets out of your estate now, reduce their present value for calculating Gift Tax, and let the funds grow for years until they pass to the beneficiaries, free of tax and, hopefully, larger. The cost to you includes the loss of income which passes to the charity, and the fact that some of your Gift Tax unified exclusion amount will be 'used up' to cover the value of your gift which isn't to charity, i.e. the present value of the future amount which will pass to your beneficiaries. The power of this trust is that the present value of your gift for tax purposes will be far less than its actual value to your beneficiaries, for two reasons. First, the value of the assets you place into the trust must be reduced for tax purposes to reflect the fact that for some period of time, the charity will be taking the income from the trust, not you or your beneficiaries. Thus, you have to use up far less of your unified exclusion to get these assets out of your estate. Second, because the trust has charitable purposes, the subsequent growth of the trust, including capital gains, dividends, interest, appreciation, etc, is all tax free. When the trust terminates, whether at your death or after a specified period of time, then your beneficiaries receive a much bigger asset, free of income tax or estate tax, and the gift taxes were already paid by the reduced use of your unified gift tax credit.

While the trust is in effect, the charity will draw income from the trust. As the trust (hopefully) grows as a result of capital gains, etc, the relative portion taken by the charity will diminish. You get to choose the income tax treatment of these payments to charity while the trust is active. A "Grantor Charitable Lead Trust" lets you take a current income tax deduction for the present value of the future income the charity will draw from the trust, BUT 1) you can only deduct it in the year you create the trust, even if the value of the deduction exceeds the amount you can deduct for charitable contributions that year (typically 20-50% of your income), and 2) the income taken each year by the charity will still be considered taxable income to you. Due to these limitations, most people select a Nongrantor Charitable Lead Trust, which gives you no current income tax deduction despite your donation to charity, but also does not attribute the income from the trust to you. Most situations call for the latter treatment to achieve the desired end.

Charitable Gift Annuity: Unlike many tools, a Charitable Gift Annuity is not a type of trust, but instead a contract you make with a charity. In exchange for giving the charity a financial donation (cash, securities or other marketable assets), the charity agrees to pay you a fixed amount of money per month for your life, or the life of you and your spouse. Some of the money you receive is considered taxable, and some is tax free. The charity is responsible to make the payments to you, and is free to use your money. State regulations require the charity to maintain sufficient financial assets in reserve to secure its ability to pay the annuities outstanding. At the end of the beneficiary's life, the charity keeps the balance remaining from the amount donated initially.

The payment to be made to you each month is usually based upon rate charts published by the American Council on Gift Annuities. The rate varies depending upon whether it is paid for one lifetime, or so long as one of two people survives, such as spouses. The age of the Donor has a huge impact on the size of the monthly payment. Just as an example, the annual payout rate under the chart for a 60 year old person, for their lifetime, is 5.5%. For a 75 year old donor, the rate is 6.7%. If the same 60 year old has a 55 year old spouse, and the payment continues as long as one survives, then the rate is 4.7%. A 75 year old with a 70 year old wife gets paid at 5.8%. *Source: 2008 American Council on Gift Annuities table.* This percentage, multiplied against the value of the assets when you establish the annuity, sets your payment for life. Regardless of the future course of the investments or assets you donate, in good markets or bad, your payment is fixed. Note that these percentages will be lower than the amount you could get for an annuity from an insurance company. It is, after all, supposed to be charity, and the difference in rates between the two roughly corresponds to the amount of benefit the charity is likely to receive when it's all said and done.

In exchange for your donation, you receive a charitable deduction based upon the residual value to the charity, you reduce the size of your estate without incurring gift taxes, and you benefit charities of your choice.

FAMILY FOUNDATIONS AND DONOR ADVISED FUNDS

One method used by families with comfortable wealth (say, over $3,000,000) who wish to engage in an ongoing program of charitable support is to from a private foundation. A private foundation is usually created by an individual or family to work towards charitable goals. These are often either formed as non-profit corporations, or simply as a charitable trust. A governing board of directors typically runs the affairs, through the structure of a trust can be more flexible regarding how the daily affairs are managed than a corporation may be. When organized by or for a family, these are sometimes called Family Foundations. Once the necessary prerequisites are satisfied, including appropriate document preparation, and recognition as a charitable organization by the IRS, then gifts to the foundation are considered charitable contributions. As such, income tax, gift tax and estate tax deductions are all available. Gifts made to such foundations usually are not subject to the annual gift tax exclusion limit ($13,000 in 2009), but instead are unlimited. For income tax purposes, however, such donations are limited in their deductibility to 20-30% of your income, depending upon the nature of the assets donated.

The appeal of a private foundation is often that the people involved have the ability to control the day to day operations and focus of the assets invested therein, and can develop a personal connection and passion with the people who benefit from the foundation's work and assets. Some foundations use income from an endowment they maintain in order to make donations to other operating charities. This use permits the foundation principal to experience capital growth for the future, while preserving the tax free treatment of most of its income. There are IRS requirements which require a private foundation to pay at least 5% of their assets in qualifying distributions each year so that these foundations aren't used simple as a place to park money. Other foundations pass through any incoming donations to the foundation each year, which are called pass-through foundations. A private operating foundation is usually formed for an organization which intends to work its charitable purpose through ongoing programs or services, using its assets to pay for employees, asset acquisition, and operating expenses.

With a private foundation, the donors retain the ability to control how the investments are handled, and how the assets of the foundation are distributed. One drawback to such a foundation is that the donations themselves (except for publicly traded stocks) are valued at their taxable cost, or basis, for determining the value of tax deductions typically, so they are not a place to benefit from an increase in highly appreciated assets, such as shares in a closely held business in a high-growth field which have already seen significant growth. The donor can still benefit to the extent that the capital gains on these assets, if sold after they are donated, are taxed very modestly to the foundation, rather than the taxpayer. Other benefits include the ability to educate, involve and even employ family members in a program of charitable works, and the preservation of a family legacy of community work for many years to come.

There are upfront expenses associated with creating such a foundation, so they are not typically used for more modest estates. In such circumstances, a Donor Advised Fund may be a more attractive option. A donor advised fund is usually established under the umbrella of an established community foundation which pursues charitable objectives. These foundations permit you to establish a fund under their charitable operation charter, and you can then participate in the administration of your fund. Most of the expensive aspects of starting and operating a charitable organization are absorbed by the charitable foundation, though it may get support from the donor advised funds too. You, and others you ask to join you, advise the foundation regarding how you would like to see the principal you have donated, and its income, distributed in the pursuit of charitable aims. The charitable foundation is not usually legally bound to your demands, but in the interest of continuing to gain donors to their network, they almost always respect the reasonable advice given by the donors, who are considered 'advisors' (thus the name, Donor Advised Fund). The foundation which oversees the fund you create takes care of the administration and investment aspects and expenses of the charity, permitting you to focus on how the funds available are ultimately distributed in pursuit of your charitable goals. Since the funds are handled by the public charitable foundation (i.e. not a private foundation), the maximum available tax deductions are available.

Charitable giving through the use of donor advised funds or private foundations can yield a double financial benefit. The donor gets a tax deduction for the fair market value of the assets donated, and does not have to pay capital gains tax on any appreciation in the assets. At the same time, the donor can see that the assets are put to good work, and have control and/or input into precisely where the money goes. For these reasons and more, many people are finding them a popular choice for targeted charitable giving.

FAMILY LIMITED PARTNERSHIPS

When is $6,000,000 not $6,000,000? Answer: when it looks like $4,000,000. Not much of a joke, huh? But it you are a person holding $6,000,000, looking for a way to transfer it to your family members without getting hit with enormous Gift or Estate Tax liabilities, making $6 mil look like $4 mil can be a nice trick, if done right. The family limited partnership might provide that punch line.

A planning tool which has evolved significantly in the last decade or so is the Family Limited Partnership (FLP). A FLP is created to permit family members to conduct business together. Planners have discovered that one useful aspect of a FLP is that it can operate to reduce the taxable value of the ownership of assets in the FLP, thereby reducing estate and/or gift tax liabilities. This is usually done through the application of 'minority interest' discounts and 'lack of marketability' discounts, discussed below.

An FLP is formed as a limited partnership, following the law of the state where it is created. In a limited partnership, the affairs of the partnership are typically run by a General Partner, while the Limited Partners have little say in the management of the partnership, and are not liable for the overall liabilities of the partnership. Accountants have realized that a limited partner owning, say, 10% of a company, with little voice in the running of the company, shouldn't have his 10% share valued at 10% of the company's overall value, because his minority interest doesn't give him the ability to make important decisions, unilaterally elect to distribute money to partners, or run the company. Thus, the value of his interest receives a 'minority interest' discount. Moreover, because the shares in a limited partnership cannot be traded on the open market, and not many people are interested in buying such a share, the value of such a 10% share is less than 10% of the overall value of the company. This is termed a 'lack of marketability' discount. Together, these discounts can work a substantial discount, say 30-35% or so, in the value of assets transferred to a FLP, and in turn owned by family members holding shares in the FLP.

Numerous traps await the unwary or careless person who creates an FLP simply to reduce taxes. The IRS is increasingly suspicious of the FLP as a tax shelter, and has pursued significant U. S. Tax Court cases to challenge those it found abusive. Some basic tips which have emerged therefrom include:

1. Don't attempt to put all of your assets into the FLP. It is supposed to be a partnership for business or investment purposes, not just an asset conduit. You should maintain credible asset levels to support you outside of the FLP for your lifetime.

2. Don't use the FLP as your personal piggy-bank. For it to be treated as a separate entity, you can't use it like a personal asset. If you use real estate that is in an FLP, you may need to pay rent. You shouldn't use FLP assets to pay your bills, buy a fur coat, or handle other personal expenses. Instead, partnership distributions will likely need to be made, which you then can spend as you see fit.

3. Don't pour all the income out of the FLP. If the IRS is to acknowledge this as a business entity, then it should retain some of its income towards growth.

4. Attend to required formalities. If your state requires meetings and records, then have meetings and records. Assets owned by the FLP should be titled in the name of the FLP. Any steps which show the independent existence of the FLP as its own entity, rather than just a fictitious extension of you and your family, can help.

5. Maintaining too much control in the family patriarch or matriarch can backfire. While the family senior member is likely the source of most of the FLP assets, keeping too much control in

their hands can provide a means for the IRS to claim the FLP is just a proxy for them, and consider its assets to be pulled back into the senior member/general partner's estate when they die, defeating one of the prime benefits of the FLP.

6.   Don't wing it. FLP's bring significant planning advantages to those with significant estate. If would be foolish to jeopardize those benefits in an attempt to save a few dollars by trying to run an FLP without input from legal planning and accounting professionals.

An example of this procedure may be helpful to understanding how an FLP could operate. Mom and Dad have an estate worth $6,000,000. They have 4 children, W, X, Y and Z. Mom and Dad want to reduce their taxable estate, and provide investment education and experience for their children. Mom and Dad create a family limited partnership (FLP), and transfer $5,000,000 in stocks, bonds and real estate to the FLP. In return, Mom and Dad receive both the General Partner and Limited Partner interests in FLP. This is a fair exchange, so no gift tax is yet involved. Mom and Dad then gift to their children limited partnership interests covering 60% of the asset value, or what would seem to be $3,000,000. Now Gift Tax issues raise their head. Mom and Dad's accountant, however, provides an expert evaluation of the FLP interests, and determines that because of the lack of control over the assets of limited partners, the lack of marketability of the shares in an FLP, and the lack of liquidity of such shares as the limited partner cannot force the FLP to give it a pro-rata share of the underlying assets, a 33.3% discount to the value of the assets is applicable in valuing the limited partnership interests. Now those assets are not worth $3,000,000, but instead $2,000,000. Conveniently, $2,000,000 is the maximum amount which can be transferred by Mom and Dad if they combine their applicable exclusion amount for gift tax. So far, about $450,000 in gift/estate tax savings has occurred.

Each year thereafter, Mom and Dad can each gift limited interests to each of the children, worth up to the annual gift exclusion amount for that year ($13,000 in 2009). With the 33.3% discount, that would be like transferring underlying assets in the partnership worth $39,000 to each of the 4 children ($19,500 from Mom, and $19,500 from Dad, reduced to $13,000 from each by the 33.3% discounts on the limited partner shares). Over $150,000 further per year in underlying assets thus could thus be transferred to the children each year under the FLP. Any growth in the value of those shares after transfer is also free from Mom and Dad's estates. After 13 years, about $2,000,000 in further assets has been transferred free of gift and estate taxes, along with any growth in the shares after each gift is made. Mom and Dad then have what's left of the $1,000,000 they set aside initially for their own maintenance, and a modest portion of value left in the FLP, which can be passed freely to the surviving spouse for further gifting, and/or take advantage of the applicable exclusion amount for Estate Tax purposes in effect in the year of their death.

Please note that this is a highly over-simplified version of how such an arrangement needs to work. Without more attention to detail, this set of facts might suffer challenge by the IRS. That is not to say, however, that the FLP isn't worthwhile. Instead, it certainly may be, but you should not, ever, attempt to do this without the involvement of competent legal and accounting advice. I can't believe that there are web sites which attempt to sell form packages to do this type of complicated transaction, but there are. Do yourself and your family a favor, and avoid the forms. If you can afford to benefit from tax saving strategies, you can afford to have a professional to give advice to do it right.

MOVING ON...

So should you give away some of your assets? Depending upon your goals and the size of your potential estate, various strategies are clearly available which can combine tax minimization techniques with tools to attain your personal, charitable and family goals. Whether you decide to do so can be a fruitful topic of discussion with your planning attorney and accountant.

CHAPTER 8

PLANNING FOR THE UNKNOWN

The Durable Power Of Attorney, Living Wills And Long Term Care Planning

---

As you have seen by now, estate planning is about more than just signing a will. Estate planning can help you prepare for the twists and turns that you can reasonably see in the long road ahead. Many times, however, people are surprised by terrible, serious situations which they did not anticipate, and their life is thrown into a confusing mess. Serious auto accidents, fast developing diseases, heart attacks and more can turn your life around 180 degrees in a moment. Fortunately, estate planning tools are available which can help to keep your affairs, and your family, under managed control while you confront the personal and/or physical hurdles that life threw in your path. Examples of these tools include Powers of Attorney, Health Care Proxies, Living Wills, and Nursing Home planning.

POWERS OF ATTORNEY

One of the most powerful estate planning tools which you may use in your lifetime is the Power of Attorney (POA). A POA lets you designate a person, or people, who have the power to act for you in ways you can limit, under circumstances which you describe. In a nutshell, it lets someone else be legally you for a while when you need them to. It can quickly, efficiently and inexpensively allow someone to handle your affairs when you cannot. It can also, however, be used to embezzle your assets, tarnish your credit, and destroy your financial future. As with most powerful things, it must be carefully considered, designed, and implemented. In the right hands, however, it is a thing of beauty.

First, a few terms of art. The term 'power of attorney' can refer to either the document, or the rights and duties within the document. The person granting the power to someone is called the Principal. The person agreeing to act on behalf of the Principal is the Agent (sometimes referred to as the 'attorney-in-fact'). Thus, the Principal uses a Power of Attorney to give a designated Agent the ability to do things for the Principal. You don't need an attorney to be your Agent under a Power of Attorney, but you should consult with an attorney before signing one.

The agent under a POA has a fiduciary obligation to the principal. This means that the agent should not use the POA for the purpose of making the agent's life better; instead, the Agent is to act for the benefit of the principal and the principal's goals. The agent can be held personally responsible for any financial damages incurred by the principal as a result of the agent's failure to act reasonably and on behalf of the principal. If, for example, the agent withdraws money from the principal's account to pay the principal's gas bill, then the agent is acting properly. Paying the agent's gas bill with that money, however, would be an abuse of the power (unless the principal was living with the agent perhaps). This example highlights one of the problems with a POA. The agent may have the ability to do things which are, in fact, wrongful. The agent in this example had the power to take money from the principal's account, but not the right to use it for the agent. Unfortunately, the remedy in this situation, when uncovered, is to require the agent to repay the money. Many times, however, sticky-fingered agents are not the type of people with assets to repay the principal with. As such, caution in the use of POA's, and selection of your agent, is warranted.

Powers of Attorney are most often used for two main types of needs: financial and medical. A financial POA can let an Agent have the power to act for you in only one transaction (such as a POA to permit a joint tenant to sign a deed on behalf of the other joint tenant so that all don't have to attend a real estate closing), or the power to broadly handle virtually all of your financial dealings. The terms Limited POA versus General POA are sometimes used to capture the relative breadth of the powers. These titles, however, have no legal meaning, and the terms of the power granted to the agent will be described in the document itself. A medical POA is typically created to provide the power to someone to make medical decisions when you are unable to. If an accident renders you unconscious, and you need a surgical procedure, someone needs to sign the hospital papers. More pressing, however, may be the cases where disease or injury leaves you in a terminal state, unable to communicate, unable to wake up, and unable to get better. A medical POA can grant someone you choose the ability to tell the doctors what to do when you cannot do so yourself.

> ➤ **What can I do with a POA?**

The dealings and transactions which can be effected by a POA are broad and deep, covering virtually all aspects of routine life. Some typical examples include power to:
1. Make limited gifts to family members to secure the annual gift tax exclusion
2. Make unlimited gifts to anyone
3. Create a trust to benefit the Principal
4. Make additions to an existing trust for the Principal's benefit
5. Claim an elective share of the estate of a deceased spouse
6. Disclaim any interest in property
7. Renounce fiduciary positions

8. Withdraw and receive the income or corpus of a trust
9. Authorize admission to a medical, nursing, residential or similar facility and to enter into agreements for care
10. Authorize medical and surgical procedures
11. Engage in real property transactions
12. Engage in tangible personal property transactions
13. Engage in stock, bond and other securities transactions
14. Engage in commodity and option transactions
15. Engage in banking and financial transactions
16. Borrow money
17. Enter safe deposit boxes
18. Engage in insurance transactions
19. Engage in retirement plan transactions
20. Handle interests in estates and trusts
21. Pursue claims and litigation
22. Receive government benefits
23. Pursue tax matters
24. Make an anatomical gift of all or part of the Principal's body
25. Appoint the Agent's own successor or successors
26. Make any health care decisions
27. Make anatomical gifts, dispose of the remains and consent to autopsies
28. Make health care decisions that conform to the Agent's assessment of the Principal's preferences and values, including religious and moral beliefs.
29. Act as formal Guardian if a court finds the need to appoint one.

Can you think of more? If a transaction you could reasonably contemplate is not within the specific list authorized in your state, then you may need to work a bit more with your attorney to find a 'work-around' to get the job done. Most times, however, the statute is broad enough to address your reasonable needs. The POA can be a very powerful tool, as you can see. That doesn't mean that you must use it to permit an agent to handle all of these tasks for you, but you can, and many choose to use it that way, provided that they have a very trustworthy agent to appoint.

➢ Who can sign a POA?

Any adult can execute a POA. Generally, a sworn or notarized signature is not a legal requirement, but many financial institutions feel more comfortable honoring a POA with a sworn and witnessed signature. In fact, many such institutions would prefer that you use their own form to designate an agent who will be dealing with them. Further, if the agent is going to deal in transaction which would require a witnessed and/or sworn signature (such as real estate dealings), then the POA may need to be executed with properly conforming formalities. If the principal is unable to sign, many states permit another person to sign it for them, provided that it is adequately witnessed and at the direction of the principal. Pennsylvania, for example, distinguishes a Financial POA (which can be signed by someone else as a convenience to the principal) from a Health Care POA (which can be signed by someone else only if the principal is unable to sign it). Execution formalities for a POA should be carefully followed in order to assure that it has the intended legal effect, and to prevent mischief and worse which can arise from loose POA practices.

➢ Who should be my agent?

Selecting an agent is a critical component of an effective and useful POA, whether medical or financial. You need to select someone with the best of the following qualities:
1. Trustworthy, to protect your interests
2. Intelligent, enough to understand what is necessary to make decisions
3. Interested, so they are willing to execute the duties of an Agent
4. Decisive, and able to make the decisions necessary
5. Educated, at least enough to make informed decisions for you
6. Like-minded, so as to make decisions in a way you would like, and
7. Any other quality you consider important.

You may find it appropriate to appoint an alternate and/or successor agent, in the event that the first agent is either unable or unwilling to continue as your agent. This permits the alternate to step into the role without the need for a new POA being prepared and signed, which is especially important during periods of your own disability or incapacity. You can even appoint more than one agent to have the POA at the same time, stating in your POA whether you want them to be able to act individually or to require their joint agreement before they can take any action on your behalf.

> **When should the POA take effect?**

When you need a Power of Attorney, you want to have one available. You do not, however, want someone using a POA to monkey with your affairs while you are still fully capable and desirous of handling them yourself. Several different drafting tools and techniques are available to help you find the balance which works for you.

The most strident POA is a Durable POA. Traditionally, a POA became ineffective if the Principal was incapacitated or incompetent. This had the advantage of decreasing the likelihood of an Agent misappropriating funds, but also led to POA's becoming ineffective precisely when the principal most needed the help. A Durable POA is drafted to defeat this problem, using language which makes is clear that the power survives even when the principal is disabled or incapacitated. (Many laws speak in terms of ' incompetency', but the more polite phraseology of 'incapacity' is considered better form in most instances). In no event, however, can a POA continue to be valid after the principal's death (except in minor circumstances, such as the ability to specify how to handle organ donation, or decline an autopsy).

Instead of a Durable POA, some people have used a Springing POA, or a Contingent POA. When a principal is concerned about placing so much power currently in the hands of an agent, the POA can be drafted so that it only becomes effective when the principal is incapacitated. This has the benefit of avoiding the temptation to mischief or malevolence that a Durable General Financial POA can bring. The drawback to this, however, is the difficulty in determining when the POA is effective. How is a bank or car dealer to know that the agent now has the power of the principal, if they don't know whether the principal is incapacitated? Who decides if the power is ready to be invoked? Thus, while this is a reasonable way to limit the harm an Agent can cause, it can also impair the efficiency and efficacy of the POA. Some attorney include language that the POA springs to life when the principal's doctor certifies that the principal is incapacitated, so those dealing with the agent can know whether or not it has sprung. This assumes, of course, that your doctor is willing to do this in the first place.

Another method for controlling the general POA is to place the POA in escrow. This process involves executing a durable power of attorney, but not giving it to the agent. Instead, the POA is given to someone else to hold onto until they agree that you are incapacitated or otherwise in need of the benefit of the POA. Thus, when the agent and the custodian of the POA have agreed that it is time to let the agent act for you, the durable POA is provided to the Agent. This prevents the Agent from being tempted to use the POA while you are handling your own affairs, but does not delay the use of the POA when it is needed, so long as your chosen custodian and the agent can agree. For example, you name your son as your agent under the POA, but your daughter holds onto the document until they both agree it is time to use it for your benefit. Alternatively, many people leave the signed POA with their attorney, and direct their agent to get it from the attorney when the circumstances warrant it.

➢ When does the POA end?

A limited POA is self-terminating usually, and is only effective so long as the described event for which it is designed is ongoing. A Durable General POA, however, can continue throughout your entire lifetime. If the POA states a time period during which it is valid, then it terminates at the expiration of that time. If the agent dies or refuses to serve as agent, and no successor is named in the document, then the POA is terminated. If a court-appointed guardian is selected to oversee the affairs of the person or finances of an incompetent person, the guardian will likely have the power to terminate the POA if it deems appropriate too.

The POA is terminated upon the death of the principal, in all but a few limited circumstances. Under many state laws, the POA can be used by the agent to authorize organ and tissue donation after your death. In addition, if the agent doesn't know that the principal has died, then the agent's actions may still be binding on the estate of the deceased principal.

The principal can always revoke the power at any time, for any reason. If, however, a third party is dealing with your agent, and reasonably is ignorant of the fact that you have terminated the POA, your former agent's actions may still be binding. You should make sure to contact the agent and anyone the agent has dealt with when you terminate, or even modify, a POA.

Finally, if your spouse is your agent, divorce actions typically revoke the POA. This is appropriate due to the antagonistic position of a divorce, which is inapposite to the fiduciary duties between an agent and principal. Some states consider a divorce filing to break the POA, while others await a final decree or interim order to have that effect, so you need to know which law applies in your situation.

> ➤ **How would a POA help me?**

Some people question why they need a POA, since they are able to handle their own affairs. The whole point of a POA, however, is that there may be a time when your affairs need handled, and you won't be able to do so. The table below discusses just a few of the circumstances where a POA would prove useful.

If you are….	…and this needs to be done…
Unconscious following an accident	A check signed to pay taxes on your house
In a coma	Your income tax returns need to be

	signed
Suffering dementia	An annual gift to your children
Incarcerated	Sign papers to admit you to long term care
Affected by Alzheimer's disease	Redeem a bond in your safety deposit box
Traveling abroad	Sell shares of stock in a troubled sector
On a long cruise	Appoint a trustee for your Living Trust
Chronically depressed	Sign your Social Security or Pension check
Aging but still able to manage your affairs	Your child wants to declare a Guardian for you against your wishes

These are just a few examples, but if you can imagine yourself in any of the conditions on the left, needing to take the steps on the right, then a POA will let your agent handle that for you. A POA is frequently advised for anyone with property or income to manage, and especially if there is any likelihood that health problems in the years ahead may make it difficult for you to handle your own affairs.

HEALTH CARE PROXIES AND LIVING WILLS

Headline-making cases over the years keep drawing our attention back to a shared fear of dying slowly. Karen Quinlan became unconscious after a party, and entered a persistent vegetative state. After spending months on life support systems, her family sought to discontinue the care to permit her to pass on. The health care facility refused to honor her parent's wishes, leading to a protracted and public legal battle. Ms. Quinlan's parent's ultimately won their case, and the life support system was removed. Interestingly, Ms. Quinlan nevertheless survived almost 10 more years in a coma before ultimately suffering pneumonia which took her life. Nancy Cruzan was another unfortunate woman, and a prominent case in the right-to-die movement. A car accident left her in a persistent vegetative state, and the hospital would not remove her feeding tube when the parents sought to enforce her prior verbal instructions to them on the issue. The case went to the United States Supreme Court after years of litigation. When the parents were ultimately able to provide 'sufficient' evidence of Ms. Cruzan's wishes for care in this type of event, her feeding tube was ultimately removed, and she shortly passed on.

More recently, Terri Schiavo lingered in a persistent vegetative state for years as her husband fought her parents over whether Mrs. Schiavo would have wanted to continue life-prolonging measures under these conditions. Who should the hospital and doctor's listen to in these situations? State and federal authorities, along with physicians and hospital personnel, injected themselves into the case and controversy over a 7 year period. Even President Bush got involved in 2005, signing legislation drafted to address her case. Her family battled through 14 appeals, five lawsuits, 4 requests for hearing by the United States Supreme Court, thousands of public news articles taking various stands on the issues, and more before her life support was ultimately removed in March of 2005. She died less than two weeks later.

Regardless of how you feel about the facts and positions of the parties involved in any of these cases over the years, perhaps the most important thing that we can take away from them as people with a mind to estate planning is this: You can spare your family the trauma, confusion, hostility and regret of making a decision about how to take care of you if you are permanently unconscious or terminally ill, simply by preparing ahead with a Health Care Proxy and a Living Will.

A Health Care Proxy is a type of power of attorney executed by a person (the principal), which authorizes a designated person to act as their agent and make various types of medical decisions for the principal if the principal is somehow unable to do so themselves. This type of document may have many different names, including a Health Care Power of Attorney or a Health Care Surrogate

Designation. The title doesn't matter. Instead, what is important is that you identify someone who can make binding decisions on your behalf, in the event you are unable to do so. Not all of these decisions will be life-or-death in nature. Even routine matters such as whether you would like a private room, which facility you should be taken to for care, or which doctor you would like to be involved in your care can be made by your agent. This document gives the physicians and health care professionals a single authority to whom they can reliably turn for decisions, permitting your treatment to move forward in a faster, more efficient fashion, and in a manner which comports which the decisions you would likely make if you were able.

Each state has their own rules regarding how such a health care proxy is to be executed. Most states are not as strict about them as they might be for other legal documents, and often they only need to be signed and dated. The mistake most often made is simply the failure to execute one until it is too late. health care proxies and living wills can't help you and your family at the time they are needed most, unless you take the time to execute them before they are needed most.

LIVING WILLS

The companion document to a health care proxy should be a Living Will. A living will permits you to identify in advance how you would like identified health care issues to be handled, in the event that you are unable to provide "informed consent" about care decisions because you suffer a terminal disease or condition or are permanently unconscious. This document may also be called an Advance Directive. If you don't make these decisions in advance about how to direct your care when you are in the most serious of incapacitating states, then the doctors must try to get decisions from your family. As the Shiavo, Cruzan, Quinlan and other cases have taught us, that is a wrenching process, and may not reach the outcome that you would have desired. Instead, you can cut through the confusion, and specify your wishes, in writing, in advance.

Every state has its own legislation to deal with this topic. Pennsylvania's is fairly typical. Your advance directive here is a legal document, and the physician's involved with your care must either respect your wishes, or transfer your care to a doctor willing to do so. This is to avoid a situation where you might be willing to let go of any fragile strands you have holding you to this world, but the physician feels a duty to keep your body going by any available methods, regardless of the personal, let alone financial, costs.

Once signed, a copy of your living will should be given to your doctor, at least one close family member, and any proxy or agent you have identified in the health care proxy. If you are admitted to a hospital or nursing home, they must ask you if you have prepared a living will, and you should give them a copy. It is important that these people know the existence of your living will, as it is not binding on someone if they don't have reason to know that it exists.

Some people get concerned that a living will is an open invitation for a hospital or greedy heir to 'pull the plug' prematurely on someone. Physicians, however, are never in a rush to implement life-ending decisions under a living will, and the document doesn't even become effective until your doctor certifies that you are (1) incompetent, i.e. unable to make or communicate decisions about your health care, AND (2) you are either in a state of permanent unconsciousness or in a terminal condition. Further, a second physician must agree that condition (2) is satisfied. As such, there is little risk of a premature implementation of a living will, but a great likelihood that its existence will bring greater peace to the patient and family if the need to consult a living will arises.

There is no specific limit as to the types of medical care which you can specifically request, or decline, in your living will. The question is a highly personal one, and goes to the issue of how much work do you want to go into keeping you alive if you are incapacitated and permanently unconscious or dying. Some examples commonly listed for consideration include: cardiac respiration, mechanical respiration, feeding/water tubes, blood products or transfusions, surgery, kidney dialysis, and even antibiotics. Many people simply conclude that once they reach this serious stage where a living will becomes effective, then they just want to be kept comfortable, and let go. A valid living will empowers you to make this happen.

Note that a living will isn't cut in stone. You can modify, or revoke, a living will at any time. There are no specific formalities to revoke one in most situations, but instead you only need to communicate it to your attending doctor, a health care provider, or even just a trusted witness. You don't even have to be fully competent to revoke a living will; the law wants to err on the side of any expressed desire to live, even if a fully competent person might have wanted to continue the living will. In addition, if you are a woman who is pregnant when a living will would become effective, the doctors may continue your care if it is likely to lead to a successful birth, though the state has to pay for this continued care.

Best practices? Execute a Living Will and appoint a Health Care Proxy, inform your primary care physician by giving them a copy, inform your Proxy and give them a copy, and let other close family members know what you have done, and where you keep the original documents in the event that they need to access them. It isn't a fun topic to deal with, but for very little time and money, you may spare your family some of the hardest decisions they could be called on to make at a difficult time.

DO-NOT-RESUCITATE/CODE BLUE ORDERS

There is one group of health care workers who usually do not have the opportunity to see a living will, and that is the paramedics and emergency medical service providers (EMS). Because these professionals are called to the scene at a time of crisis, and are not usually in a position to determine the existence or applicability of a living will, they are permitted to treat an EMS patient in accordance with their typical life-saving protocols. This may, however, be counter to the wishes of a terminal patient, such as one undergoing Hospice care at home. To remedy this situation, many states have passed Do-Not-Resuscitate statutes. Pennsylvania's is now the Out-of-Hospital Nonresuscitation Act. These acts typically provide that if a person has executed a living will, is suffering a terminal condition, and doesn't want CPR from any EMS workers if they suffer cardiac/respiratory arrest, to obtain an order from their doctor confirming their wishes. Proof of a valid Do Not Resuscitate order, approved by a physician, is typically given to the EMS workers by way of a DNR bracelet or necklace. This necklace or bracelet will include the patient's name, the name and signature of the doctor approving the DNR order, and the date it was signed. In most other respects, a DNR order is treated the same as a living will, described above.

NURSING HOME PLANNING

Many of us fear it, and many of us don't want to think about it, but the possibility of spending time in a nursing home as we age is substantial. Nearly everyone can expect to experience at least a period of temporary disability at some time in their life. According to the National Center for Health Statistics, the number of residents in nursing homes grew from about 1.1 million in 1973 to 1.6. million in 1999. Paying for this type of care is a major concern of many clients seeking estate planning advice, and with good reason. Medicare only covers short stays in a nursing home (typically 90 days), and Medicaid only pays for nursing home care for those which have become impoverished under Medicaid regulations. Medicaid and Medicare together cover the majority of the expense for approximately 70% of the people admitted to nursing homes. Long term care can pay some or all of these expenses, if you have planned ahead and purchased such coverage, however this coverage is expensive, and its quality and benefit levels vary greatly. If you don't fit into one of these categories for payment, then nursing home care comes out of your pocket, your assets. With the average nursing home cost running between $7,000 and $8,000 per month, it is easy to see why so many of us fear paying for nursing home care. But do not lose hope, as there are options to discuss.

➤ What is Long Term Care?

First, it is important to understand the nursing home beast, before we can conquer it. If you mention nursing home care to someone, they immediately think of an elderly person spending years of their life languishing in a wheelchair parked in the corner of a room. Statistics show us, however, that most people (over 70%) are in a nursing home for less than three years, and 42% are there for less than one year. This is because nursing homes aren't necessarily someplace the elderly are just sent to die. Instead, the trend in this field is shorter stays, with the goal of returning people to their homes or other locations where less focused care and attention is required, such as assisted living or home-based care.

There are different types of long term care which a person might need in their lifetime. A person may need assistance with the activities of daily living (bathing, dressing, eating), health care in their home, care to recover from a heart attack or stroke, monitored and structured activities in an adult day care, assistance with some, but not all, daily activities in an assisted living facility, or near-the-end care and support through hospice care. Someone with physical disabilities are more likely to need medically trained support working with them on a daily basis, while mental and cognitive impairments like dementia or Alzheimer's disease may need care focused more on support, protection and supervision.

➤ How expensive is Long Term Care?

The costs of long term care increase every year. Getting accurate numbers is difficult, due to differing levels of care and service from a facility, patient needs, and geographic differences in pricing. For the purpose of getting your arms around your planning needs, however, some rough numbers will suffice. Nursing home care will likely cost around $85,000 per year. Assisted Living facilities cost around $35,000 per year. Part time basic home health care can be expected to run about $25,000 per year. Round-the-clock home health care is much more expensive, varying widely depending upon the level of care required. Statistically, more women than men end up in nursing homes, and for longer periods. One reason is simply women's' longer life expectancy. Further, they are more likely to be left alone due to the death of a spouse, which is a critical factor leading to nursing home stays. Nevertheless, paying the bills for nursing home stays is a significant concern for aging men and women. What options are available to shoulder these expenses?

LONG TERM CARE INSURANCE

Undertaking to pay for long term care in the United States falls mostly on the shoulder of the individual. If you have the money to pay the bills, you do. If not, you go broke trying, and only then does Medicaid pay. Not much of a system. Recognizing the growth in the number of citizens over 65 in the U.S. in the coming decades, and the longer lives which we enjoy the benefit of living, the insurance industry has been increasing its efforts to make available and encourage long term care insurance. This insurance will cover some or all of the expense of long term care which isn't otherwise covered by health insurers or Medicare.

Unlike many other insurance products, long term care insurance is not uniform from insurance company to insurance company, and all companies are not equally strong, so if you decide that long term care insurance may be appropriate for you, you still need to use caution to identify the proper company, product line, and benefit level which is best for you.

A common concern among elder law clients is the preservation of their lifetime of assets, and the prospect of seeing their collected wealth reduced, or entirely consumed, by Medicaid in order to pay for nursing home care is a tangible one. Such impoverishment can harm the health, longevity and lifestyle not only of the nursing home patient, but also their spouse and their children, which are deprived of support or an inheritance which might otherwise have been available. Other clients considering LTC insurance hope that having a private source of funding a nursing home stay will increase their options and ability to get into a 'nice' home. This concern stems from complaints from home operators that they lose money treating Medicaid patients, and that they cannot 'evict' a Medicaid patient except under stringently regulated circumstances. Thus, a prospective resident with insurance may indeed seem more welcome in a facility which has spent its own resources to remain modern.

The current generation of long term care insurance products has evolved beyond simple nursing home care. Home care, adult day care, assisted living, and part time nursing care are all likely to be available for reimbursement. The typical policy provides for a certain daily rate of benefits payable, and a threshold where benefits run out. For example, a policy might pay up to $150.00 per day, for a maximum period of 3 years. Such coverage, however, does not come cheap. It is not uncommon to see premiums of several thousand dollars per year or more for the example cited above. Usually rates are cheaper if you buy the coverage when you are younger (say in your 50's) than older (say, in your 70's). Many companies will guarantee, or freeze, your premium against increase for a period of years, though such an option comes at a cost. More important may be to obtain a rider which allows for benefit levels to increase, tied to an index of medical expenses. Otherwise, the $150.00 in coverage you purchase today will pay far less of your nursing home care in 10 years when the expense of nursing home stays increases from $85,000 per year to $175,000. Such riders are often called an 'inflation protection benefit'.

You also should be aware of whether you are purchasing simple or compound inflation protection. These two different methods can yield substantially different benefit levels in the future. Simple inflation protection merely increases your initial benefit level by a set amount each year. If a $100.00 per month benefit has a 5% simple inflation rider, then that benefit will go up 5% each year, measured from the initial benefit, or 50% total after 10 years, for $150.00. Compound inflation protection works like compound interest, in that you get inflation protection measured from the immediately prior year, so the inflation figures build up on one another, or 'compound'. A 5% compound inflation protection on a $100.00 benefit will pay 105.00 in year 2, 110.25 in year 3, and builds thereafter, which with longer periods of time and/or higher inflation rates can lead to significant differences, as the following chart shows:

Inflation's Effect Of Inflation on Cost of Daily Care					
COMPOUND INTEREST					
Inflation Rate	2000	2005	2010	2015	2020
5%	$150	$191	$244	$312	$398
6%	$150	$201	$269	$359	$481
7%	$150	$210	$295	$414	$580
8%	$150	$220	$324	$476	$699
SIMPLE INTEREST					
Inflation Rate	2000	2005	2010	2015	2020
5%	$150	$188	$225	$263	$300
6%	$150	$195	$240	$285	$330
7%	$150	$203	$255	$308	$360
8%	$150	$210	$270	$330	$390

Inflation protection, however, isn't cheap. You can expect it to add 20 to 40% to the annual premium.

As with many insurance products, there is a conflict of interest inherent in the sale of this insurance product, as the salesman may be best served simply by getting you to purchase the product, not by getting you to purchase the best product for you. While the article is dated, there was a report in Consumer Reports magazine in the early 1990's of sending an insurance expert 'undercover', posing as a long term care insurance customer. He saw 14 salesmen representing the largest insurance companies in the field then. He reported that every salesman misrepresented something about the product, the insurer, or the competition. How can you expect to protect yourself? In my experience, the best option is to consult with someone knowledgeable about such insurance who does not have a financial interest in getting you to buy the product. No offense to insurance salesmen, but they are, by definition, there to make a sale. Let an informed and impartial planner or insurance consultant review the product information with you to help you decide what seems best for you.

> ➤ **What should I look for in a**
> **Long Term Care policy?**

The better long term care policies are likely to contain the following features, provided that they are available in your state:

1. Available inflation protection to increase benefit levels
2. Predictable and/or level premiums that don't increase because of inflation or aging
3. Coverage for in-home care
4. Skilled nursing home care coverage
5. Intermediate nursing home care coverage
6. Custodial nursing home care coverage
7. No requirement that you be admitted to a nursing home before you are eligible for home-care benefits
8. No requirement that you be admitted to a hospital before you are eligible for nursing home benefits
9. A Guaranteed renewal provision, regardless of changes in your age or health.
10. Benefits payable at least for a period of one year, or more as you select
11. Elimination period (time before policy begins to pay after care begins) of less than 100 days (i.e. after Medicare is exhausted).
12. Coverage for mental illness, including dementia and Alzheimer's disease
13. Any limitation on pre-existing conditions in coverage expires within 6 months.

While your proposed policy may not contain all of these factors, they are often still available as a rider if you ask the agent involved. You can decide to purchase a policy without any of these features, but you need to know what you are getting, and what you are not. The agent selling you this policy, or trying to, is well paid for doing this job, so don't be afraid to ask him to provide information about the expense of each option you might consider on your policy. Getting proposals from multiple sources is also an excellent idea.

➤ How do I decide whether to buy insurance?

Should you purchase long term care insurance? Like many insurance products, if you need the benefits, you are glad you have them. If you don't, then you feel like you wasted your money. I prefer to look at it as a calculated risk, i.e. if I don't get the coverage, can I live with the possible outcomes? Alternatively, if I do get the coverage, can I afford to pay the premiums, now and in the future? Finally, am I even eligible for the coverage at my current age and health status? Let's look at how to consider these questions.

If you don't get the long term care coverage, then what might happen? One possibility is that you don't need to go into a nursing home at all. You might die without needing those types of care, or you may require care which can be provided by available family or some other support network in your life. This possibility means you did well for yourself: saved the premiums, and didn't have to pay for care. Another possibility is that you need some long term care, which you would have to pay for. Medicare will pay for about 90 days of rehabilitative long term care after a hospital admission, but other than that you may largely be on your own. Many people do find that they are able to be sent back home, with or without family to provide for some of their care needs, at or near that 90 day limit. Even if you needed another month or two of care, that $7,000 to $16,000 or so is likely less than 6 or 7 years of insurance premiums. Finally, you might require extensive long-term care for an extended period, whether two years or ten. Now, you are going to be spending serious money. If you estimate nursing home care to average around $85,000 per year, then you can see these bills adding up. The odds, in my opinion, are in your favor, in that most people don't need this level of care. For this analysis, however, the underlying question is "can you live with that outcome?"

If you have enough assets to pay these bills and still maintain a sufficient lifestyle or inheritance for your loved ones, then I'd suggest you might find you can accept this risk. If you have very few assets to begin with, which this would rapidly consume, then you'd likely end up on Medicaid anyway to pay the bills, and the insurance would be too costly for you to pay for in the first place. If you can't afford to pay an $80,000 nursing home bill from your assets, then why protect your modest assets with thousands of dollars in insurance premiums. Get rid of the assets via attorney-directed planning, and go on Medicaid if you need the care. The difficult case scenario, in my opinion, is the person, or couple, who could probably afford a few years of nursing care, but not necessarily 10 or 15 years, or 8 years for both spouses. Such a situation, with available resources of perhaps $500,000 to $1,500,000, might find it difficult to engage in adequate planning to qualify for Medicaid early on, but also would find their estate completely dissipated by an extended stay. Such people, living in the gap between clearly wealthy and clearly not-wealthy, face the toughest choice in deciding whether to purchase long term care insurance. It requires a balancing of interests, between spending substantial money for security or peace of mind, and preserving their assets in the hope of staying healthy. Remember, however, that long term care insurance isn't a total fix. While 'unlimited' benefits may be available in the marketplace (I've never looked, to tell the truth), most policies with benefit payments for a period of 3 to 5 years are considered pretty good. Thus, your coverage doesn't protect you completely against extended stays: It just cushions the blow substantially.

If you get the coverage, can you afford the premiums? Hopefully, you are considering a level-premium policy, so that your premiums don't rocket out of sight as you get older. Still, you must consider if you are going to have that money to pay the premiums in 10 or 15 years. Otherwise, just as you are likely to need the coverage, you risk seeing the financial need to let it lapse. Will your income level at that time be adequate to make the payments? In my experience, if you can't reasonably afford the premiums, then you can't afford the luxury of long term care insurance. Don't lose hope, however. You simply need to target your focus now on planning to increase your Medicaid eligibility to the earliest reasonably time, using the services of an experienced Medicaid planning attorney.

Finally, are you eligible for long term care coverage? An insurer selling long term care insurance is not required to issue you a policy when you apply. Instead, your medical history is carefully reviewed by the insurance underwriters to determine whether you are an acceptable risk or not. If you already suffer from Alzheimer's disease, or Parkinson's, or other conditions likely to need long term care soon, you probably will not find much available to you in the way of insurance for long term care. This does not mean that you have to be in perfect health when you apply, but the younger and healthier you are at the time of application, the more likely you are to be accepted, and the lower your premiums will likely be. Unfortunately, that also means that you will likely be paying those premiums for a longer period of time before you might expect to be at risk of needing nursing home care. The insurance companies have experienced actuaries (number crunchers) working for them to decide how much they need to charge you, and everyone else, and still make a handsome profit after paying benefits, administrative expenses, sales commissions and the like.

In addition to the financial analysis, you should consider personal factors in your own life. Do you have a spouse who could help care for you if you needed assistance? Is your family in a position, geographically, financially and/or circumstantially, to assist you? How is your health, for your age? What is your family medical history for needing long term care? Do you suffer from any conditions which are reasonably likely to deteriorate significantly, leaving you incapacitated or disabled but not terminal?

> ### What details should I examine
> ### in a policy proposal?

The following chart may help you to organize your thoughts and observations about any long term care policies you are attempting to evaluate.

Factor	My Comments
Strength of Insurer	standardandpoors.com, ambest.com, moodys.com, or written information from the agent

Factor	My Comments
	may suffice
Agent presenting proposal	Don't be afraid to get bids from other agents
Rate Increase History of Insurer	Ask the agent or the State Insurance agency (see appendix)
Benefits for skilled nursing care	How much per day/total payable/how long
Benefits for personal care a/k/a custodial care	How much per day/total payable/how long
Nursing home stays which aren't covered?	Ask agent to point out the exclusions
Limits on which facilities you select	Who picks the facility you can go to?
Home care benefits for: • **Skilled nursing** • **Home health aides** • **Housework assistance** • **Other support services**	How much per day/total payable/how long
Assisted living coverage?	How much per day/total payable/how long
Adult daycare coverage?	How much per day/total payable/how long
Other important coverage?	What is important to you?
Daily benefit Levels • **Skilled nursing** • **Custodial nursing** • **Assisted living** • **Home care**	As of 2009, the average cost of a nursing home stay was approximately $250.00 per day. Assisted living is about half as expensive.
Limits on benefits • **Per year** • **Number of years** • **Lifetime benefits**	The average stay for a person over 65 is about 2 1/2 years. 90% of people over 65 stay less than 5 years in a nursing home. Some people may be in-and-out of nursing homes for various conditions as they age; will the policy treat these separately?

Factor	My Comments
When do you begin to receive benefits? **i.e. doctor certification, admission to facility, limited ability to perform daily activities, prior hospital stay required...**	How does the policy describe what has to happen before the insurer will start to pay the benefits?
Waiting period for benefits to pay after you are eligible? • **Nursing care** • **Home health** • **Assisted living**	How long do you have to pay your own way before the benefits will begin? It should be measured in days or weeks, not months.
New waiting periods when care level changes?	If you go up or down in your care needs, do you have to start a new round of eligibility determinations and delay?
Pre-existing conditions covered/limited/excluded	If they are completely excluded, is the policy going to likely be of use to you?
Inflation protection included in premium? • **Simple or Compound?** • **Using preset number or index?** • **Expected benefit level in 10 years?**	If you are young and healthy enough to get reasonable coverage rates, then it will likely be a long time before you start needing the benefits. What will care cost then? See chart.
Option to increase coverage without physical examination at later dates?	If you decide later to get a higher benefit level, for a higher premium, can you?
Premium in first year • **In 5 years** • **In 10 years** • **In 20 years**	
Premium waiver during benefit receipt?	Will you still have to pay the premiums while you are getting the

Factor	My Comments
• **Nursing care** • **Assisted Living** • **Home health care**	benefits?
Refund of premiums benefit?	If you drop the policy, will you get money back? You likely pay a significant amount for this feature, which may be an unnecessary expense.
Nonforfeiture benefit?	If you can't pay the premiums, can you get a lower level of benefits still? Again, you likely pay a significant amount for this feature, which may be an unnecessary expense.
Coverage for spouse?	A joint policy can be less expensive than two individual policies.
Policy tax-qualified? **Will you reasonably benefit?**	Required for benefits to be tax-free. Also, while there is a tax deduction available for qualified policies, many people can't use it because it counts as a medical expense (over 7.5% of Adjusted Gross Income required), and the amount deductible may be limited.
Discounts available?	It's always worth asking!

There is no easy answer to whether you should purchase long term care insurance, but investigating the factors discussed herein can at least help you make an informed decision, rather than one based on ignorance or fear.

MEDICAID: NURSING HOME/LONG TERM CARE BENEFITS

For individuals requiring long term care in a nursing home environment, Medicaid is the dominant payer. Also known as Medical Assistance, Medicaid is provided for people with low incomes, and very low levels of available assets, as well as to the blind, disabled workers, or orphans. Nursing homes prefer 'private pay' residents, because they can charge them a higher rate; however government payments are the bread and butter of most nursing homes. To qualify for Medicaid coverage, you will need to demonstrate that your income and asset levels are sufficiently low that the government has to step in to cover your bills. This rescue, however, may come at the expense of a lien against remaining assets which you hold onto, which will have to be used to repay the government after your death. For some, these restrictions can be worked around, but the earlier planning is done in this regard, the better.

> ## ➢ Who can get Medicaid to pay for long term care?

Medicaid will only provide payments if your income is below a certain level, which changes annually. Pennsylvania, for example, states that all of your monthly income, minus a $65 allowance you can keep, has to be paid towards your nursing home care. You must also have assets, called countable resources, of less than around $2,400. The secret to being on Medicaid, and not being impoverished, is to have your assets fit within the exclusions to what are considered countable resources, and get as much of the rest out of your hands using methods which Medicaid won't penalize, or won't penalize much, well before you may reasonably need the nursing home benefits.

Examples of excluded resources include term life insurance policies, modest whole life insurance policies, an automobile (even a very nice one!), prepaid funeral/burial accounts, and your home (equity limited to $500,000 to $750,00). Other exclusions can be found in the value of personal effects and furnishings, jewelry, business property, some (few) trusts, spousal retirement accounts, and a spousal resource allowance (a moderate sum, usually less than $110,000 of joint assets, which the spouse of the applicant can set aside to avoid spousal impoverishment). Joint property is considered as the asset of the Medicaid applicant, unless you can establish the contribution of the other owner, so just listing your child on your deed isn't going to shelter property from Medicaid.

When you are the beneficiary of a trust established by someone else, the issue of whether your trust fund will count as an asset precluding Medicaid eligibility gets tricky. In a nutshell, if the trust makes it clear that (1) you are not entitled to demand such benefits as you desire, and (2) the benefits are intended by the settlor to supplement, not duplicate or replace, any government assistance benefits, your chances of successfully arguing that the assets are not a countable resource is greatly improved. Otherwise, Medicaid can argue that you can and should use the trust assets before government assistance is sought.

Without good advice from an estate planner who understands Medicaid well, you can easily get yourself disqualified from Medicaid nursing home benefits for quite a long time. As an oversimplified example, if you gave $120,000 to your son as a 'gift', or to 'hold onto for you', and nursing home care costs around $6,000 per month in your state, the state agency can disqualify you for benefits for a period of 20 months (120,000 / 6,000 = 20). In days of old, the penalty months started to expire when the gift was made.

More recent changes have made the penalties more burdensome, and often start the months of ineligibility from the date when you apply for and need the benefits. Under this newest approach, your 'penalty months' do not start to expire until you are in a nursing home and eligible for Medicaid otherwise (i.e. impoverished), so you don't serve your penalty time until you desperately need the benefits. There is a 'look back' period, which specifies how far back Medicaid will look to see if assets were disposed of by you for less than fair market value (gifts, or discounted transfers). As of 2006, the look-back period was extended to 5 years! If you dispose of assets for less than fair market value less than 5 years before you need to go into a nursing home, you are in danger of being assessed penalty months by Medicaid. Professional guidance is most highly suggested.

Medicaid agencies will seek repayment from any legally available assets in a nursing home benefits recipient's estate following their death. Substantial limitations and exclusions to this right are contained in the laws of many states, and vary based upon the timing, title and transfer method of the assets in question. For example, Pennsylvania limits its estate recovery efforts to the assets in the probate estate, so proper planning can get assets outside the reach of the estate recovery program.

> ## ➤ Planning can increase your Medicaid eligibility

So, is planning for Medicaid nursing home benefits a useless gesture? Not by any means. Quite to the contrary, it can be an effective way to secure the family fortune stays in the family. It does, however, call for creative, but not crazy, planning techniques. Examples which have been successful include:

- ➤ Making gifts or discounted transfers years before nursing care may reasonably be required.
- ➤ Timing the taking out of a loan shortly before applying for benefits, to increase assets set aside for a spouse not in a nursing home
- ➤ Paying down mortgage debt,
- ➤ Investing in needed home repairs at the proper time
- ➤ Funding trusts for blind or disabled children
- ➤ Properly timed and drafted 'income only' discretionary trusts
- ➤ Annuity purchases which provide income to you within permitted levels
- ➤ Annuity purchases which provide spousal support income within permitted levels

Medicaid planning is a classic example of an area where your planning lawyer can provide crucially valuable advice to help you maximize the value of your life's savings, while at the same time maximizing your eligibility for these valuable government benefits. Do not try to engage in Medicaid planning on your own. Instead, consult an attorney who practices in this area.

All of us will continue to experience highs and lows as we journey through our lives. The assistance of an effective planning attorney can help to smooth out the roughest spots for you, taking advance steps to minimize the harmful effects on you, your family, your business, and your assets.

MOVING ON...

Now that we've looked at steps you can take to make yourself look poor to the government, let's examine the use of life insurance to efficiently increase the wealth you leave for your family.

CHAPTER 9

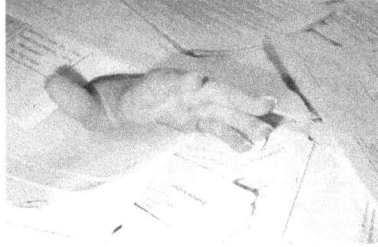

LIFE INSURANCE: THE GREATEST GIFT?

Understanding How To Harness The Power of Life Insurance To Secure Your Estate

---

Life insurance is a topic which almost everyone must confront, so we might as well be able to laugh about it and then move forwards. Life insurance has the ability to bring large sums of money to its beneficiaries at a time when it is likely needed and appreciated. Unfortunately, it is also a complex yet boring field, wherein the possible insurance products seem endless, the explanations are frequently hazy, and the sales tactics have, at time, varied from 'high pressure' to 'downright fraudulent'. Nevertheless, there are a plethora of useful insurance products, and helpful, honest insurance agents. I suggest that clients first develop an understanding of what type of insurance needs they might have, and how they might fill them, before they invite the agent into their home. Today, you can even buy insurance directly from companies on the internet, saving time and hassle, though without the benefit of the information an experienced agent may provide. Hopefully we can make some progress here, because in my opinion, life insurance may be one of the greatest gifts you can make. You pay for it all, and the beneficiary reaps the windfall from the tragedy of your death. I don't know anyone who was ever ungrateful to be the beneficiary of a life insurance policy.

In discussing life insurance, several key considerations are:
1. What type of insurance to purchase
2. What is the insurance for
3. Who should be the 'owner' of the policy
4. Who should be the beneficiary

TYPES OF LIFE INSURANCE

Whenever the discussion turns to life insurance, it is important to distinguish the two main types: Term, and Whole Life. All of the other products and options you hear about are variations on these two themes. Term Life policies are the least expensive and easiest to understand. You pay your annual premium. If you die, the insurance company pays the benefit. If you don't, the company just keeps your money, and then you can do it again the next year, and on and on it repeats. Whole life policies are more complex, and require more cash paid up front, but contain the benefit of building value. Essentially, the insurance company takes your whole life premiums, uses a portion of them to cover the expense of Term insurance on your life, and uses the rest to fund investments which it holds onto for you. Oh, and it pays s decent commission to the agent who sells you the policy. Still, at the end of the day, if you live a while, a whole life policy still has money for you in something akin to an investment account, which will continue to grow tax free, while a term policy will not.

There are advantages and disadvantages to both types of insurance. Boiled down, term insurance is cheaper to purchase at the beginning, but gets more expensive and then runs out at the end of the 'term'. Whole life insurance consumes far more cash, but builds value for you, and has tax-advantaged saving features.

USES FOR LIFE INSURANCE

Life insurance can serve several important functions. You may wish to consider which of these, or others, is applicable to your life as you consider how much insurance, or which type, to purchase.

1) Replace Income from family wage earner: When the primary income producer for the family dies, turmoil almost inevitably ensues. Families wonder what they will do in the long run, and what are they going to do right now, to get by. These needs need to be met as part of your plan.

2) Payment of Estate Taxes: for an estate where taxes are reasonably expected to be due, insurance may be a useful method to generate cash to pay them. Many people forget that estate taxes are due, in cash, within 9 months of the death. If a substantial portion of your estate is not in easily marketed products (cash, stable stocks, redeemable bonds, etc), then your heirs might have to do a 'forced sale' of estate assets to generate this money. Such rushed sales are unlikely to generate a Fair Market Value return for the value of some of the assets. Instead, a life insurance policy can be purchased to cover these expected expenses, and conserve your estate for your heirs.

3) Payment of death related expenses: It isn't always cheap to die in America. Funeral costs, unpaid medical bills, burial expenses and the like can quickly eat up a chunk of your estate. Moreover, they reduce the cash available for your family. Insurance can accommodate these needs.

4) Providing liquid assets to estate: Many a family business owner has children who do want to take over the business, and those who don't. Some people have a child who wants to keep the old family homestead or mansion. To be fair to your heirs who do not participate in ownership of such assets, you can leave life insurance proceeds to fill their share, or to permit them to buy each other's ownership shares outright.

5) Income to you: Whole life policies, which build value over time, can be used as either a savings vehicle, or to generate annuity-like income to you in your retirement.

6) Fund charitable bequest: Many people need their insurance during their lifetime, but find that at death, it will not be needed for their estate. Thus the plan may provide a vehicle to transfer this asset to a worthy charity.

The function of life insurance in your estate may fit into these categories, or others as well.

WHO IS THE POLICY OWNER

Every life insurance policy is 'owned' by someone. Many people wrongly assume that the policy owner is the person whose life is insured. That is frequently the default position for a life insurance contract, if no estate planning has taken place. With a bit of forethought, however, you may find that someone else should be the owner of the policy on your life, and perhaps you the one on theirs too!

For purposes of taxation, several principles about ownership come into play. First of all, the value of the death benefits paid by the policy is included in the estate of the 'owner', not the beneficiary. If you own your own insurance policy, payable to your spouse, then she receives the insurance benefits income tax free, but the value of those benefits is a portion of your estate. Because those benefits pass to your spouse, they will enjoy the unlimited marital deduction. Now, however, your wife's estate is that much bigger than it already was, and those benefits will become taxable when they pass on her death to her heirs.

If, however, your children, or a trust, 'own' your life insurance policy, then on your death, the benefits are a part of your children's 'estate', not yours, and thus are not subject to estate tax at your death nor your spouse's. We will discuss below one of the well established tools for effecting this savings, the Irrevocable Life Insurance Trust.

You can change the name of the owner of a policy which is already in effect, but care must be taken. If you transfer ownership to another, you have given them an item of substantial value. 'Give' = gift, and gift = gift tax liability, unless care it taken to mold your gift within an applicable exclusion. Note that the creation of a new policy, naming someone else as the owner, is not a taxable event, since the brand new policy doesn't have value to be taxed. The other risk in transferring ownership of your policy to others lies principally in the loss of control you suffer. If someone else owns your life policy, they can change the beneficiary, surrender the policy for cash, cancel the policy, let it lapse by nonpayment of premiums, or borrow money against the policy. Thus, care must be taken before transferring ownership to see that the new owner is stable enough to handle this position of trust. Speaking of trust, the Irrevocable Life Insurance Trust (discussed below) can mitigate most of these problems too.

Finally, you should know that if you transfer the ownership of a policy from your name to someone else within three years of your death, then the value of that policy gets pulled back into your estate for tax purposes. This three year pull back is inapplicable in the event a new policy is issued however.

WHO ARE THE POLICY BENEFICIARIES

Every life insurance policy benefits someone when the insured life ends. You might assign the benefits of a policy on your life to your wife, children, charity, estate, or a combination of these and others. Insurance companies will pay the beneficiaries listed in your policy, unless you fail to name any, in which case it will pay your estate. Note that when you get divorced, your policy naming your former wife may, or may not, be changed by operation of law to disinherit her. The best course is to make sure that your policy lists the beneficiaries you actually want to benefit, at all times.

If your listed beneficiaries are already dead, then the benefits go to your alternate beneficiaries. If you don't name alternate beneficiaries, then the payments would go to your estate. Failing to name alternate beneficiaries can result in the benefits ending up back in your estate, increasing the expense of probate and diluting the asset value. I suggest you always keep your beneficiaries, and alternate beneficiaries up to date as part of an annual "state of the plan" review of your financial planning documents. Remember that you can also leave your benefits to a trust, which may permit you to enjoy a level of control over those assets after your death which you wouldn't otherwise have.

Life insurance is a part of modern life, and a part of many responsible estate plans. If must not be looked at in isolation, however, but instead as one part of your overall plan. Consultation with your planning expert or attorney is often the best way to get to the multiple answers needed to make your best insurance decisions.

IRREVOCABLE LIFE INSURANCE TRUSTS

Q: How do you eat an elephant?
A: One bite at a time. (insert laugh here…)

The awkward, imposing title of this planning tool does a disservice to the incredible value it can provide some people. Any of its key words alone may induce one to turn away. Irrevocable; no one likes the sound of that. Life Insurance; here come the salesmen. And Trusts; snooooze…

Stop. Wake up, and pay attention. If you might have an estate where taxes are an issue, then this is a beast you should really try to tame, because it may have substantial value to you and your family. If you don't have the confidence to attack it, however, you will be inclined to reject the power it brings.

What if I could craft your estate in a way that permitted you to place a virtually unlimited amount of money outside of your estate, free from estate taxes and most income taxes, free from attacks by creditors, impervious to the frittering demands of immature beneficiaries, and still subject to some control by you? Would that be worth tackling a few tough terms? Let's give it a try.

> **Understanding the irrevocable life insurance trust**

So, what is this creature? First, it's about life insurance. This is a way to handle the policy contract, ownership, premiums, benefits and beneficiaries. Second, it is a Trust. In a trust, you don't hold the ownership, nor does anyone else. Instead, it is held in the name of a trust, and controlled by a trustee who you name. We tackle trusts more fully in their own chapter herein. Finally, it is Irrevocable, so once you create it, you can't change its terms or take it back. Except, however, that you may be able to with careful planning, discussed further below. So, it is an Irrevocable agreement to put your Life Insurance into a Trust, in order to get the benefits I described above. Hopefully that is a little easier to digest.

When one of your planning goals is to avoid federal estate tax on the proceeds of a life insurance policy, or policies, creating an irrevocable life insurance trust (ILIT) to own your policies can be the most effective means. They are broadly accepted by planners, attorneys, and the IRS, so long as care is taken to properly draft and implement them. This ILIT utilizes the principal that what you have validly given away should not be considered a part of your estate. Herein, you give your life policy to the trust, or have the trust purchase one with money you have essentially provided. You must technically surrender control over the policy, and revocability of the trust, in order to get the advantage of this tool. All is not lost, however, as you still can provide for adequate protection against changes in circumstances, discussed later.

The trust is funded when you transfer a policy to the trust, or see that one is purchased. For ease of discussion, we'll focus now on a trust set up to purchase a new policy, though the key principles are the same. Further, a new policy cannot be pulled back into your estate if you die within three years of the trust taking ownership, while the transfer of a policy may be confounded this way. The IRS didn't want to see people on their deathbed throwing valuable policies into trusts to shield them from estate tax, and thus the rule. For your new policy, you can give gifts of cash for the beneficiaries to pay the annual premiums. While the gift tax rules provide a $13,000 per person (2009) exclusion from gift taxes, for the purpose of this trust, the limit is also the greater of $5,000 or 5% of the fund per person/beneficiary.

Ordinarily, a gift of money to pay life insurance premiums wouldn't qualify as a gift tax exclusion, because of a requirement that a gift be of a 'present interest', whereas life insurance premiums purchase a 'future interest' in the benefits at death. A gentleman named Crummey battled the IRS in the late 1960's to establish that if you have the beneficiary of a gift to a trust a 'window of opportunity' to take the gift out of the trust entirely, then the recipient of the gift had a 'present interest' in the money, even if the recipient didn't exercise that right. So, in a Crummey trust, you give an amount (let's use $5,000) to the trust for the trust to pay the insurance premiums. The beneficiary of the policy is advised that he can withdraw the $5,000 during a 30 day window that year. The beneficiary understands that if he leaves the money in, the policy will be funded, inuring greatly to his or her future benefit, and thus does not withdraw the money. Instead, the insurance premium is paid by the trustee, and the policy continues, without taxable event.

What if the beneficiary is rash and decided to withdraw the money during his 30 day window? The good news is that it almost never happens. If it does, the trust only has to provide the beneficiary with the current year's gift ($5,000 in our example), not prior years' amounts, thus limiting the damage which can be wrought. You can always go ahead and make the payment yourself in such circumstances to keep the policy 'in force' in the worst case scenario, though you may not get the gift-tax exclusion for the amount of the premium that year, while you get your beneficiary 'back on target' regarding the goal of your trust.

You can specify in your trust document who you wish to serve as the trustee. Your spouse can serve, though that increases the risk of the trust being attacked, and results in any income from the trust being imputed to you for tax purposes. Since the trusts purpose, however, is not to produce income but instead to hold premium gifts briefly and then pay for the policy, income taxes shouldn't be an issue. You must provide for the trustee and any successors in the initial trust document, and those cannot be changed at a later date.

The ILIT tool can be used with virtually any of the life insurance products sold, whether from the term or whole life families, or the numerous products within and between. In order to avoid the three year pull-back rule discussed above, it may be best to have the policy purchased initially by the trust in your name, rather than transferring the policy over, just in case you die within 3 years. If, however, there are enough financial incentives attached to the current iteration of a policy you own, transfers into a trust can be reliably made. Further, the trust can provide that if the pull-back event occurs, then the proceeds will be held for the surviving spouse, which will keep them tax free until the surviving spouse later dies with them as a part of his or her estate.

When you arrange for this type of insurance policy, care should be taken in completing the forms. It is important that the insured person not fill out the application as the owner; instead, the trust must be named as the owner. The insurance company will permit you to undergo the necessary physical examination in order to ensure insurability and determine the precise rate before the formal policy application is set, so as to permit your trust document to properly reflect what the policy, and trust, provisions will be. If the insurance company insists on payment of the premium with the application, then you must get the trust document signed in advance so that the trustee can open a checking account from which to draw the premium, and notify the beneficiaries of their Crummey rights to withdraw the premium instead, prior to payment of the premium. Remember that the trustee, in the capacity of trustee of the ILIT, must sign the application as owner/applicant, not you.

Finally, this 'irrevocable' trust has one last failsafe. The trust is irrevocable, but the insurance policy doesn't need to be. In the event that you decide that this arrangement is no longer a viable part of your estate plan, you can cancel the policy. If it is a term policy, then that simply terminates the usefulness of the trust, with no distribution to be made. With a whole life policy, policy value may be returned to the trust, which can be disposed of consistent with whatever wishes you describe at the time of making the trust, though usually such funds are distributed to the ultimate beneficiaries for tax purposes.

Life insurance, in or out of an Irrevocable Life Insurance Trust, is a part of many estate planning discussions. You must decide whether it will be a part of your plan, hopefully with a bit more understanding now about how it works than you had before.

MOVING ON...

Life insurance can achieve multiple important goals in an estate plan, if it is carefully planned, purchased and implemented. Now it is time to take a look at what happens when you ultimately pass on, as we examine how a Will operates in your estate plan.

CHAPTER 10

EXPLORING WILLS

How Your Will Can Work To Protect Your Family And Fulfill Your Estate Goals

WHY DO I NEED A WILL

It is always amazing to me how many otherwise responsible people don't have a Will prepared. Truth be told, I went for many years, even after becoming a lawyer, without signing one. The decision whether to make a will or not essentially comes down to a decision about whether you want to control your estate and affairs, or just leave it up to the government. Hmmmm.

You can use your will to direct what will happen to your property, how to avoid taxes with your estate plan, and who will serve as representatives and fiduciaries of your estate after you pass, as well as to construct trusts which serve your goals for your family, all of which are worthy achievements.

➤ What is a will?

A will is your opportunity to express in a binding legal document exactly how you want property, and some other items, to be dealt with after your death. It provides the plan to guide an executor, and the courts if necessary, regarding what to do to see that your wishes are fulfilled. You can describe who gets your property, what they get, how much they get, how they own it, when they receive it, or even what they can do with it. You can also describe your wishes regarding care of minor children, pets, and more.

First, a few terms are worth describing for clarity in the discussion which ensues. The person who is making the will is called the Testator. When a person dies with a valid will, they are said to die 'testate', and if you die without a valid will executed, then you are 'intestate'. When the testator is dead, they are also the decedent. A gift to someone in the will is called a devise, a legacy, a gift, or a bequest. The person receiving something in the will is called a devisee, a beneficiary, or occasionally a legatee. If you died testate (with a will), the person who will oversee the administration of your will is called the Executor, since they 'execute' your plan. An "heir" is technically a person who would be entitled to your estate if you died intestate, though it is frequently used more loosely to include someone who takes property even under your will. If you die intestate, the court must select a person to implement the state's plan for your estate, typically called an Administrator. If either an Executor or an Administrator is a woman, they become an Executrix or Administratrix, at least in formal days of old. The more modern usage is to dispense with the 'rix' nonsense altogether. Either the Executor or Administrator is frequently referred to as the Personal Representative of the estate. A Codicil is a supplement to a will, used to make minor changes in lieu of executing a new will.

So, a will is a written expression of the testator's intent to distribute property to one or more beneficiaries.

> ➤ **What happens if I don't execute a Will?**

If you die without an executed will, you have abandoned your right to control who gets your property, and all details thereof, in favor of whatever plan the legislature in your state has put in place. This is known as dying intestate, or intestacy. Each state is a little bit different, but the basic outlines are similar.

First, someone has to go to the courthouse to open an Intestate estate, i.e. an estate with no will. The court may have to hold a hearing before it takes the next step of selecting someone to serve as the administrator of the intestate estate. This administrator will take responsibility for overseeing all steps required to implement the intestate succession rules, i.e. the rules about who takes what and how if you are intestate. Almost no tax saving steps are available in this administration, and instead the property is collected, your debts, expenses and taxes all paid, and whatever is left is distributed to your 'heirs at law'. Frequently that means that if you are married with kids, they all get a portion. Married without kids; wife gets it all. Unmarried with kids, the kids get it. Unmarried without kids, parents and/or brothers and sisters get it.

Any property left to a minor will go into a custodial or trust account, which will be overseen by a custodian or trustee selected by the court. Moreover, if no natural custodial parent of your minor children remains, then the court will get to select who looks after their health and safety, and who looks after their money. Please note that all these people selected by the court will be entitled to be paid for their efforts, and paid from your estate or from money which you leave your children, typically at whatever their 'customary and reasonable' rate may be.

So, which sounds better to you; Execution of your plan to distribute your assets in the most tax efficient manner to whomever you select and the manner you choose, overseen by people you know and trust, OR letting the court sort it out under the statutory scheme when you are gone? If you care enough to be reading this, then the question should be rhetorical at best.

> ### ➤ Can I just do it myself?

Yes, Virginia, you can do your own will. The better question is, Why? Because you know more about it than a lawyer? Because it doesn't matter if you get it wrong? Because you want to save a few dollars? Most mistakes which you make in life you will live to be able to live to fix, or at least to apologize. Wills are unique; they don't legally speak until your death, and it would have to be a pretty neat trick for you to come back and fix it then. Your will should be done, and done right by a competent lawyer. If you don't have many assets, then your will should be easy and inexpensive to do. Just because you don't have a lot of money doesn't mean you have to neglect having a crafted plan for what happens after you die.

If you do have enough assets to even consider tax saving techniques, minors trusts, or some of the more involved procedures, then you can afford the miniscule fraction of a percent which a competent lawyer will charge you to do it right. If you have a few million dollars, and spend a few thousand on a decent will and/or trust set of documents, you've spent 1/1000th of the estate value to see that it is protected. Compare that to how much you spend each and every year just to insure the car sitting in your driveway. $500.00 in insurance on a $50,000.00 car (1/100th of value) is ten times more expensive, and you pay it each and every year! A good estate plan, once in place, needs only inexpensive monitoring as your life circumstances change, with changes made when necessary.

I heartily discourage the use of will forms, and internet wills from various web sites. These are usually just form documents, created with absolutely no consideration of your own life and circumstances. You are not a 'form', nor are your family, life and finances. Why should you expect to have a form take care of all of this in a comprehensive fashion? Many times these forms aren't even drawn to satisfy the specific requirements of wills in your specific state. Even the websites which let you 'customize' your documents are, at their best, barely adequate, for one quintessential reason; Confidence. Since you never actually meet with an attorney to explain your situation and goals, and you never meet with an attorney to let them explain to you how your estate planning documents implement your goals in light of your situation, you can never have the confidence that your estate plan does what you want it to. In the face of such a lack of confidence, many people simply don't bother to execute these 'forms', and thus they remain intestate, though with a few less dollars now because of the fees they paid for the forms.

When you hire a lawyer to aid in your estate planning, you are buying more than someone to print a form off of a word processor. You are hiring someone who has taken the time to understand the legal ramifications of wills, trusts, probate, taxes, and other estate planning issues. You are hiring someone who has experience in taking all of these issues, combining them with the facts of your own life and situation, and crafting a plan which works well specifically for you. Perhaps most importantly, you are hiring someone to explain what all of this means to you, what was done, why, and how to implement it now and in the future. Finally, you have hired an expert who can serve as an important resource when you have questions in the future about how life's inevitable changes affect your plan. Over the lifespan of a typical will, a person may get married, have children, get divorced, get an inheritance, purchase or cancel life insurance, get remarried, sign a prenuptial agreement, create retirement accounts, have grandchildren, withdraw from retirement accounts, lose a spouse too soon, become disabled, lose some of their mental or physical faculties, suffer incapacitating illness, and on and on. Our life paths are filled with joys and sorrows, ecstasy and suffering, and many of these have an impact on how we want to plan our future. Wouldn't it be nice to have someone you can call with confidence to answer a quick question about how these changes affect your plan? With a lawyer, that confidence is only a phone call away, and for far less than that insurance on your car for yet another year. Ever try to call a website?

So can you do it yourself? Yes, but then again, you can stitch up your own wounds too, but it isn't recommended. Likewise, I strongly do not recommend that you do it alone. Anyone suggesting otherwise is most likely just finding a way for them to get money out of you themselves by selling you a form or package of forms. Finally, resist the temptation to take advice from other untrained advisors who want to share their 'knowledge' with you. This includes your nosy mother-in-law, your brother who has read a lot on the topic, your coworker who just had their will done, or the friend of yours who knows someone who knows someone that works at the courthouse. I'm not saying that you must ignore them entirely, but don't accept their advice instead of consulting with an attorney. A good attorney can quickly tell you whether what these people are saying makes sense in your situation, or not.

WHAT MAKES A WILL VALID

Preparing the most basic of wills requires few formalities. In most jurisdictions, any document in writing, demonstrating an intent to dispose of property at death, and signed at the end, will do. The most interesting story I heard from the people actually involved was about a couple of attorney who I knew from Pennsylvania. They were on a small chartered plane coming back from the courthouse in another state, and the plane encountered severe turbulence in a thunderstorm. The pilot couldn't get above the storm apparently, and they just had to ride it out. The plane would periodically drop what felt like a hundred feet in a second, and then shoot back up. Both attorneys were green, and scared. When the plane finally landed safely, and they got off the plane, one of the partners noticed a matchbook on the floor. Bending to pick it up, he saw that his fellow partner had written a will on the inside of the matchbook, dated and signed. It didn't say much, but it got the job done. I don't know what was specifically written, but something as simple as "Joe Smith leaves all property to his wife" would do it. This simple language shows whose will it is (Joe's), which property is covered (all property), demonstrates an intent to make a will ('leaves'), and identifies adequately the beneficiary ("my wife"). Signed, dated, and ready to go. It's not a great will, but it's a will.

Traditionally, a will had to be signed at the end. If there was any material part of the will which came after the signature, then the will was invalid. Many states, including Pennsylvania, still require a will to be signed at the end. Modern revisions to the statutes, however, provide that provisions following the signature are merely ignored, rather than serving as a basis to completely invalidate the will.

Some jurisdictions are even less restrictive. In some states, a will needn't be signed if it is in the Testator's own handwriting. Others permit unwritten wills, such a recordings or videos under certain circumstances. Nevertheless, resorting to such extreme practices must be avoided if one it to prudently plan for your estate. The good, old fashioned printed will, signed, dated and witnessed, is the way to go.

WHAT GOES INTO A WILL?

A will typically starts with an exordium clause at the top, which states who the testator is and where they live, makes it clear that this is "my Will", and revokes any prior wills. You want to revoke prior wills explicitly to avoid any unintended contradictions or ambiguities from prior wills or codicils. The will usually then goes on to describe specific bequests, which are items of specific tangible personal property which you wish to leave to someone ('my 2 carat diamond ring I leave to ...'). Alternatively, some wills refer to and incorporate a separate written document you might prepare, and change over time, which is limited to describing which items of tangible personal property go to which beneficiaries. (This document itself will be signed, dated, and may be witnessed.)

Your will should name the executor for your will, who will carry out the will's instructions for distributing your property, creating or funding trusts, and any other instructions. This section will also describe if the executor is to be paid for his efforts, or is expected to do it for free. Make sure that your executor is willing to be your executor before assigning this role, and discuss compensation requirements. There is no sense naming an executor to serve without compensation who is unwilling to do so. All that will do is thwart your efforts to select that executor, and instead a named alternate/successor executor must be appointed if identified in your will, or one selected by the Court if a back-up isn't named. This section should also describe any special powers given your executor, such as whether the executor can sell real estate you own to generate cash for the estate without court approval, and if the executor is excused from filing a bond to secure their faithful execution of the duties of an executor.

This initial material may be followed by the bequests of property to others, creations of trusts, and other actions intended to give your assets to others. The final dispositive paragraph will deal with the residuary estate, which is whatever is left when all of the other bequests identified in your will have been made. This clause typically describes to whom "all the rest and residue" of the estate is to pass.

A will may also exercise a power of appointment, which is essentially when someone has given you use of an asset or property during your life, with the power to appoint in your will to whom it should pass. Frequently, if you fail to exercise this power in your will, then whoever gave it to you in the first place will have specified somebody else to take the property instead when you die. Other times, failure to exercise a power of appointment over an asset leaves it to pass as a part of your estate.

The will may describe how bequests to incapacitated beneficiaries or minors will be handled, whether by trust, custodial arrangement, or otherwise. Trustees, guardians and custodians can be appointed in the will as well.

A will often describes how the debts and expenses of the administration of the estate should be handled, such as which assets the estate should pay them with, or whose assets to use for such purposes before the remaining portion passes to them. Similarly, the taxes which will be due on the estate can be taken from specific assets in the will if it so describes. Otherwise, taxes, and debts and expenses, will be paid from assets in an order described in the probate statutes in that state. For example, if you leave a house, a car, $5,000, a donut shop and an uncut 8 carat diamond, your will can provide that the taxes and expenses should be paid first by the cash, then selling the diamond. If, on the other hand, you really want that diamond to go to your beneficiary, your will can direct that other assets be used first to fund estate obligations if necessary. This is discussed more fully in the chapter on probate proceedings.

Any trusts which you create in your will (called testamentary trusts because they are created in your last will and testament), will be described in detail here. Trusts are discussed more fully in a later chapter in this book.

Your will should have an 'attestation clause', which states, and therefore raises a presumption in your favor in the event your will is challenged, that you did what you had to do to execute the will competently, that the witnesses did what they had to do, and that the will is to be 'self proving'. A self-proving will is one which can be submitted to the court for probate all by itself, without witnesses having to appear to prove that this is the will you signed. In most jurisdictions, the notarized signature of two witnesses on the will, and on the affidavit which establishes that they properly witnessed the signing of the will, is enough to take care of this.

WHAT CAN'T A WILL DO

While the law recognizes the concept of freedom of testament, the freedom to leave your estate as you desire, there are nonetheless some limitations on what you can do with your will. A will cannot change how property is handled which is not part of your probate estate, such as life insurance benefits paid to a beneficiary other than the estate, or property held as a joint tenant with rights of survivorship. Those 'self planned' assets will be governed by their own title or contract.

A will can not readily address the disposition of body organs or tissues for donation, due to the time delay between death and probate, during which these organic materials will be rendered useless. Instead, such matters should be dealt with in a separate writing made known to those close to you, or on your driver's license in many states. A health care proxy or power of attorney might also give someone the authority to make that decision following your death. Similarly, funeral arrangements should be spelled out in a document your family can locate and read before, or right after, your death, whereas a Will is not usually consulted until after the grief of the funeral has subsided.

You cannot disinherit a spouse in most states. You can try to cut your spouse out of your will, but if you do it without their informed consent, the surviving spouse can usually obtain what is known as the 'elective share'. The elective share is describe in the relevant probate statutes in each state, and provides that if a surviving spouse is omitted in a will, disinherited , or even receives only a small portion of the estate, the surviving spouse can 'elect' to take a share of the marital assets and/or probate estate, as described in the statute. The surviving spouse may be able to set aside, or recover, certain types of gifts made by the deceased spouse in the several years before his death, or at least claim a portion of the value of those gifts to be paid from other remaining assets. A typical formula requires the surviving spouse to get at least 1/3 of the assets, but each state sets its own law on this topic. Remember that this only applies when the wife is cut out without her consent. So long as the wife consents to the disposition in the will in a properly signed writing, after full disclosure of the assets she may be giving up, then she can waive her right to claim this elective share. Obviously, an attorney's help is called for in preparing these types of documents.

WHAT CAN I DO WITH MY WILL

Setting aside all the technical information, many people want to know what they can do with a will. Presented with a smorgasbord of options, you can identify the ones you already considered, and also get ideas for some things you never thought of. So, what can you do with a will? Common examples include:

1) Give property to your wife and children
2) Give property to your grandchildren
3) Give property to anyone you want
4) Give property to people to share
5) Give property for someone to use until they die, then send it to someone else

6) Give away your real estate, financial holdings, and tangible personal belongings
7) Donate property to charity
8) Donate property to charity, but provide income for someone else from it
9) Exercise a power of appointment previously given to you
10) Pour over property into a living trust
11) Create a trust to save taxes using the unified credit
12) Maximize the benefit of the marital deduction
13) Create a trust to prevent beneficiaries from squandering their inheritance
14) Create a trust to preserve money for future generations
15) Keep your spouse from giving your assets to a new spouse if they remarry
16) Fund accounts for minor children
17) Disinherit your children or others
18) Provide for children which haven't been born when the will was drafted
19) Identify your executors and their powers
20) Identify trustees
21) Create a trust for virtually any purpose
22) Name proposed guardians to care for your children
23) Identify guardians to care for your children's money
24) Create an QTIP trust to save taxes and limit the risk of your spouse dissipating the inheritance before it passes to your children
25) Enforce a prenuptial agreement
26) Provide for future care of a pet
27) Keep a family owned business going in the family
28) Describe what funds should be used to pay estate expenses and taxes
29) Describe what to do if property in a bequest is no longer in your estate at death.
30) Clarify if someone gets property before or after any loan on it is paid.
31) Provide a trust for disabled or special needs children
32) Penalize greed if someone contests the will
33) Incorporate flexibility for tax planning after your are gone

34) Protect a beneficiary who may be incapacitated when your Will is probated.
35) Avoid complications if you and your spouse die shortly after one another
36) Make almost any personal statements you want
37) Make your will self proving to ease its administration
38) What other ideas might you have about what you'd like to do?

As you can see, the power to create and enforce your wishes in a will can be extremely broad. The more you try to do with a will, the more complex you make your scheme of disposition, the more expensive it will likely be, and all the more care is required to make sure it will do what it is intended to. Nevertheless, the world is your oyster when you begin to plan your will plan. Let's discuss the items identified above.

- **Give property to your wife and children**

If there is a single dominant purpose for most wills, it is likely to pass a person's lifetime accumulation of real estate, financial holdings, personal effects, and anything else to their spouse and/or their children. Recognizing this, anything which you leave to your spouse is free of estate taxes, under the marital deduction. Children don't get the same tax break, but nevertheless are frequent beneficiaries under a will. You can split property between your spouse and children, or even put it all into a trust for them to share equally, unequally, or perhaps based on their individual lifetime needs and desires.

- **Give property to your grandchildren**

Many grandparents want to give something to their grandchildren. People who either dislike or distrust their own children may want to give a lot to grandchildren rather than see their own children destroy the estate's value. Education funding is a common goal, and you can bequeath money into a tax advantaged 529 College Savings Plan, or a prepaid tuition plan, or even into an education trust created in your will or before. Sometimes people give assets to their grandchildren simply because their own children don't need the money. In any event, whenever you have a gift which you plan to use to skip over your children's generation and instead benefit your grandchildren's generation, you risk having your plans altered by the generation skipping tax. The GST, discussed elsewhere in greater detail, basically attempts to tax you twice when you skip down to grandchildren, because the government losses the opportunity to tax the property in the estate of your own children some day. The tax is very onerous, and should be avoided. Fortunately, with the Unified Credit available, gifts to this generation are still very much within the reach of most people planning their estate.

- **Give property to anyone you want**

Testamentary freedom includes the ability to give your estate, or portions thereof, to anyone you want. While the law will not permit you to leave your spouse destitute, or leave minor children without support, you are otherwise largely free to dispose of your estate. Unfortunately, you cannot use this opportunity to thwart creditors to who you owed money at your death, as the creditors have the right to claim payment from your estate before the estate assets are substantially distributed to the beneficiaries. Still, you can give property to friends, neighbors, strangers, lawyers, employees…anyone you want to benefit. I recently read a story about a childless couple who died with about 3 million dollars. They arranged their estate to provide gifts to almost all of the residents of their small community, based upon the nature of their relationship and/or their needs. One family was able to save a farm from foreclosure, a young man went to college as the couple intended, the church got enough to secure a mortgage for the balance of its new construction needs, and so forth.

- **Give property to people to share**

Whenever you bequeath property, you can give it to more than one person to share. With liquid financial accounts, it is more common to leave each person their respective amount, or share thereof. With less liquid items, such as a house, you can leave it to the beneficiaries as tenants in common or as joint tenants. The relative merits of these are discussed in the chapter on property ownership. Leaving property for people in a co-tenancy like these has several effects. First, it enables them to decide to hold onto the property until such time as they may find a buyer willing to pay fair market value, rather than a rushed 'estate liquidation' at whatever price can quickly be found. They may also benefit from any appreciation in the asset if they hold onto it long enough for it to appreciate. The beneficiaries receive the benefit of their taxable basis in the property being 'stepped up' to its value at the time of ultimate sale, and thus owe taxes only on the gain since they received it. You can even arrange for the property to stay in the family (say, a favorite vacation home), under terms so that one person can't sell it unless the others agree too. The cautionary note here is to consider if the people involved are a good match for joint ownership. Leaving a cabin to two siblings who don't get along well, use the cabin far different amounts, or have different ideas regarding its future (renovation, rental, demolition or even just redecoration) may do more harm than good for your beneficiaries.

- **Give property for someone to use until they die, then send it to someone else**

People can bequeath property, whether real estate or other financial assets, to one or more person to use for their lifetime, and then to others when the first passes on. This is known as a Life Estate (use of the asset during someone's life). For example, if you have a child who hasn't married, and still lives with you, perhaps tending to your medical needs, you might give that child the right to live in the house during their lifetime, but provide that on their death, it goes to any remaining siblings or their children. Or you can further provide that the one child can live there as long as they want, but upon their death or decision to vacate the home, it then is to be split among all of your children. In most instances, if you can think of how you would like your estate to reasonably work out, a good attorney can find a way to plan for it. There may be advantages or disadvantages to doing so, but you can address those in the planning process.

- **Give away all types of real estate, financial holdings, and tangible or intangible personal belongings**

Your will is able to pass title and ownership in all manner of things that are a part of your estate. Example include real estate, savings accounts, CD's, bonds, stocks, investment accounts, retirement accounts, loans and debts people owe you, patent rights, royalties, many contract rights, and on and on.

- **Donate property to charity**

Many people want to benefit a charity, but don't want to run out of money during their lifetime. A will is a fine place to make charitable donations. You certainly don't need the money any longer, and the charity will do a better job of putting the money to work than it would if you give it to the government. Charitable donations are fully effective to reduce your estate size prior to calculation of the estate tax payable.

- **Donate property to charity, but provide income for someone else from it**

With a little planning, you can have your cake and eat it too by making donations which benefit a charity and someone else in your life. You can provide what amounts to an interest in the income from property during a beneficiary's life (such as the interest and dividends and such on an investment account, rental income from a commercial property, or the right to use a vacation home for life), and then have the asset pass on to charity following the beneficiary's death. You can still get a substantial deduction in your estate taxes, based upon IRS regulations which calculate the value today (so called Present Value) of the charity receiving the property in the future. This is discussed more fully in the section on charitable trusts.

- **Exercise a power of appointment previously given to you**

A will is the final place to exercise a power of appointment which was given previously to you. Suppose your Uncle Ted left you his family home to use as you wished during your lifetime, but provided that if you didn't decide who would get the property on or before your death, then the property would pass to a particular charity. You have been given a Power of Appointment, or the power to point out in a legal document who should take title to the property. This is known as exercising a power of appointment. If you don't, then the power of appointment is unexercised, and instead passes as your Uncle prescribed previously. If you have been given a power of appointment, then you'd best exercise it no later than in your will, or you lose control over it.

- **Pour over property into a living trust**

If you have established a living trust during your lifetime, frequently referred to as a revocable living trust (see the Trust chapter), you may or may not have funded the trust by placing property or assets into it. Even if you did transfer all of your assets into the trust, there is a substantial likelihood that you have acquired some type of property or asset between that time and your ultimate death. Your will in this case may provide to "pour over" some, or all, of your estate into the living trust, which will then be administered by its trustee under the terms of the trust you prescribed earlier.

- **Create a trust to save taxes using the unified credit**

Most of the tax planning steps which people take advantage of during their lifetime can just as easily be dealt with in their will. For example, you can use your will to create upon your death a Credit Shelter Trust, or Bypass Trust, into which your executor will deposit as much of the Unified Estate Tax credit as can be sheltered therein. In 2008 and 2009, the amount is $2,000,000 and $3,500,000 respectively. This trust can then be used to provide income and security to, for example, your spouse for their lifetime, and then be kept in trust or the property distributed to other heirs you designate in your Will.

- **Maximize the benefit of the marital deduction**

The marital deduction for estate tax purposes is a valuable tax shelter, though not one without disadvantages. The good news is that any property which you pass to your spouse is entirely free of Estate Tax. The burden there is that the property is now in your spouse's estate, and thus subject to tax at their death. Nevertheless, where your spouse is a primary intended beneficiary of your estate plan, the marital deduction will let you give them as much as you want, tax free.

- **Create a trust to prevent beneficiaries from squandering their inheritance**

Children, it seems, never get too old to make mistakes in judgment, and the area of personal finance is one rife with opportunities for missteps, or disasters, to occur. Many a person has received an inheritance, only to watch it disappear to an ex-wife in a divorce, a partner in a failed business, or a creditor collecting on unpaid loans. Greater trouble follows if the beneficiary has problems with drinking, drugs or gambling, which may only be fueled by an inheritance. Thus, a protective testator may leave property and assets in Trust for a beneficiary. Then, the trust can hold onto the money and just pay it out to the beneficiary over time.

The risk in such a trust is that the funds in the trust can still be attacked, or attached, by a persistent creditor, or given away by a beneficiary who may pledge the payments from the trust as security for a loan they don't intend to repay. You can add a "spendthrift clause" in most states, which prevents such foolhardy waste of your generous legacy to them. The spendthrift clause provides that the assets cannot be pledged or attached directly, and is usually coupled with language giving the trustee discretion about whether and when to make distributions from the trust. Such language provides a high level of security again the wayward acts of your intended beneficiary.

- **Create a trust to preserve money for generations**

You can use your will to put money into a trust to benefit your children, your grandchildren, even your great grandchildren. In some jurisdictions, the length of a trust is limited by an ancient "Rule Against Perpetuities", which acts to prevent money staying in trusts forever, and requires that a trust end at or before the death of someone related to the trust who is living at the time the trust is created, or within some period of years thereafter. Many states have eliminated the old Rule entirely, and most of these have substituted a specific number of years a trust can last, such as 90 years. This discussion oversimplifies a complex topic, but suffice it to say that you can control what happens with your estate for a long time after you have passed on, if that is your intent.

- **Keep your spouse from giving your assets to a new spouse if they remarry**

Many a grieving widow has found at least some comfort in the fact that her late husband left her financially secure with his estate. Many a grieving widow later finds another man to share her life, and the late husband's assets are, perhaps unfortunately, now in a new family. The surviving spouse is free to use this money to send her new husband's kids to college and buy them cars, while ignoring the children of her former marriage, if she wants to. She can also leave these assets to her new husband in her will, which may be very unlikely to provide for the children of his wife's former marriage, and instead leave the money to his own. You can control this in your will by having your executor place the money into a trust under terms you describe in your will, such as paying her a reasonable amount of the income and/or principal in the trust annually, with the remaining balance to go to your children when your surviving spouse passes on. Obviously, the wife can, and often does, have similar language in her will governing the assets in her probate estate if she predeceases the husband. The variations abound, but with careful and precise planning, you can exercise control to keep your estate assets in your family, not another.

- **Fund accounts for minor children**

If you leave money to your children, or any children, who are still minors when your will is probated, the court cannot give the money directly to them. If you take no action, then the court will appoint a guardian to oversee the minor's property. The guardian will make decisions about management of the property, will be tightly limited in what benefit the minor can get from it, will have to account to the court for actions taken, will likely charge a fee for the service, and will turn the property over to the minor upon attaining the age of 18 typically. Your will, however, can utilize tools far more refined. One simple method is a Uniform Transfers to Minors Act transfer (UTMA), valid in almost all states. Some states instead still refer to Uniform Gifts to Minors Act accounts (UGMA), but the basic premise is the same. UTMA transfers let your will name an adult custodian, and successor custodian, responsible to supervise the property, and often let you state an age later than 18 for the child to receive the property outright, sometimes as late as age 25. The custodian has a broader range of discretion in this arrangement regarding the management and distribution of the assets, provided it acts in the best interests of the minor. If the custodian handles the property in a manner to benefit the custodian instead, it is liable to the child for damages under the law.

You can also create a trust for a child, or several children, and provide the trustee with instructions regarding how the money is to be managed, what it is to be used for, and when the children are entitled to a portion of the income or principal of the trust. Examples such as individual Trusts and Family Pot Trusts are discussed more fully in the Trust section.

- **Disinherit your children or others**

For many people, their children are the joy of their lives, while for others, perhaps not. There is no requirement that you leave property to your adult children in a will, and you are free to disinherit them. In most states, you cannot disinherit a minor child, but instead a portion of your estate, described in the statute, will be the minimum you can provide. In my experience, however, most people have no desire to disinherit their young children. Instead, it's those Twenty-somethings and up who are at risk of disinheritance. Common reasons cited by parents for disinheriting children include concern that the child will be listless if easy money is provided, because the parent had to work hard for it and the experience of hard work was important, the child's conduct has been akin to abandonment or rejection of the parent, or the child is stricken with a drug, alcohol, gambling or other addiction that an inheritance would only fuel. Disinheritance is by no means the only, or perhaps even best, way of confronting these problems, however it is an option available to you. You should make sure to be explicit in your will that you are not leaving anything to your children, or else they may argue under state laws that you accidently forgot to include the 'natural objects of your bounty', and thus should receive a portion of the estate. Where you have made clear your intent to disinherit them, such a challenge can be thwarted.

- **Provide for Children which haven't been born**
  when you sign the will

Your will is a classic example of a dynamic document, which is a document which may change before it takes legal effect. There is always a time lag between execution of your will by signing it in front of witnesses, and the time of your death. While in unfortunate circumstances that time lag may be very brief, there may well be a period of decades between when a will is first signed, and when the testator dies. In the meantime, a will can be changed as often as you want. Moreover, your life circumstances can change. Suppose your will leave a portion of your estate to "My children, Matthew and Samantha", but several years later, young Nicholas is born. He is one of your children, as stated in the will, but he is not one of the named children. Under the law, Nicholas would be considered a pretermitted heir, born to you after execution of a will. As a pretermitted heir, most jurisdictions would permit Nicholas to claim a specific portion of your estate, even if it is greater than that left to the children identified in the will. Sometimes, a court may find that your will clearly meant to include 'all your children', and just reform the will to include Nicholas with Samantha and Matthew. Any of these resolutions, however, involve time and money in the court system, family members squabbling, and hurt feelings at the end. Fortunately, you can provide in your will for this eventuality by making clear what you want to do for any children born after the will is executed.

I hope, however, that you will have the prudence to revise your will, or at least recheck if it is still reflective of your intent, when life events occur. Marriage and divorce, births and deaths, buying and selling significant assets, a move to a new state, may all affect your will. To keep its dynamic qualities useful, you would be better advised to keep you will up to date.

- **Identify your executors and their powers**

The executor is the person who carries out the tasks required by your will, as described in the chapter on probate proceedings. In your will, you get to choose the person you think is best suited to this position of responsibility and trust. An executor needs to be organized, smart enough to know whether to hire an attorney to aid the probate of the estate, oversee preparation of tax returns, and more. If you don't select the person by naming them in your will, then the court will pick someone to do it. The court doesn't have to let a family member be the executor, and may choose someone representing the interest of one of your creditors, or just a local attorney or fiduciary with whom the judge is friendly. It would be better for you to exercise this power, naming one or more executors, and one or more successor executors in the event that your first pick is unable to serve, or at some point is unwilling to continue. Make sure to talk to your proposed executors first, however, as there is no sense naming someone who doesn't want the job to begin with.

- **Identify trustees**

Just as it is important to name executors in your will, you are well advised to appoint trustees for any trust you may establish in your will. The failure to name a trustee to oversee and administer a trust created by your will isn't a fatal flaw, and the trust will still be created and given effect. The court will select a trustee for you, typically either an attorney or a trust officer at a bank nearby. If you've taken the time to set up a trust in your will, it is the best practice to take the time to establish a trustee too. As with executors, you should check with the proposed trustee first, and explain what you need done, and your general intent, as well as clarifying what fees should reasonably be paid, if any, for the trustee's involvement.

- **Create a trust for virtually any purpose**

Despite the endless advertising which has emerged in the last decade or so urging the absolute necessity to create a trust in your lifetime, there are often no compelling reasons for people to create a trust while they are alive. Most types of trust you ordinarily might want to create can be included within your will, which is then described as a Testamentary Trust. A testamentary trust can provide a wide range of intents and goals, including commonly credit shelter trusts, marital trusts, minors trusts, spendthrift trusts, and many more. The sellers of 'living trust' packages and forms go to great expense to point out all the wonderful things you can do with a trust created in your life, but seldom fail to address the issue of how you are better off incurring that expense and inconvenience now, rather than just providing for it in your will. Be very careful of anyone hawking legal documents as though they were selling hot dogs at a ball game. Everyone's situation is different, and there is no true "one size fits all" legal solution for any problem, especially for estate planning.

- ## Name proposed guardians to care for your children

If parents of young children had no other incentive to execute a will, its ability to provide a guardian for the children in the event they are orphaned by the parents' deaths should be enough to make it a top priority. Too often, though, it still isn't. When a child's parents die, whether in a joint accident, or separated by years, someone has to still care for the child. If the parents don't express their wishes on this topic before they die, then a court has to make the decision based upon its own judgment. With the increase in single parent homes, sole custody awards following divorce, and unique adoptive situations, there may not be an obvious choice about who should be selected. Even where the orphaned children have natural family available, they often vary in suitability depending upon where and how they live, their age and health, their economic situation, mental instability, or even just disinterest in taking care of your children. Asking the court to enter this fray and pick a guardian isn't the most loving gift you can give your children.

Instead, use your will to make clear who you would like to be their guardian. Your opinion as the parent is almost always the single most powerful piece of evidence to aid the court in its selection. You should know that your designation isn't binding on the court though, particularly if the court finds that the proposed guardian is either unwilling to accept the role, or is unfit for serious reasons (suppose since you signed your will, your sister went to prison, or dropped in and out of rehabilitation for drug abuse…). Still, in almost all cases, your choice will prevail. Placing this information in your will is helpful to the court because of the formality of a will. Judges know that people think hard about what they include in their will, and thus your designation of a guardian therein is given great weight indeed.

- ## Identify guardians to care for your children's money

You can name two different types of guardians for your minor children, if you desire. One type of guardian cares for your children, and the second type is responsible to manage their money. Sometime these two roles are handled by one person, but other time people find it helpful to separate the roles in order to assure that estate assets they leave to their children aren't 'inadvertently' squandered by the guardian of the children's care on other types of expenses, such as care for the guardian's own children and family, cars and homes, etc. If this is a concern, designating a separate guardian, or even a trustee, for financial matters can be useful.

- **Create an QTIP trust to save taxes and limit the risk of your spouse dissipating the inheritance before it passes to your joint heirs**

Sometimes people are rightfully concerned that their surviving spouse may not manage the estate assets in a way consistent with how the Testator spouse would have liked to see it managed. Due to the unlimited marital deduction for estate taxes, and sloppy use of will forms, many people just leave all of their property to their spouse without further thought. Once you leave money to your surviving spouse, however, they are free to do with it as they wish. This includes giving your estate money by gift or in her own will to a new husband, the new husband's children, her family members, The Church of Magic Rainbows, etc., rather than who you thought and preferred it would go to someday, such as your own children.

One method to avoid this is a QTIP Trust (Qualified Terminable Interest in Property). Such a trust essentially gives the surviving spouse the use of assets from your estate during her lifetime, including income from the assets and even some of the principal too, but provides that on her death, the property passes to whom you have already described in your will, not whoever she may choose. This is particularly useful for potential young widows, second marriages where one spouse or the other has children, and for those surviving spouses which are either uninformed about money management or unreasonably lavish in their spending habits. This vehicle is described more fully in the Trust section, if you want more information.

- **Enforce a prenuptial agreement**

For better or worse, prenuptial agreements are a part of the fabric of marital life in America. Commonly, such agreements provide not only limits on divorce asset splits, but also for limits on what property might pass to a surviving spouse if the other, perhaps richer, spouse dies. Such agreements, however, are contracts which are only useful if they are enforced. Frequently, the surviving spouse has no interest in enforcing the prenuptial agreement which may limit her portion of your estate. Since you will obviously not be around to raise the prenuptial agreement issue, you should describe it in your will, or at least make explicit reference to it so that your executor can enforce its provisions as part of the administration of your estate.

- **Provide for future care of a pet**

Animals in our homes are frequently considered members of the family, and treated with due care. Under the law, however, animals are not the same as people. Traditionally, they have been considered property. As such, pets can be given away to someone in a will to do with as they see fit, and pets typically could not be left money or a trust fund any more than you could leave money to a chair. Nevertheless, even under the traditional rules, you can at least state to whom your animal should go. If you don't, the animals technically pass under the residuary clause of your estate, where you leave all the 'rest and residue' of your estate.

Frequently overlooked in estate planning are the needs of your pets. Who is going to take care of your animals if you are no longer around? Will they provide a loving home, and be willing and able to shoulder the financial burden of pet care? I've seen reasonable estimates of $5,000 to $50,000 to care for a dog, for example, over its lifetime. Asking someone to take care of your animal is asking them to shoulder payment for food, vaccines, vet bills, treats and toys and equipment, flea treatments, repairs to damaged items, occasional kennel boarding, etc. Is it fair to ask someone to care for your animal and simply saddle them with the cost? If in your situation it isn't, you can create an enforceable Pet Trust in over half the states, which lets you leave money specifically for the animal's care. In the other states, you can create a so-called Honorary Pet Trust, which isn't strictly enforceable (i.e. the trustee can take the money and neglect the animal), but nevertheless is typically followed by the person you choose to take the pet.

- **Keep a family owned business going in the family**

For many family owned businesses (FOB's), the business itself is one of the biggest assets in the estate when the person primarily responsible for it dies. As a taxable asset, it can generate a significant estate tax bill, and yet they frequently are part of an estate that can not readily pay that tax within 9 months of the business owner's death as would be required. The family who wants to continue the business is left with options of using most of the other assets in the estate to pay the estate tax, taking out a large loan if they even qualify for one, or abandoning the business.

Congress has provided, in its own convoluted way, for a special Qualified Family Owned Business Interest deduction to the estate tax, largely separate from the spousal exemption and the Unified Credit. The details of a QFOBI deduction are too complex to discuss here, so we'll over-simplify it for illustration purposes only. In a nutshell, you can give about $675,000 of fair market value in a FOB tax free, in addition to your other exemptions. Due to tax law changes in 2001, this exemption is unavailable from 2004 until 2010, but will be reinstated in 2011, unless Congress again changes the estate tax code (enter your own saying about the Pope being Catholic, bears in woods, etc here !). The business must have been family owned for 5 of the last 8 years, located in the U.S., a significant part of the estate, and be given to either a family member or a longtime employee. This is one of the areas of planning which absolutely requires help from an attorney or experienced advisor, due to multiple complex aspects. The transfer of family owned businesses is worthy of its own book which specifically addresses those issues.

- **Describe what funds should be used to pay estate expenses and taxes**

After your plan for how to provide to give your estate to others is well established, another part of the planning is ready to begin; how to pay the estate taxes. If taxes are expected to be due on your estate, then they must be paid within 9 months of your death. Pretend that you give your house to your brother, your expensive car to your sister, and your cash and investment account to a friend, and that taxes are due. Where would the tax money come from? You can't give the IRS a car or house, but is it fair for the friend to have to pay just because he got marketable securities or some cash? Do you expect your executor to sell the car if needed to pay the taxes instead, and give what's left to your sister? Maybe the home should be sold first, since your brother already has one? Whose gift is going to bear the tax burden, alone or with others? Any of these solutions may make sense to you, but you should specify your intent in the Will.

If you take the time to think this through with your planner, you can come up with a method that makes the most sense, taking into account the nature of your estate, and your planned intent for passing it on. If yours isn't likely to be a taxable estate, then this isn't important. If, however, it is, then a failure to specify which assets should be used for the taxes will leave it up to the executor and the statutory requirements, which may radically change your dispositive scheme. In some states, the intestate succession property, if any, is used first for taxes if you don't specify, then the residuary clause dispositions, then general and specific bequests from the will. This process is known generally as Abatement. In others, all the gifts bear a portion of the tax burden, and the recipient can pay the tax into the estate to avoid a sale of the asset to pay its share.

- **Describe what to do if property in a bequest is no longer in your estate at death.**

Sometimes the property you mean to give to someone in your will is gone before you die. Then what? Suppose your will states that you intend to leave your sports car to your son, who always loved it. The car is stolen from you, insurance pay you, and you purchase a truck to replace it. If you die owning the truck, but not the car described in the will, what should your son get? This is known as Ademption, or the potential failure of the gift intended. In our example, most states follow what can be called an 'identity' rule, under which if you don't have the identical property described in the Will as a part of your estate, then the gift fails, and someone else will get the truck (such as whoever gets the estate residuary at the end). Some states follow an intent rule, where if it seems the intent was to give Son your vehicle, then the truck can be substituted for the car. Best practice would be for you to state in your will what to do it you no longer own any property described in the will, in order to avoid the issue altogether.

- **Clarify if someone gets property before or after any loan on it is paid.**

Payment of estate debts for loans on property in the estate is known as exoneration. In days of old, if I left you my home, and I owed a mortgage on it, it was presumed that you would get the home free and clear, and my estate would pay the mortgage from other assets. The modern rule is that you take title subject to any liens on the property; in other words, you inherit the debt with the property. In practice, this isn't often a problem because most loan agreements from banks and institutions contain 'due on death' clauses requiring that they get paid back in full if you die during the loan. This is because the bank issued the loan based upon your credit, not the credit of whoever you gave the property to. It remains an issue, however, when private financing is involved, such as when a friend or family has loaned money to help someone by a home, and the homeowner then dies. The loan will be repaid; the question is whether it is paid by the estate, or by the person who wants to take gift of the home. You can make this clear by stating it in your will.

- **Provide a trust for disabled or special needs children**

If you have a child with a physical or mental disability, or other special needs, a frequent device used to protect their finances, and maximize eligibility for government benefits, is a Special Needs Trust, though more properly it is called a Supplemental Needs Trust. This trust holds assets for the beneficiary to provide "supplemental and extra care" beyond that which is provided by governmental benefit programs, such as Medicaid. It is not a trust to provide for "basic needs", or else the government will require that the trust funds be used before the beneficiary is eligible for benefits. The trustee has discretion about whether and when to provide money from the trust, and as such, the trust is not considered an asset of the special needs individual. This is important, because most of the governmental benefits are connected to Medicaid, which requires a person to be impoverished (assets less than a few thousand dollars) for many benefits. This trust further acts to protect the special needs individual from wasting money, as the trustee keeps control of the distributions.

Moreover, it is protected from claims of creditors in most situations, provided it is properly drafted. This type of trust can be amended or terminated under limited circumstances, but generally must be irrevocable in order for it to not count against them in determining benefit eligibility. The government may require language in the trust to provide for repayment to Medicaid when the trust is no longer needed (i.e. upon the death of the special needs beneficiary), but only under specified circumstances which can be avoided when someone other than the person with special needs creates and funds the trust, such as a parent or relative in their will.

- **Penalize greed if someone contests the will**

When you take the time to draft an estate plan, you don't want your beneficiaries coming in and mucking it up after you're gone by contesting the provisions in your will. A will contest involves an 'interested person' objecting to probate of the will, setting forth reasons the will should be invalidated, usually so that the interested person will increase their inheritance. In general, 'interested persons' are those people who would take your estate if you didn't have a will (Spouse, children, grandchildren if your children have died, parents and/or siblings if you have no children). State statutes usually define the challenges which can be made to the will, such as claiming the Testator was incompetent when the will was signed, the will was improperly signed or witnessed, the will was the product of fraud, mistake or undue influence, or that it just isn't the true Will at all. Most wills aren't contested, and most will contests are not won by the contester. Still, the delay, aggravation, and expense of a will contest to the estate and your beneficiaries can be substantial. To avoid this, you can provide language to discourage your beneficiaries from contesting your will, essentially penalizing them for fighting your will by either reducing or eliminating, the property and assets your will would have left for them. If they succeed in invalidating your will, then the 'no contest' clause will be rendered moot, but if they lose, most jurisdictions will enforce the clause and reduce or eliminate the contesters share in your estate. This is a powerful tool to prevent people from threatening to contest the will merely as an effort to increase the size of their recovery, and should be in many wills where it is not.

- **Incorporate flexibility for tax planning after your are gone**

Good estate planning attempts to establish an estate scheme which will accomplish your goals, but life doesn't always go as you've planned. Therefore, in some circumstances it is appropriate to leave some flexibility to your executor to make decisions about some aspects of your estate after you have passed on. As an example, many people are understandably unsure at the time their will is drafted about just how much of their property can fit under the Unified Credit to be tax free, and what remaining amount will need to be sheltered under the unlimited marital deduction. You can provide a formula in your will which permits the executor to calculate how much to give to your spouse versus a credit shelter trust which benefits your wife. You can also empower your executor to make decisions regarding whether to implement a QTIP trust (see discussions in the chapters on Trusts and on Probate), and qualify some or all of it as being tax free. The point here is that in planning a will, you can include tools which let your executor and beneficiaries make decisions about the best format for some of your gifts after you've died, when the financial and tax aspects of your estate will be clearly established.

- **Protect a beneficiary who may be incapacitated when your Will is probated.**

What if someone you give property to under the will suffers an incapacitating stroke, or develops Alzheimer's disease, or is otherwise unable to reasonably manage their affairs at the time of your death and probate of your will. Absent planning, the court will require that a custodianship be created, with strict limits on the use of the property until the beneficiary regains capacity. You can instead provide for a contingent trust in your will for all beneficiaries, placing their assets into their own simple trust if the contingency (being incapacitated) is in effect when the will is probated. You can identify who is to manage their money rather than the court, permit payment of the money for their needs, and even specify what happens to the money if they don't escape their incapacitation prior to their death, if you so desire. Such a trust is far less burdensome for your beneficiary and his loved ones than a court imposed custodian would be, further enhancing the quality, if not quantity, of the gift you make with a will.

- **Avoid complications if you and your spouse die shortly after one another**

Too many families have witnessed the tragedy of losing both parents at or near the same time. Whether simultaneous deaths from a horrible accident, or deaths separated only by days due to differing injury severity, or even just broken hearts, the loss of a husband and wife at once is an enormous sorrow. This sorrow can be further complicated by the law, which has to address how property passes. Suppose Husband's will leaves everything to his wife, and if she predeceases him, then to his children. The Wife's will leaves everything to her husband, and if he predeceases her, than half goes to her children, and half to her church. If both parents are killed in an accident, who gets the property? According to the Husband will, it's the kids, but the Wife's will sends it to the kids and the church. This becomes an enormous tangle if the couple have different planning needs (such as children from a prior marriage, different charitable bequests, etc), or if one spouse survives the other, say from an accident, but only for a few days. In this last scenario, where one spouse lingers, the assets of the first spouse to die would all go to the estate of the second spouse to die, and then be distributed under the second spouses will. This can waste substantial tax planning opportunities, and deprive one spouse of the opportunity to be assured that any of the testamentary plans will be achieved except for giving assets to the barely surviving spouse. This mess can be avoided, however, by including language in the wills which address the so-called 'simultaneous death' situation, including deaths which are close enough in time that it doesn't make sense to treat either estate as though one spouse had survived. Most simultaneous death clauses provide for each person's estate to be handled as though the other spouse died first. Under such a clause, each spouses separate assets pass under their own will provisions, and their joint assets typically are split in half, with each person's will controlling their respective half.

- **Make almost any personal statements you want**

The right to make a will includes an enormous amount of flexibility about what you include in it. Not everything you say in a will has legal effect, but you can still include information about your intentions, goals, or opinions in your will. For instance, you can leave $10,000 to your granddaughter, stating "it being my hope that she will further her education with this." This precatory language doesn't put a mandatory condition on the gift, and she doesn't have to use the money for that purpose, but it can explain what you meant it to be. Some people even take a parting shot from the grave, such as leaving "my gun to my worthless brother-in-law, and all of my bullets, with the hope that he will use it on himself and spare my dear sister further grief." It's not nice, but you can say it. There are some limitations, as some jurisdictions do recognize the concept of libel or slander by will. If you were to state that a banker were a dishonest thief, such harmful language could give rise to a claim against your estate, however not every bruised ego will have such a claim. Finally, you can include a letter which you keep with your will, expressing all the same intentions, goals, and opinions instead. This method has the advantage of keeping your will neater, cleaner and easier to read, and keeps your comments out of the official probate file at the courthouse, but some people can't resist the temptation to directly link the gifts in their will with the chance to have the ultimate 'last word'.

- **Make your will self proving to ease its administration**

If a will is to be probated, it must first be proven to be your valid will. Absent proper documentation in your will preparation, your beneficiaries will be required to provide the court your will, accompanied by testimony to the court to establish that it is, in fact, your will. Even if this is not a contested issue, the court is still required to have your family or others take the time, expense and delay of attending a hearing to testify about their relationship to you and their knowledge of your will. You can streamline this process substantially by making your will 'self-proving'. A self proving will can be simply offered to the probate clerk by your executor, without the need for testimony thereon. To achieve this, you need to include an affidavit stating that you and the witnesses to your signature of the will followed the necessary steps. Typically, this will include language that demonstrates that you signed the will in front of the witnesses, that you were competent of mind and signed the will voluntarily, and that the witnesses watched you do it. The requirements vary slightly from state to state, but the core concept remains the same. This affidavit, usually notarized with sworn signatures, then makes your will 'self proving'.

- **What other ideas might you have about what you'd like to do?**

As I've said, we have testamentary freedom in this country. If you can dream it, you can probably plan for it. That doesn't mean that your plan is a good idea, makes sense, or is tax efficient, but it does mean that you have a significant range of freedom about how you craft your plan. You estate planning attorney can help to take your thoughts, explain the risks and benefits, modify them with you into something which addresses your goals in a way which makes sense under the applicable probate and tax laws, and provide you with the document or documents necessary to implement the ultimate goal; YOUR estate plan.

WHAT MAKES FOR A GOOD, VALID WILL?

All good wills share a number of characteristics. The language chosen should be as clear and straightforward as possible, permitting easy and unmistakable identification of the testator, beneficiaries, bequests made, divisions of any property, and executors to be involved. Trust should be described clearly, and trustees identified. The will should be in writing, and signed at the end in the manner required by state statute. The signatures should be witnessed, and an attestation by the testator and witnesses as to the validity of the will sworn and signed. All of the property owned by the testator should be included somewhere within the provisions of the will, though this isn't a legal requirement, and any property not transferred by a provision in your will instead passes under your state's intestacy laws created for those persons who die without a will. The testator must be over 18 years old, and "of sound mind", or legally aware that they are executing a will, who they want to benefit, and what the will does, at least in a general sense. If the testator owns property, especially real estate, in more than one state, the will should satisfy the requirements of each state involved. The will doesn't have to be typed, just written, but a typed will is far easier to probate efficiently. Any modifications to the will after it is signed should be in the form of a Codicil, or will supplement, which is executed with all the formality of a will itself, and which makes it clear that the prior will is still valid except for changes in the Codicil. The will should be tax efficient, and otherwise no more complex than necessary to achieve the planning goals for the testator. Finally, the will should be kept in a safe but accessible location, as described below.

WHERE DO I KEEP MY WILL?

After all of the work and planning that may go into executing a Will, it is important to store it safely. There is no single 'best' place to keep it, but I have suggestions. It is important that your will be stored somewhere **secure**, so that it isn't taken or altered without your permission. It should be somewhere **safe** from destruction or defacement by water, steam, fire or insects. If should be somewhere **accessible** to you and to one or more people who can take it to your attorney when it needs to be probated. A bank safety deposit box may not be the best place, because many states seal them upon your death until a court approved inventory of the contents can take place (to make sure no one steals your valuables, and to make sure that no one takes the gold and diamonds you've collected there without accounting to the Court for them for estate taxation). Some states have modified these procedures to provide streamlined access to your safety deposit box under bank supervision, provided the only thing taken or examined is your will. Further, some states will permit your spouse to continue to have access to a box held jointly with you, even after your death, but check your bank for its specific procedures before you store your will there. Your own safe or fireproof box can serve this purpose, provided you make the combination or means of access known to one or more people you trust so they can get to your will when necessary. The will's location should be **disclosed** to a few close people, so that someone knows where to go to get your will when it is needed.

You may also choose to leave it with your **attorney** for safekeeping. Your attorney will have access to his firm's safe when the will is needed, can be trusted to keep your confidences, and is already aware of what is in the will. Thus, your attorney can handle keeping your will secure, safe and accessible. Then you just have to make it known, or easily discoverable, what the name of the attorney is, so that your interested people can appropriately contact him. One further benefit of this is the attorney's ability to provide quick, comforting counsel to your family or friends regarding what needs to be done next. You may keep a copy of your will around your home in a location you consider appropriate, for ease of reference if you want to examine it, but make sure that it prominently notes that it is a 'copy' on each page so that it isn't accidently submitted in a probate attempt. This copy is another good location to record the location of the original, signed copy. Your attorney may also provide you with an estate planning information document (See Appendix 1), which your family will have access to, which can contain information regarding the location of the original will.

WHAT IS AN ETHICAL WILL

The term "will" has been bandied about loosely in the last few decades. We now have 'living wills' to describe how we want our medical care to be governed in serious circumstances where we cannot direct our own care. More recently, the concept of an 'ethical will' has developed. An ethical will is essentially a statement of your thoughts, beliefs, values, hopes and dreams which you leave behind for your family and friends. It is important to note that there is nothing official, binding, or of legal effect in an ethical will. Instead, it is akin to leaving a letter to your family with your thought on, well, anything. Your ethical will has absolutely no impact on your estate planning documents, however you are free to prepare one if you desire to do so.

MOVING ON...
Many wills utilize the power of a trust to achieve planning goals, while other times, a trust created during your life may be a better choice for you. We'll explore both in the next chapter.

CHAPTER 11

EVALUATING TRUSTS

Knowing What Trusts Do Is The Key To Deciding Whether A Trust Is Right For You

Trust. As a verb or adjective, it is a word which creates a warm feeling of security, confidence, hope and reliability. The people we trust are our closest friends, family members and confidants. When you trust another, you share a strong emotional bond not to be taken lightly, but treated preciously. Yet, you take this wonderful word, and turn it into a noun, as in "do I need a Trust?", and it becomes cold, scary and unapproachable. Now it is a fiduciary relationship between a Trustee and a Beneficiary pursuant to instructions from a Settlor. Brrrr. If, however, you take the time to understand the purpose and function of a Trust (there, I said it again), you will find that a Trust can indeed provide the type of security, confidence, hope and reliability that you would like to associate with the word. Let's have a look.

WHAT IS A TRUST

Think of a trust as asking someone to hold something for you, along with instructions about what they are to do with it. If you gave ten dollars to your son to go buy candy for all of your children and bring you the change, you could almost call that a trust. Technically, a trust involves a Grantor or Settlor transferring assets to a Trustee, who manages the assets for the Beneficiaries. Let's look at what those mean, and then apply them to our candy purchase.

> ➤ The **Grantor**, also referred to as a Settlor, is the person who creates the trust, and usually puts their property into the Trust, whether to benefit themselves or someone else.
> ➤ The **Trust Assets** are the property owned by a Trust. It can be financial assets (bank accounts, investment accounts, stocks, bonds), tangible assets (gold, antiques, cars), real estate (homes, land, apartment buildings) or almost any other type of asset.
> ➤ The **Trustee** is the person responsible to hold and manage the trust assets, taking care of the property not for themselves, but for the Beneficiaries.
> ➤ The **Beneficiary** is whoever will get the benefits from the trust, whether income generated by the Assets, or some or all of the Assets themselves. The beneficiary may be someone the Grantor wants to give support to, a charity, or even themselves.
> ➤ The **Trust Agreement** or **Declaration of Trust** is the document which typically spells out the terms of the trust itself, including all the above items, how the Trust is to be run, what it is supposed to do with the assets, and how and when it will end.

In our candy example, you were the grantor, giving assets (ten dollars) to a trustee (your son) to transfer assets to the beneficiaries (all your children). There is no written trust agreement, but there was sufficient expression of your (grantor's) intent that the money given to the son was not a gift to him, but money for him to hold and manage for others. Thus, he is now holds the ten dollars as your trustee. The ten dollars will be managed by the trustee according to your expressed terms to benefit the beneficiaries (you hope). The trust agreement you created with him directs him to take the initial trust assets of $10, convert it to candy, and then distribute the candy to the beneficiaries. See, kids and candy. What could bring warmer feelings about the concept of a trust than that? (cautionary note: not to be a killjoy, but I have to point out that this technically isn't a trust, because you didn't actually give the son 'title' to the assets, just possession, so it is more likely a custodial bailment type of relationship, but the core principal works out just fine. I only insert this clarification for the nitpickers in the crowd).

We could even draft up a Trust Agreement with all sorts of formality if we so desired. Actually, that might help in your understanding if you ever had to look at your own trust someday, so let's do it.

> The Mark Coulter Candy Trust
>
> I, Mark T. Coulter, have this day conveyed and transferred TEN DOLLARS to Junior Coulter, Trustee, and said Trustee shall agree to hold this property in trust and subject to the following uses and benefits. First, the property shall be held and managed by the Trustee. The Trustee shall use the trust principal and such income as the Trustee shall generate therewith to purchase Candy in a reasonably prompt fashion. Upon completion of said purchase, the Trustee is hereby directed to terminate this trust, and distribute all candy purchased thereby to the beneficiaries hereunder, being each of my children. Any assets otherwise remaining from the trust shall revert back to the Grantor, Mark T. Coulter.
>
> It witness whereof, I set my hand and seal this ___ day of ___, 200_.
> Signed: Mark Coulter

Obviously a bit more goes into a trust for estate planning purposes, but these core elements run through them all. With that in mind, let's take a closer look at some of the terminology and distinctions in the Trust field.

REVOCABLE OR IRREVOCABLE TRUST.

Sometimes when you give assets to a trust, you want the ability to get them back out of the trust if you change your mind. This essentially distinguishes Revocable from Irrevocable trusts. If the grantor who creates a trust can substantially change or revoke a trust, then it is considered revocable. If you give up ownership and control over the assets, except for what is spelled out in advance in the trust agreement, and don't retain the right to take it back, then it is an irrevocable trust. Many people are scared when they hear that a trust is irrevocable, because it speaks to losing control over something they have established. This fear is often poorly founded, however, as the grantor does have significant control. First and foremost, you control the assets in the trust from the very start by controlling the terms of your trust agreement. The trust agreement can be filled with all sorts of directions, suggestions, and contingent actions to be taken by the Trustee. It requires a bit of foresight by you and your attorney regarding how you generally want the trust to proceed, but you don't have to plan for everything. Second, by carefully selecting the right trustee to hold the property (see discussion later in this section) you help to assure yourself that the trustee understands the intent you had in creating the trust, and thus will take steps in furtherance of your intents as he decides how to exercise the discretion granted to him in managing the trust, including how investments are made, how the assets are managed, and how distributions to the beneficiaries take place. Finally, in many situations where an irrevocable trust is appropriate, the grantor can still have the power to make decisions about how the trust is managed, and even alter the beneficiaries. Thus, you should not automatically put up a fear curtain to shield yourself from advice that an irrevocable trust may be a proper planning option for you. Instead, listen to the advantages and disadvantages, and try to make a rational, informed choice based on intellect, not instinct. Trusts are a creation of man, not nature, so your natural instincts may serve you wrong in this field.

But why would anyone want to use an irrevocable trust instead of a revocable trust? The main reason is to get protection from claims by the government, or sometime from creditors. In many instances, the law considers property in a revocable trust to still belong to the grantor, even though it has been given to a trustee, because of the fact that the grantor can get the property back if they wanted it. Thus, if someone is trying to qualify for Medicaid benefits to pay for long term nursing home care, to cite a common example, they cannot give their money away to a revocable trust and say they are poor. Similarly, if you try to escape an obligation to pay your debts to others by placing your money in a revocable trust, the courts would frequently say that since you have access to the money by exercising your right of revocation, then you have to use it to pay your debt. As a final example, a revocable trust is treated as property of the grantor for income tax purposes, so any income and capital gains generated from the trust assets are taxed to the grantor, whereas with an irrevocable trust, the burden of the taxes is shifted to the trust itself, or even the beneficiaries. Many other reasons exist which can favor the creation of an irrevocable trust, while other situations appropriately call for a fully revocable one. Part of the planning process is understanding the difference, and then understanding why one is being suggested over the other. With a good planning attorney, and good listening skills on your part, you should be able to make this decision on an informed basis.

LIVING TRUST OR TESTAMENTARY TRUST

Much ballyhoo has been made about the magic of the living trust. Who hasn't seen at least one article titled something like "5 reasons you must have a living trust". You read about them in newspaper ads, seminars have bloomed to preach their healing powers, books line the shelves touting them, and the internet sites make them sound like the best thing ever. But what is a living trust, and why are they useful?

The distinction between a living trust and a testamentary trust is the difference between life and death. Literally. A living trust is created while you are alive, while a testamentary trust is created in the terms of your will. Those are basically the two options you've got. Another term for a living trust is an Inter Vivos Trust, which is just substituting the Latin phrase for 'during the life' in the place of 'living'. Perhaps someone can bill extra by calling it 'inter vivos', but it is the same thing.

If the main reason for creating a trust is to properly handle the distribution of your assets after you have died, or to manage them for your beneficiaries after you are gone, then it usually makes no difference whether you have a living trust or a testamentary trust. in either case, your assets will ultimately pass to a trustee to manage for your intended beneficiaries. If instead you want to manage your assets in a trust for various reasons or benefits during your lifetime, then obviously a living trust is the stronger choice. For example, some people use a living trust to make sure that someone is available to manage their assets if the grantor should become incapacitated and unable to manage their own affairs for themselves or their family. Some also do it in an attempt to minimize the expense of probate of the assets necessary with a will. These are not bad goals, or even bad uses of trusts, but they aren't often the only available means. A power of attorney can provide for asset management if you are disabled, and in most states, probate is not the time and expense monster that some make it out to be. Notably, most of the information about the horrors of probate seems to come back to people selling books, forms or other information about living trusts. Go figure.

GRANTOR OR NONGRANTOR TRUST

If you look into the information about trusts long enough, you reach discussions about Grantor or Nongrantor Trusts. These terms are poorly chosen, I think, since all trusts are created by a grantor, so confusion can follow. The distinction between these two is primarily based upon who benefits from the trust. If a living trust is created for a primary benefit of the grantor, such as giving the grantor the income from the trust during his lifetime, and/or the power to give property in the trust to others during the grantor's lifetime, then it may be considered a Grantor Trust. By who? Mostly, the Internal Revenue Service. If it is a grantor trust, then the income from the trust is taxable income to the grantor, even if he doesn't use it all for himself or take it all out of the trust. The fact that the grantor had the ability to access the income in a trust the grantor created is frequently enough to have the income from the trust, distributed or not, considered taxable income for the grantor. If, on the other hand, a trust is set up so as to be a Nongrantor Trust, then the trust is its own taxable entity. The income to the trust is taxable to the Trust. Moreover, any income which the trust distributes to the beneficiaries is a deduction to the trust, such that the trust has no taxes due so long as it distributes all of its income and/or recognized capital gains. In the right circumstances, your planner may recommend that a nongrantor trust status is important to achieve then to achieve your planning goals.

WHAT ARE TRUSTS USED FOR?

Trusts unquestionably involve some amount of administrative hassle and expense to set up and administer, and may limit your control and enjoyment of your property, so why bother? There are a number of uses for a trust, but the most common ones can be grouped by the following general descriptions.

1. To Manage Assets

There are times in most peoples' lives when they are not readily able to manage their own affairs. For some, it is during periods away from home, such as military service, or extended travel abroad. For others, it may be the result of deteriorating mental faculties from aging, or perhaps a serious accident. Depending upon the nature of your assets, you may have routine banking which needs tended to, rents to collect, portfolio balancing to be done, shares to be voted, business decisions to be made, or a host of other items. In a trust, you can provide for you to be trustee when you are able to, and keep control over your affairs, and yet provide for one or more trustees to step in and take control for you, on terms you describe, when you are unable to.

Trusts are also used to manage assets for others. If you place property in a trust to benefit your children, whether in living trust or a testamentary trust, you and your successor trustees can manage the property for the beneficiaries. If you want to give property to your children, for example, but they are too immature in age or experience to responsible handle it, you can give it to them in a trust. Properly done, the asset is then out of your estate, and thus avoids the Estate

Tax, and yet you and/or your trustees can retain control to manage the assets and distribute money from the income and/or principal of the trust in accordance with your directions in the trust agreement. That direction may be strictly scheduled, such as providing that all income will be paid monthly, with the principal to be paid in equal installments when the child turns 25, 35 and 45. You may go to the other extreme too, and provide that the distribution of income or principal is at the exclusive discretion of the trustee (you or someone else.). Or you can land anywhere in between with how much direction you give the trustee in the trust agreement. It is a very flexible tool for those looking to have efficient yet powerful estate planning.

2. Tax Savings

The old saying about the certainty of 'death and taxes' can these days be shortened to 'death taxes'. The relevant principles of estate taxation are discussed separately herein in the chapter on estate taxes, and the details of using trusts to avoid them are also addressed a bit further below. For now, suffice it to say that by using a trust properly, you can get assets out of your estate during your lifetime, and into a trust, and thereby avoid having these assets count for the calculation of estate taxes.

Trusts can also be used to minimize income taxes to you, such as when you place property into a trust for another's benefit, and the tax burden of the property transfers from you (say at a high income tax bracket) to them (presumably at a lower income tax bracket). You have also shifted the future growth in that asset to the trust and beneficiaries, instead of having it continue to grow in your estate where it may increase potential estate tax liabilities. By making this transfer to a trust instead of as an outright gift, you can still retain control of the property, provide for management of the property after your death until they are ready to take it, and protect the property from being lost to life events like bankruptcy, tenacious creditors, divorce, or just poor choices by your beneficiary.

3. Minimizing Probate Expense and Delay

The average American was often unswayed by the forces attempting to push them to use trusts for management during times of incapacity or for tax savings, as the former seemed to remote, and the latter was an expense for 'the rich'. Time has shown both presumptions to be false with increasing frequency, however the living trust industry created a third to motivate its customers; the goal of avoiding probate. Probate does take some time, and does involve some expense. The extent of the time and expense depends upon a number of factors, including the size and nature of your estate, the state you live in, the experience of your executor/attorney, and others.

With a living will, the trust agreement can provide that the property be transferred to your beneficiaries at your death in the same manner as in your will could. In either a will or trust, you can give property outright to your intended beneficiaries, create trusts for minors or spouses or anyone's benefit, etc. In a trust, the trustee can transfer the assets directly to these beneficiaries without the need for probate, since the assets are 'owned' by the trust, not by you. Thus, the argument goes, expense and delay is avoided. The extent of this savings, however, is often not well explored. Just as an executor under a will needs to prepare and sign documents to transfer property from your estate to the beneficiaries, the trustee will have to do the same. The total costs, when it's all said and done, may not be significantly different. Depending upon the expedience of probate in your jurisdiction, and the skills of your respective trustee or executor, the transfer of property from a trust may be similar, or a lot faster, than from a probated will. I understand that California is expensive and slow. Pennsylvania, by contrast, where I live, is relatively speedy and inexpensive. You will need to examine your own situation with your planner.

The final aspect of probate avoidance deals with privacy. For various reasons, people may not want their estates made public after they die. When you probate an estate, you need to file an inventory of the property in the estate, typically recording its value so that taxes can be assessed. This document is technically a public record, so if someone wanted to stop at the courthouse, they could see the inventory, and the will too. Many courts are declining to make these records available on-line, in an effort to minimize the intrusion of the merely curious, but some courts will no doubt make records available online. Perhaps your spouse doesn't want it to go on record that he or she is the recipient of a large sum of money after your death, or you don't want it known that your children are now to be recipients of a trust fund. Under such circumstances, transfer of your assets to a living trust during your life can avoid examination of your affairs by the public, as Trusts usually do not need to be recorded as public records. Some exceptions to this privacy exist, such as some real estate transactions, but they can be discussed with your planning attorney if it is a concern.

4.   Ancillary Benefits

There are other miscellaneous nuances to a trust which may be of value or benefit to you. One advantage is that most trusts are valid in any state if they were valid in the state you lived in when you executed the trust agreement. If you later move to a different state, the Trust is valid since is its validity is measured at the time it was executed. With a will, however, the will usually must be valid in the state where you reside when you die, and/or the state where some types of assets, such as real estate, are located. If you move after signing a will, you will need to check the laws in your new state to assure it is still valid, though most states have similar provisions which protect the vast majority of wills written by attorneys today.

There is also the issue of a will contest. As described in the wills chapter, a person might try to contest your will if they feel underappreciated or slighted. Because a will may have more technical features to its execution, some feel that a will is more subject to attack than a Trust. On the other hand, a will requires only very modest mental competence to be validly signed, while a trust agreement usually requires a more stringent examination of competency, though the successful management of your trust by you after its execution can help buttress this. More important, perhaps, is the fact that potential heirs must be notified of the probate of a will, but not the administration of a trust, such that those receiving little or nothing under a trust don't have something to remind them that it is time to complain, and further don't necessarily have access to the terms of the trust. The will, however, will be public record for them to examine. In most instances, however, even an excellent living trust will still be accompanied by a will which at least puts any assets the grantor/testator still owns at their death into the living trust, such that the heirs will still be notified of the death and have access to the (abbreviated) will. Simple fact is most wills, and most trust, are not contested by anyone so long as debts to creditors are paid.

A final advantage mentioned for trusts is the ability of the grantor to observe the conduct of the trustee in handling the trust while the grantor is still alive. If the trustee should demonstrate themselves to be incompetent or otherwise unsatisfactory to the grantor, then the grantor can exercise his right to replace them with another if the trust so provides. Obviously, a deceased person can't so observe a Trustee named in his will to oversee a testamentary trust. This trust advantage, however, would require the grantor to give the trustee control during the grantor's lifetime (seldom done) and ignores the ability of the grantor to observe the trustee in management of assets which remain owned by the grantor after the trust is created and funded. Nevertheless, some may find it a material benefit, and it is worthy of mention here.

WHAT ARE THE COMMON TYPES OF TRUSTS

Trust language can be modified and molded to address a wide variety of planning needs. Trusts may be intended to generate tax savings, control the future handling of property, reduce exposure to creditors, or a number of other reasons. Usually, there are tradeoffs which have to be made between different types of trusts. The more control you retain over property, the less likely there are to be tax benefits. The more access you have to the property in the trust, the less protection from creditors there may be. There is no single 'best' trust, and instead the merits of any trust must be measured against your planning goals. Here are some of the typical trusts used today.

> ## Credit Shelter Trust

The typical purpose of a Credit Shelter Trust is to shelter the unified Estate Tax Credit which every estate is given, making sure that this credit is used to its maximum benefit before the rest of a person's assets are given to their surviving spouse. Thus the name Credit Shelter. The assets qualifying for this credit are placed into a trust, which usually provides for the surviving spouse to have access to the money, as described below, but for the trust to distribute the assets to someone else (frequently the children) after the death of the surviving spouse. Couples often want to minimize the overall estate taxes they pay on their collective estates, without impoverishing the surviving spouse, and this trust provides a means of doing both.

As an oversimplified example, if Husband and Wife have $5,000,000 in assets, all jointly held, and the husband died first, he could leave everything to his wife, tax free under the spousal exemption. When his wife later dies, however, if her estate still is worth $5,000,000, then her estate is taxed (2008 values) on $5,000,000 minus $2,000,000 (unified credit value), or on $3,000,000. At the 45% tax rate, that is $1,350,000 in taxes, leaving $3,650,000 for the couples' heirs. If instead, the Husband's will gave $2,000,000 (2008 value of unified credit) to their heirs at his death, then the wife later dies with the remaining $3,000,000 left, then she can use her own $2,000,000 unified credit to reduce the taxable portion of her estate to $1,000,000, resulting in $450,000 in taxes, saving $900,000 in taxes, and leaving the heirs $4,550,000 total between the two estates. Clearly, one doesn't want to waste the Unified Credit on the first estate.

Many people, however, are reluctant to give that substantial sum represented by the Unified Credit directly to their children or other descendants instead of their spouse, due to concern that the spouse could be subject to circumstances which made access to that money important. Other people simply want their spouse to enjoy the benefit of that money represented by the credit during her life, permitting a much more comfortable standard of living. Here enters the credit shelter trust. In our example, when the Husband dies, a credit shelter trust is established with assets from the estate, up to the amount of the unified credit ($2,000,000 in 2008, $3,500,000 in 2009). The balance of the estate may go to the wife tax-free, or to other beneficiaries as the husband saw fit to plan. The money in the credit shelter trust is held on terms which typically provide for the wife to have access to the income, and as much of the principal as she may need, during her lifetime, with the balance to be paid at her death to their children, or whomever. Because this credit shelter trust was funded by money easily excluded under the Unified Credit, there are very few restrictions on how this trust operates. It can be for the wife's lifetime, or longer or shorter. It can benefit the wife, charity, children, strangers, whoever. There are a few restrictions necessary to avoid giving the wife so much access to the credit shelter trust assets that the IRS considers it to be in fact her money, which would then place the value of the trust back into her estate and eliminate the tax advantage. These restrictions, however, are not very onerous.

Finally, while it is a very useful tool, it isn't always necessary. If the surviving spouse will have plenty of assets available to her from the rest of the decedent spouse's estate, coupled with her own assets, then you can forgo this trust and just give the proceeds to the ultimate beneficiaries. For many couples, though, this solution is ideal. Frequently, a credit shelter trust is coupled with a Marital Trust, discussed next.

> **Marital Trusts**

As you've no doubt realized by now, a person can leave an unlimited amount of money to their spouse completely free of estate taxes. For many people, after the Unified Credit, the marital deduction is the only other significant estate tax escape available, so it is frequently used. In some situations, however, one, or both, spouses are interested in keeping control over the property which they leave to their spouse. The reasons vary: Some want to protect the spouse from frittering it or mismanagement, while some second-marriage couples with children want to assure that their children, including from prior marriages, get their money after the surviving 'new' spouse dies, and some just want to see that their plan for ultimate disposition of their assets is not thwarted by a surviving spouse changing their will later to invoke a new estate plan. Enter the Marital Trust.

A marital trust is designed to take advantage of the marital exemption, and is not taxed as a part of the estate of the first spouse to die. The assets in the trust, however, are taxed as a part of the surviving spouse's estate when they ultimately die. When this trust is created, because the first spouse to die has avoided, or deferred, taxes on the property under the spousal exemption, but not actually given the property outright to the surviving spouse, the IRS has strict limitations on how this trust can be set up. Make a mistake here, and the assets placed into the Trust will still be taxed as a part of the first decedent spouse's estate AND the second decedent spouse's estate too.

There are three main types of marital trusts which conform to the IRS regulations in this area.

1) **Marital Trust with a General Power of Appointment** : In this trust, the income generated by the trust assets must all be payable to the surviving spouse. The surviving spouse can access the principal in the account, and no one except the surviving spouse can let anyone else access the principal. Finally, the surviving spouse must be permitted to exercise a power of appointment, during her life and at the time of her death, to direct the trust to someone she chooses. If, however, the surviving spouse elects not to exercise this power of appointment, then the trust assets will pass on to the beneficiaries as describe by the first decedent spouse which created the trust.

2) **Qualified Terminable Interest Property Trust** : This trust, commonly called a QTIP trust, permits assets to pass to the surviving spouse in a Trust, under terms controlled by the grantor who establishes the trust, i.e. the first spouse to die. The phrase "terminable interest" refers to the fact that the surviving spouse's interest in the trust terminates at their death. It is Qualified as being entitled to use the Marital deduction when the first spouse dies because it adheres to the IRS regulations constricting it. Principal among these regulations is the requirement that the wife be the sole person entitled to the income generated from the trust, which must be distributed at least annually. No one but the surviving spouse can receive any of the principal of the trust from the trustee. It is essential that the executor of the first deceased spouse make a proper election on the Estate tax return to qualify some or all of the trust property as being QTIP property.

One interesting tax quirk of a QTIP Trust deals with how it is taxed at the death of the second spouse. It is a part of this second estate, and thus taxes are then due. Where, though, does the second estate get the money to pay to taxes, since the assets were in the trust, and are payable to other beneficiaries upon the death of the second spouse? The IRS provides that the trust is to be invaded to pay any taxes due on the estate of the second spouse, to the extent that the QTIP property increased the estate tax.

3) **Estate Trust:** The least common trust for the marital exemption is known as an Estate Trust. This trust does not require that the surviving spouse receive anything from the trust while the surviving spouse is alive. It does require, however, that the trust assets be paid to the estate of the surviving spouse upon her death, where they can be disposed of under the formerly-surviving-spouse's own testamentary scheme in their will.

These various types of marital trusts, with or without an accompanying credit shelter trust, are likely the most common trusts used in estate planning.

> **Living Trust**

When you discuss estate planning with most people, and they have some information about trusts, the most commonly referred to one is the living trust. living trusts have received a lot of attention in the media in the last few decades, and in advertisements. With the onslaught of the fiber-optic internet, the sales pitches for living trusts have increased to the speed of light. Unfortunately, many people pitching living trusts are taking advantage of misunderstandings and misinformation that the public has about estate taxes, the process of probating a will, and the delays, complexity and expense thereof. Pouncing on the ignorance and fear of anyone, and especially older people, the unscrupulous purveyor will advertise living trust 'kits' and 'forms'. For most people, even if the forms are marginally adequate, the consumer doesn't have enough information to correctly and confidently implement them, so they sit in a drawer, unused. Worse, some people find their personal or financial information sold by the salesman or internet site to others. Finally, for some people, a Living Trust makes perfect sense. So, what's a person to do?

The first step is to understand what a living trust is. A living trust is created while you are alive. You transfer some or all of your property into the living trust, and you then own it as trustee of the trust, rather than in your own name. The trust agreement says that you will be trustee of the property during your lifetime, typically with as much control over and access to the assets as your desire. At your death, a successor trustee named in the trust agreement will step in and transfer your property according to your expressed wishes in the Trust. This may include giving property to others, creating trusts, making charitable donations, etc.

Despite all the wonderful things that you may hear about a living trust, their main advantage is that they permit your assets to pass according to your estate plan without having to go through formal probate. The drawback to a living trust is the expense and administrative work to create and maintain it. Counter-arguments to each point have equal validity, i.e. probate is not that difficult these days, and even with a living trust you usually probate a small will, but with a living trust you shoulder the burden of organizing and orienting your assets during your lifetime, making it easier on your heirs after you die.

What living trusts don't do, at least not any better or worse than other options, is save income or estate taxes, or insulate your assets before or after your death. Nevertheless, these are often selling points stressed by the marketers of forms for living trusts. As far as Estate Taxes go, you can make use of most of the exclusions and deductions in your will just as well as you can with a living trust. There is no magic in the living trust which creates new tax saving opportunities. (One important exception to this is the Irrevocable Life Insurance Trust discussed elsewhere in this book, but that isn't what most people mean when they are talking about a standard living trust). You also do not uniquely insulate your assets with a living trust: Your access to the funds during your life almost always makes them available to your creditors, and while you can protect the assets in a trust after your death, that protection does not come from the living trust, but from use of other trust devices described in this book. These other devices just happened to be mentioned in the living trust, but could as well appear in your will.

In my opinion, the main advantage to a properly planned living will is the fact that it forces you to stop, think and compile information and plan your estate. Hopefully, you are doing this with the benefit of the advice of someone who truly understands this field and can lead you toward the best options for you from the wide range available. At the end of this process, the living will may not be your best choice, however if the prospect of making one helped you generate the momentum to plunge into your estate planning, then it has value. Its value can be obtained by other means, certainly, but it can serve a purpose.

Who are living trusts more likely to be appropriate for? The wealthy, the old, and the sick. Wealthy people benefit from living trust planning because it makes them confront and anticipate how to conquer the Estate/Gift/Generation Skipping tax hurdles in front of their estate. It doesn't magically fix the issues, but it makes a person at least plan how to handle them with other tools. Older people are more likely to use a living trust because there is less time during which they will have to shoulder the hassle of living inside a trust, such as keeping all assets titled to the trust, transferring property in and out of the trust, and so forth. People who are sick and at risk of becoming incapacitated may like how a living trust can provide for a successor trustee to jump in and manage their assets while they are incapacitated, rather than requiring a court proceeding to declare them 'incompetent', and appoint a guardian for their financial matters.

There are a host of factors which are variously touted for and against living trusts, depending upon who is trying to convince you. I've attempted to list a few of these arguments above, but you really should consult with a planner to address the specifics of your situation. I, and anyone who practices this field of law, could craft an argument for or against a living trust for just about anyone, depending upon my motives. Instead, you'd be better served to use this information simply to enable you to ask yourself and your planner informed questions about whether one makes sense for you.

> ➤ **Minors Trusts**

People give money to children for various reasons. Besides shear generosity and benevolence (let's take those for granted), other reasons include shifting income-generating assets to a lower-income-tax-bracket owner, decreasing the estate size to minimize or avoid estate taxes, keeping property away from creditors, etc. Anytime a significant gift is made to a minor, either during the donor's lifetime, or afterwards in a will or from a trust, a critical issue to be addressed is whether they should receive it outright, or in a trust. Most children, by virtue of inexperience, ignorance, enthusiasm or a combination of all of these, are not well equipped to handle financial issues. The risk that money given to them will be squandered on trivial items, depreciating property rather than appreciating ones, poor investment choices, theft and chicanery, or even misplaced generosity, is very real for children. Minor children are not typically permitted to take title to assets directly as a matter of law.

As such, trusts are often used to hold such property for the minors, and for their benefit, until the giver finds that the minor is ready to take it as their own. The advantage of using a trust over a UGMA/UTMA account is the increased flexibility and control you get with a Trust. A trust for a minor can hold any type of asset you desire, for as long as your reasonably desire, be subject to specific directions regarding its management and distribution, or be completely flexible subject to the trustee's discretion. The trust can include protective devices to shield the trust assets from creditors, courts, and even future spouses (or future ex-spouses).

Sometimes people refer to very specific types of Minor's Trusts. A Section 2503 b or 2503 c Trust is used to hold property given to a minor which might otherwise fail to qualify for a Gift Tax exclusion. As you will recall, the annual Gift Tax exclusion permits you to give up to $13,000 (2009) per year to anyone, and not owe any gift tax on it. Usually, to qualify for this exemption, the recipient has to get a 'present interest', or a present benefit, from the gift, and the right to get the money sometime in the future when they are older is not enough of a 'present interest' in the gift to qualify the donor (giver) to use the annual Gift Tax exclusion. Enter the 2503b and 2503c Minors Trusts. Congress provided a special trust form for minors to accommodate this aim, but with a choice for the donor to make in order to keep the Gift Tax exclusion. Either the trust must make annual distributions from the trust to the minor (2503b), or the trust must provide that all of its assets can be distributed to the minor at age 21 (2503c). Conversely, a 2503b trust can continue for many years after a minor turns 21, and a 2503c trust can withhold making any payments to the minor, accumulating value until they turn 21, or elect to make payments to, or on behalf of, the minor beneficiary prior to age 21. Either of these trusts must be irrevocable by the donor. To avoid adverse tax consequences where trust income is imputed to the donor, the donor should not serve as trustee. An annual Trust Form 1041 will need to be filed each year.

A nearly-trust situation is created by opening an account under the Uniform Transfers to Minors Act (replacing in most states the Uniform Gifts to Minors Act). The UTMA permits you to place assets for a minor in the name of a person to hold "as custodian for Named Minor under the Transfers to Minors Act". The Custodian is responsible to exercise his power over the property for the benefit of the minor. At the age of 21, the money must be given to the no-longer-minor absolutely free and clear of restraint. Note that if the donor names themselves as custodian, the property may still be deemed a part of the donor's estate if they die, with potential adverse tax consequences depending upon the size of the estate and the UTMA holdings.

> ➤ **A Crummey Trust For Minor**

Despite its name, a Crummey Trust is a unique and effective method for addressing planning needs where the accumulation of property in a trust is desirable, including for minors. As we discussed, the Gift Tax exclusion is only available to the donor if the beneficiary gets a present interest in the property. A trust which doesn't let the beneficiary, including a minor, access the trust assets isn't a present interest. To make it one, special provisions can be inserted in a trust which give the donor a window of opportunity to get benefits from the trust each year, thereby making the gifts to the trust a 'present interest', but the trust's goals are more powerfully implemented if the beneficiary declines to exercise their Crummey power.

The advantage of a Crummey trust for a minor is that it can be much more flexible than some others. The trustee can have the right to make discretionary distributions to one or more beneficiaries, of income or principal, at any time. It can last for decades, and doesn't automatically vest in a beneficiary at any particular age.

A Crummey trust does not usually give the minor any right to demand income from the trust. Instead, a window of time each year, often 30 days, is provided, during which the beneficiary has the right to demand the value of the gifts given to the trust during the prior year. In fact, the beneficiary has to be advised of the gifts each year so they can decide whether to exercise this right. If the beneficiary does not elect to take the money, it is thereafter a permanent part of the trust, and subject to whatever the other trust provisions may be. If you fund such a trust with regular gifts over the years, you can end up with a very large pot of money accumulated here. If the beneficiary understands this math, and the likelihood that if he or she disrupts this plan by withdrawing money in a given year then the gifts to the trust will stop, most people find that the Crummey rights are not exercised, and the trust grows for their later benefit.

In practice, you can examine the case of a married couple with 3 young children. They both can contribute up to $13,000 (2009) to a Crummey trust for each of their children, or combine them into one multiple beneficiary trust. 2 parents times 3 children times $13,000 exclusion yields $78,000 per year which could be shifted from the parents into a Crummey trust, to grow and grow. For a person with the assets to do so, and in need of estate tax planning, such a tool is not to be overlooked.

> ### Irrevocable Life Insurance Trust

Even for people who don't have enough assets to worry about estate taxes, the addition of assets from a life insurance policy may be enough to send their estate into the taxable realm. Life insurance policies are free from income tax, but people often forget that they are an asset which may be taxed to the estate of the policy owner (who, not coincidentally will be newly dead when the benefits are paid to someone else), and not to the beneficiary. An irrevocable life insurance trust (ILIT) is an effective vehicle to make sure that these insurance benefits stay out of the deceased's estate so as to avoid estate tax, as well as increased probate fees and costs.

If your life insurance policy is transferred to an ILIT, naming the trustee as the policy owner, then it is effectively removed from your estate. Thus, no taxes or probate. If, however, you die within three years of transferring the policy to the trustee, it is pulled back into your estate as though you owned it, for purposes of calculating estate tax, though the benefits will still go to your beneficiary. If you wish, you can also, or instead, have your trustee purchase a new policy on your life, using funds you typically provide as described further below. Moreover, a 'new' policy is not subject to the three year pull back rule. You can even transfer your interest in a group life insurance policy issued by your employer in many circumstances. Check with your benefits or human resource coordinator at work if you want to see whether your policy permits this.

It is important that the trust be Irrevocable, or else it is considered a part of your estate. The beneficiaries cannot be unilaterally changed by you, nor can the trustee, though a person may agree to resign and permit a successor trustee you've described previously to take over. This lack of control makes some people uneasy, but if you are in the group that may need the tax break, it is a valuable tool.

In order to fund the trust's operation, which essentially is payment of the annual insurance premium, you would usually make an annual gift to the trust for the amount of the insurance premium. We just discussed Crummey trusts above, and this discussion follows on its heels because the same Crummey structure is required to preserve your annual $13,000 (2009) gift tax exclusion. The beneficiaries of the trust are permitted once per year, usually for 30 days, to withdraw from the trust the amount of the current year's gift. Unfortunately, that leaves the trust without assets to pay the premium. Thus, if a beneficiary does withdraw the gifted payment, it would be necessary to make a second gift to the trust to cover the premium, and to the extent that the combined amount of the gifts exceeded $13,000 (2009) in value, it would be reportable for gift tax purposes. That would use up a portion of your Gift Tax unified credit, but likely only a very small portion. Moreover, if your beneficiaries are aware that the money is intended to benefit them in the future, and understand that you won't be able to fund the policy if they make any withdrawals in the future, experience shows that most beneficiaries leave the trust to operate as intended.

The donor, trustee and their attorney must be careful not to explicitly pronounce that the children should leave the money alone, because the annual gifts aren't really for them, but for the policy. The reason for this is that the IRS has attempted to challenge some ILIT's, charging the gifts as taxable for lack of a present interest by the recipient/beneficiary, arguing that since everyone is clear that the intent is not to make a gift, despite the Crummey rights of access, but instead only to fund the policy, then it isn't an excludable gift. The IRS does not win a lot of these fights, but it is better to avoid the issue by due care.

What are the uses of an ILIT? For some, it is just a way to make gifts of money to benefit their children at a later date, while reducing estate tax liability. For those with larger estates, the ILIT provides one vehicle for assuring that money is available to pay Estate Taxes when they are due. Remember that Estate Taxes are due 9 months after death, so some fairly liquid assets are needed to pay them. You don't want your family to have to sell your home to generate the money for the taxes, nor to take out a loan from a bank. Instead, an ILIT trust, flush with cash benefits from your policy, can either loan the estate the money to pay the taxes until other assets are sold, or can buy the assets, leaving the cash in the estate (to pay taxes), and the assets in the trust (to be distributed to whomever you provided in the trust agreement.

Some have wondered if it wouldn't be easier to simply transfer the policy to someone else, say a beneficiary, and avoid the trust altogether. While you can do that, it comes with substantial risk. When you give the policy to a trust, it is managed by a trustee you selected, guided and constrained by the trust agreement. When you give the policy to your children, for example, it becomes their property. If the policy names them as the policy owner, then they can redeem the policy to collect its cash value anytime they want. If they are sued, the policy is available to creditors. In a divorce, it may be a countable asset. These risks are all avoided by putting the policy in the trust.

Who should be the trustee? For starters, not you. The IRS may find that if you are the trustee in all this, then it is still essentially your policy, not the trusts, and place it back in your estate. Instead, a trusted financial advisor, attorney or bank trust department may be best. You can name a family member not insured by the policy, but you may want to add a co-trustee with more experience to give the benefit of expert guidance. Also, name a successor trustee in case your first choice becomes unwilling or unable to continue.

As for the payment of the insurance benefits upon your death, you are free to set up that trust any way you want. The money can go straight to beneficiaries, be paid over time, be paid on certain terms or at a Trustee's discretion. After the death of the person insured under the policy, the multiple restrictions imposed by the IRS are lifted, and your estate plan can finally blossom.

> ➤ **Pot Trust**

A Pot trust, sometimes called a Family Pot Trust, is a rare example of a legal term reasonably describing what it does. A pot trust is usually created for your children, and it is funded by a common pot of money for all of them to benefit from. The trustee is frequently vested with significant discretion to determine which children receive money, when, and how much, within the confines of the directions in your trust. The advantage of a pot trust is that it permits the trustee to treat the children differently, depending upon their situations and needs. If a child has a medical emergency, or decides to go to college, the trustee may increase payments to that child, while a child in an established career with no great needs may receive less. This gives the parents who have created this trust peach of mind, knowing that the family resources for the children will be available to support them.

Usually, a pot trust is drafted so as to terminate when the youngest child reaches a certain age you select, and the remaining assets in the trust are then split among the children. The pot trust permits the trustee to act in a semi-parental role, providing funds in response to your children's needs, rather than treating them all equal. The disadvantage for the trustee, however, is determining how to make the numerous choices about how much to pay the children, and which requests to honor or deny payment for. You can help reduce this burden by giving instructions in a letter to your trustee, or talking with the trustee, to instruct them about how you have approached making decisions about your family finances. Moreover, you can be the trustee of a pot trust while you are alive, with a successor trustee waiting in the wings until you pass on.

For example, suppose a married couple has a son and daughter, aged 4 and 14 respectively. If something were to happen to the parents, then a pot trust can provide for the children's educational expenses. The trust will pay tuition and expenses for the daughter when she goes to school, and then hold the remaining money until the son goes to school years later. If the assets will not be enough to satisfy the needs of both, then the trustee will exercise his discretion typically about how to balance the two. After both have finished college, or when the youngest reaches a certain age if one doesn't go to college, then the balance of the trust may be distributed. The concept is fairly simple.

> ➤ **Sprinkle Trust**

A Sprinkle Trust, or sometimes called a Spray Trust, is the same concept as a pot trust. It draws its name from the ability of the trustee to 'sprinkle' principal or income of the trust among the beneficiaries at the Trustee's discretion.

> ## Generation Skipping Trust

Once a tool used to preserve the fortunes of the super-rich for many generations, the Generation Skipping Trust has become more commonly used today by comfortable, if not rich, people. The purpose of a generation skipping trust is to avoid dissipation of assets by estate taxes as family money moves down through generations. If you imagine you had a great grandfather with $10,000,000 in assets beyond the exemptions (Unified Credit/Marital/etc), and he leaves it to his only child. The IRS takes 45% or so, and $5,500,000 remains. The child takes only the income from the money, and leaves the principal alone. The child passes it on to their child. Again, take away 45%, and now about $3,000,000 is left. Child of child (your parent) again doesn't touch the principal, and leaves it to you. Give the IRS 45%, and you, the great grandchild of the donor, are down to $1,650,000 of the initial $10,000,000. Almost 85% of the property was dissipated by taxes. This wasn't popular with the super-rich.

Suppose instead that Rich Great Grandfather put that $10,000,000 in a trust. The trust provided that his child got the income, but not the principal. Upon death of his child, then the child's child (your parent now) gets the income, but again not the principal. Upon the death of the child's child (your parent), you get the income. The only taxable event here was the initial $10,000,000. If that was $5,500,000 after taxes, then after Great Grandfather's death, that money is still ultimately available to you. The principal has skipped through the generations without ever paying taxes again. These became known as Dynasty Trusts, preserving the wealth of the Rockefellers of our country. This wasn't popular with the IRS.

Enter the Generation Skipping Tax. In a nutshell, anytime the property skips a generation, it is subject to tax at the maximum estate tax rate in effect in the year of the skip. Now the trust is more like the first example, dissipating rapidly with the generations. But, to their credit, Congress has permitted a Generation Skipping Tax exemption, worth about one million dollars in assets, which can be transferred to benefit 'skip' generations (i.e. grandparent to grandchild, skipping the child in between) free of Generation Skipping Taxes. Further, the growth of that exemption money after the time of the transfer remains free of the Generation Skipping tax. (This is known as 'zero inclusion ratio property'.) If Great Grandfather was hoping to get money to you eventually, he could put $1,000,000 into a Generation Skipping Trust, and let it ride until it got to you when you were born. If that was, say, 70 years after the trust was started, that $1,000,000 could grow to, say, $30,000,000 (70 years, at 5% real growth, net of inflation). Wow.

Most GST's do not operate to generate this kind of wealth, because the intervening generations do have access to the income on the assets, and even to the principal. To the extent that they don't take the income or principal, however, it can continue to pass to successive generations for quite a while. Most trusts can't last forever, and due to statutory limitations, it is tough to stretch a trust in most cases beyond about 100 years, but that is still an awful lot of time for growth and benefit by family members, even at lower sums for initial creation of the trust.

So, in a nutshell, a generation skipping transfer may be taxed when the creator dies, though $1,000,000 in assets can be exempt from taxes, which can otherwise skip through the generations for about 100 years, benefiting future generations with income and/or principal, as your trust agreement provides. Note that for a couple, if you both use your Generation Skipping Tax exclusion, you could put $2,000,000 ultimately into the trust, free of generation skipping tax. Remember also that this tax is in addition to the Estate and Gift Taxes, so the $1,000,000 exemption does not shelter additional money beyond the exemptions for Estate and Gift tax. Instead, it is a method of protecting some money from all of them. Thus, if the Estate exclusion amount is $3,500,000 (2009), then you can exclude $1,000,000 from both Estate and Generation Skipping Tax, and $2,500,000 from Estate Tax but subject to the GST if those assets pass to a 'skip' generation.

> ## Qualified Personal Residence Trust

Gifting a personal residence to a Qualified Personal Residence Trust (QPRT) is used to remove the value which you have in your home from your estate before Estate Taxes might be due. A QPRT can provide substantial reductions in Gift taxes and Estate Taxes, while still permitting you to enjoy the use of the home. You can shelter your home this way, and even an occasional residence (vacation home) too. Once your home is into a QPRT, the value of the home is out of your estate, and the subsequent appreciation on your home is as well. It is established as a grantor trust (see discussion earlier), so that you can continue to enjoy tax benefits of home ownership while you have the home, such as mortgage interest deductions, and capital gains exclusions for home sales.

In a QPRT, you transfer the title of your home to the QPRT trustee. You can still keep the right to live in and use the home for a number of years which you decide, rent free, though you pay to keep up the home just as you ordinarily would. At the end of the time period, your children can take title to the home without paying estate taxes. You may even continue to stay in the home, though the IRS requires you to pay market rate rent to stay longer than the trust initially provided, in order to avoid a gift of the rent value being imputed from your children back to you by letting you stay for free.

As an example, suppose that you owned a home worth $1 million today, which might appreciate to $1.5 million in the next 10 years. You transfer the home to a QPRT, which provides that you can live in the home for 10 years, and then it goes to your children. You haven't given the children a $1,000,000 house, or even a $1.5 million house. Instead, you've given them a $1,000,000 house MINUS the value of you living there for 10 years. The IRS has actuarial tables which permit an accountant to evaluate this reduction. In our example, the value of the gift you have made is about $500,000. Your $1 million dollar Gift Tax lifetime exemption is reduced by the $500,000 gift, but you owe no taxes. You live in the home for 10 years like you always would, and after 10 years, the children have received a home worth $1.5 million with no taxes due. One drawback to transferring your home via a QPRT is that the tax basis in the home is not 'stepped up' at your death, and instead your basis, or cost, is transferred to your children. If they decide to sell the home, they will owe capital gains taxes on the difference between the basis and the sales price, but the applicable tax rates for capital gains (15%) are far better than estate taxes (45%). Moreover, if they don't sell the home, but instead you or they continue to live there, then there is no taxable event.

If you don't live until the end of the time your trust provided for you to live in the home when you created the QPRT, then this vehicle doesn't work. Essentially, the IRS treats is as though it didn't happen. Your home is back as an estate asset, and the portion of your Gift Tax exemption which you used is restored for your estate. If you decide to sell your home, the trust can sell the home and purchase another with the assets. Provisions in the IRS regulations deal with what happens if your new home is more or less expensive than the one you sell, but for current purposes, suffice it to say that it can be readily dealt with in several ways.

If you are married, your trust can provide that at the end of the term in the trust, the home can remain in the trust for the spouse to use for her life, rent free, and then to pass to the children.

> ➢ **Personal Residence Trust**

You'll note that a Personal Residence Trust doesn't have the word "qualified" in front of it. A non qualified personal residence trust (PRT) can yield some of the same benefits as a QPRT, but the home in the trust cannot be sold during the term of the trust. PRT's have less technical requirements than a QPRT, but the lack of ability to sell the home for a pre-set period leads most people to utilize the QPRT structure instead.

> ➢ **Special Needs Trust**

A Special Needs Trust, sometimes referred to as a Supplemental Needs Trust, is used to manage and protect the assets of people with physical or mental disabilities, while preserving the beneficiary's eligibility for important government benefits such as Medicaid healthcare and long term care, and Social Security Supplemental Security Income benefits. These programs usually require that the recipient first exhaust their own assets, essentially impoverishing themselves, before the government will start to pay the benefits. Unfettered receipt of money, such as an inheritance or family gift, can disqualify someone for these important benefits, even if they have already qualified and receive the benefits. Moreover, the government has been working hard to make it tougher for people to get rid of money or assets in an attempt to qualify for benefits. Once the assets are in the name of the person needing these special benefits, they often lose the benefits for a long time. Use of a special needs trust empowers you to leave money for a special needs individual, without risking their eligibility. If you have a special needs person in your life, you know how critical this eligibility is for them.

Just placing a gift or inheritance in a trust for a special needs person is inadequate. Care must be taken, starting with whose money is funding the trust. A person who's assets go into their own special needs trust creates what is known as a first-party, self-settled trust, which is judged more strictly as an asset of the person than one created with someone else's assets (parent, grandparent, inheritance), referred to as third-party trusts.

- **First Party Special Needs Trusts**

First party, self settled trusts (i.e. using the beneficiary's own money) which retain the ability of the special needs person to qualify for federal and most state benefits share one common theme: The government will get any money back it can from the trust at the end. To the extent that government benefits are paid to the trust fund beneficiary, the trust must provide for the government to be paid back for all benefits paid, to the extent funds remain in the trust, at the termination of the trust, which is usually the death of the person with special needs. During the trust's existence, however, the income and principal of the trust can be used by the trustee to provide for the special or 'supplemental' needs that the government doesn't pay for. It is important that the trust not provide for general care of the beneficiary, or the trust may be required to be used up before eligibility can be established. Three types of such first-party, self-settled trusts are generally recognized in the federal statutes (42 U.S.C. 1396p) as acceptable for maintaining benefits:

1) **A 'd4A' Trust**, which is created by a parent, grandparent, legal guardian or a court, using the special needs person's own assets. The beneficiary must be under age 65 when the trust is started, and be disabled as that is defined by Social Security (inability to perform any substantial gainful activity). This trust may be used, for example, when a person is injured in a serious accident, and receives insurance money for their injuries. The court, or the parents, may establish a trust under d4A to protect the proceeds, at least while the person lives.

2) **A 'd4B' trust**, sometimes called a Miller Trust (the name of a legal case), which protects income received by the special needs person, including Social Security benefits, pensions, and other income. It is used in those states which limit how much income a person can receive without impairing benefit eligibility. This is sometime referred to as a Utah Gap trust, based upon a disability advocate's observation that the difference between the high expense of nursing home care and the low level of income which bars eligibility for people seeking benefits results in a gap as big as than between Utah mesas.

3) **A 'd4C' trust**, called a Pooled Income Special Needs Trust by some, wherein the person's own assets are given to a qualifying non-profit association to manage in their master trust, which includes accounts for numerous special needs people. The assets are kept track of separately, so the person receives the benefit of their assets. At the end of the person's life, the remaining money either stays in the trust for other uses, or goes back to the government for benefits paid. This trust account can be created by the person themselves, or by parents, grandparents, guardians or a court.

- **Third Party Special Needs Trust**

Third-party trusts, created by someone other than the special needs person applying for benefits, have different, more relaxed rules regarding the structure of a special needs/supplemental benefits trust. So long as the trust assets are not coming from the beneficiary, but instead from another person (or third party in legal parlance), then most trusts which provide for discretionary payments by the trustee can be drafted to assure continued benefit eligibility. The key inquiry for these purposes is whether the trust is available to the beneficiary. Where the discretion to make distributions lies with the trustee, not the beneficiary, then the trust is deemed not an available asset for government benefits. Such trusts will often provide for the trustee to pay for 'special or supplemental' needs of the beneficiary, to make it clear that the trust is not meant as a primary means of support, such as food and shelter payments. Others will give the trustee broad discretion, provided that the trust payments do not operate to make the beneficiary ineligible for the benefits. There are, however, cases where a change in situation of the beneficiary, their needs, or the government programs could make the use of the trust assets for the beneficiary of greater importance than continued benefit eligibility. In light of this, the trustee may be given discretion to make such payments despite its effect on benefits.

A third-party special needs trust does not need to be irrevocable, and the donor can provide a means to recover the assets in the trust if planning goals change for any reason. It cannot be, however, the power of the beneficiary to terminate the trust or demand payment from the trust. Finally, despite the relaxed rules the government applies to third party trusts, the government does not need to be repaid for the benefits paid, even after the trust is terminated.

➤ **Spendthrift Trust**

The phrase 'spendthrift trust' is a bit of a misnomer, but the usage is quite common. It is not so much a type of trust as it is a type of protection which can be incorporated into many types of trust. A Spendthrift Trust is a trust (of almost any type) which includes language to protect the trust assets against being dissipated, paid, used or otherwise diminished by anyone other than the trustee operating pursuant to the terms of the trust declaration. This trust language gives the trustee the authority to decide whether and when to make payments for the beneficiary. The beneficiary has no absolute right to claim or demand payments from the trust. As such, the assets in the trust are generally not available to creditors for payment of the beneficiary's debts, such as gambling debts, litigation liabilities, or most liens.

Moreover, language in a spendthrift trust can also bar attachment of the trust by a creditor. Attachment occurs when a creditor gets a court order that orders someone who owes money to a debtor must instead pay the creditor. Attachment orders can be issued after a debtor refuses to pay a legally established debt, usually after a suit on the debt is won by the creditor. Attachment orders are powerful collection devices, because the debtor never gets the money otherwise owed to him; it goes straight to his creditors. A spendthrift trust, however, can have language barring attachment of the assets by creditors. This way, the creditor has to wait until the money is in the beneficiary/debtor's hands, and then try to collect it. Such collection is far more time consuming, difficult and expensive than attachment, and most creditors will quickly write off bad debt if they don't find substantial assets for attachment.

Spendthrift language is also useful for beneficiaries who may have trouble in their personal life, such as gambling, drugs, alcohol and other lifestyle issues. A spendthrift clause gives the trustee discretion whether to give the beneficiary money. If the beneficiary is simply going to fritter it away, then the trustee can decide to make no further payments, withdrawing the fuel from the beneficiary's self-destructive engine, and conserving the trust assets for a time when the beneficiary is more likely to use them appropriately, and/or for the use of any other beneficiaries who have an interest, currently or after the beneficiary's death, in the trust assets.

You can leave or give money into a trust with spendthrift language to protect someone else, but you can not ordinarily put your assets into a trust for yourself, include a spendthrift clause, and expect to insulate your assets from creditors. In almost all states, such a trust you make for yourself, called a self-settled trust, could operate to defraud creditors of rightful payment due. If, for example, you injured someone in an accident, and then put your money into a spendthrift trust to avoid payment of your liability to the injured person, the court can ignore the trust language and order the trustee to pay the injured party the debt due.

A small but notable exception to the absence of spendthrift protection for self-settled trusts is known as an Alaska Trusts. Alaska modified its laws a number of years ago to permit self-settled trusts to include spendthrift limitations, which were enforceable for trusts located in Alaska after a 4 year waiting period. Nevada more recently modified its laws in similar fashion, but permits the spendthrift language protecting a self-settled trust to be effective after only a 2 year wait. These waiting periods are intended to prevent quick-and-dirty attempts to defraud current creditors, while permitting people who want to seek asset protection to have a vehicle to do so conveniently. Many people who might risk large personal liabilities, such as physicians concerned about medical malpractice liability, have put their assets in Alaska or Nevada institutions with one of these types of trust. The thorn in the ointment here, however, is what might happen if a court in a different state finds the trust language unreasonable or unenforceable. While the court may not be able to reach across state lines to the financial institution in Nevada or Alaska, there are other pressure tools available to the court. A court could issue a Civil Contempt order against a debtor in, say, Pennsylvania for failing to respect a court order that the beneficiary/debtor tell his trustee to give him money to pay the debt or take other steps to secure assets from the trust. These Alaska Trusts are not completely without risk.

> ### ➢ Grantor Retained Annuity Trust

Include the word 'annuity' in a planning discussion, and many people make the same face as they do when they think about meeting with an insurance salesman. Annuities have a sometimes underserved poor reputation, brought about by the unfair and deceptive practices of some salesmen who push expensive annuities on people they are poorly suited for, simply to gain a large commission. A Grantor Retained Annuity Trust (GRAT), however, is not that type of annuity, so read on without fear.

A GRAT is used to give property to a beneficiary at a reduced value to minimize the use of the grantor's lifetime gift tax exemption, while preserving to the grantor an income flow from the property. Due to an expected difference between the interest rate which the IRS uses to evaluate the gift into the trust, and the expected growth or return on the assets anticipated by the grantor, substantial benefits can be obtained.

A GRAT begins with a grantor transferring assets into the GRAT. The terms of the trust provide for payments to be made to the Grantor of a certain set amount, with or without annual increases limited to 20%, for a certain number of years. When that time is over, the balance in the trust passes to the beneficiaries. If the grantor doesn't survive to the end of the term set in the GRAT, then the value of the remaining trust property is pulled back into the grantor's estate, and some of the tax benefits lost. If however, the grantor plans the GRAT so that the grantor has a reasonable chance of surviving the described term of years, then substantial tax savings are available.

Unquestionably, the transfer of assets into the trust, to the extent they will go to some beneficiary after the years of payments back to the grantor, is a gift. The GRAT magic lies in how that gift is valued. Suppose you placed $500,000 into a GRAT, with payments for 10 years back to you of $40,000, and after that, the property goes to your children. The value of this gift can't be $500,000, because you are keeping the income on the property for ten years. Instead, using the actuarial tables from the IRS, one can calculate the value of the residuary interest in the Trust which will pass to the beneficiaries at the end of the term. It is possible to draft a GRAT in a way that the value of the income you will take back from the trust is just about equal to the money you put in. In such case, the value of the remainder to the beneficiaries at the end is actuarially valued at next to nothing, and little or no gift tax consequences are present.

The GRAT works because the rate of return which the IRS assumes the trust assets will create as they are invested is a relatively small number compared to what the actual return on the investments might be. For example, since 2001 the rate of return assumed by the IRS has never been above 6%. In 2008, it was close to 3%. These are called IRS 7520 rates, after the section of the IRS Code which provides for them. With the IRS actuarially assuming that the trust assets will create a low rate of return, the value of the money you take back for a period of years is relatively high, in turn decreasing the value of the residuary available at the end of the term. Provided that your trustee manages the assets in a fashion which exceeds the IRS rate in effect when the trust is created, then all of the excess income, and remaining principal, can pass to your beneficiaries completely free of gift or estate taxes. The lower the Section 7520 rate is, the better a GRAT looks, since the actuarial value of the money you take back is proportionately higher.

In our example above, if a trust was established at the end of 2008, the 7520 rate was 3.45. Using that rate, the present value of $40,000 per year for 10 years is about $334,000. Thus, of the $500,000 you put in the trust, only $166,000 is a gift. If you increased your payments annually from the trust to $60,000, then the value of the residuary gift drops to zero. Some call this a 'zeroed-out GRAT'. If the trustee is able to generate a return on the assets of in excess of the Section 7520 rate (3.44% in our example) then there will still be assets at the end to contribute despite a 'zeroed out' formula for valuation. As such, to the extent that you place higher-appreciating assets into a GRAT, you increase the likely size of the residuary which can pass freely to your beneficiaries. In our examples above, the trust would have to return about 12% per year to avoid touching the principal on the zeroed out GRAT paying $60,000 per year for 10 years. The $40,000 example would require a return around 8% to save the entire principal. Returns in excess of these percentages will serve to further increase the residuary value, while returns less than these will diminish the principal available for the residuary.

A GRAT may be appropriate in a number of different situations. Where a person has a large estate and wants to maximize the use of the lifetime Gift Tax credit, then a GRAT permits him to put substantial assets into the trust, with actuarially decreased value, and effectively leverage the credit to greater power. A person who has already consumed their lifetime gift tax credit but still wants to make further gifts to decrease estate tax liabilities could use a zeroed out, or nearly zeroed out, GRAT with minimal tax consequences. Assets which might explode in value, such as venture capital stock or a risky biotech investment, can go into the GRAT and be evaluated at current values, with the explosive growth, if it occurs, passing to the beneficiaries rather than being in your estate. Even garden variety stocks (not bonds usually) in which you have a measure of confidence that they will significantly exceed the Section 7520 rates can benefit from this type of a trust to pass the growth beyond the 7520 rate to your beneficiary.

In all of these examples, if your assumptions regarding the asset performance are correct, then you have won, successfully passing what turned out to be under-valued assets. If your trust assets don't beat the 7520 rate, then your actuarial value of the residuary to pass on will turn out to have been too high, and thus too much of your gift tax exclusion used. Where, however, you calculated a nearly zeroed out GRAT, the downside of this risk is minimal because you didn't use up much of your lifetime credit anyway.

There are technical details to a GRAT which aren't worth getting into in this discussion, and your planner can address those with your plan if a GRAT is recommended.

> **Charitable Lead Trust**
> **Charitable Remainder Trust**
> **Charitable Gift Annuity**

All three of the above devices are used to give some benefit to a charity, while preserving the use or enjoyment of the assets for either yourself, or beneficiaries which you choose. Because these were already discussed in the prior chapter on gifts to charity, I'll just refer you to those pages for a discussion on these topics.

SELECTING A TRUSTEE

Whether you create a trust while you are alive, or in your will, every trust will need a trustee to manage it. A Trustee is a fiduciary, which means generally that the trustee owes duties of good faith, trust, confidence and candor. These qualities make trustees sound like pretty good folk, and properly selected, they are. A bad trustee selection, however, can impair or ruin a trust, destroying the intent of the person who sets up the trust, and impairing or eliminating the value of the trust for the beneficiaries. As such, selection of a good trustee can be as critical as the selection and creation of the trust itself.

At its core, a good trustee needs to be someone you can trust. The trustee will be responsible to collect and manage assets, invest money, pay bills, file accountings, take care of taxes, make investment decisions, know when to consult other professionals, and other duties. You need to be able to rely upon your trustee's willingness, qualification and ability to get these tasks done. While a bad trustee may be legally liable for harm caused, that is no substitute for avoiding harm in the first place by selecting someone worthy of the trust you place in them.

If you tried to make a laundry list of factors about a trustee to consider, you might look for some of the following:

- Honesty
- Education
- Experience
- Judgment
- Involved
- Insured
- Available
- Geographically close
- Attentive

- Hard working
- Discrete
- Prepared
- Prudent
- Resourceful
- Fair
- Impartial
- Responsive
- Healthy
- any others important to you

Many trustees are given very wide discretion in how they handle your trust. Our world is complex and frequently changing, and a trustee who is hamstrung by stringent limitations in how he handles the assets may find it more difficult to produce a return on the assets which those involved would consider reasonable. It is difficult to remove a trustee when one person is unhappy with their performance, as others may find it satisfactory, especially where the Trustee was selected by the grantor of the trust. Instead of placing strict limitations on how a trustee is to implement his duties, you may be better served by giving the trustee wide latitude, coupled with explicit trust provisions about who can remove the trustee, under what circumstances, and who will step in then as successor trustee.

Trustees can come from several sources. You can be your own trustee for many trusts. You can frequently use your spouse, or another family member. Friends or business acquaintances can qualify as trustees. More professionally, you should consider an attorney knowledgeable in the field, or a responsible planner. Finally, institutional trustees can be appointed, whereby instead of naming a person, you have a company serve as trustee, in the form of a qualified banking or trust institution. Which is best for you may not be an easy question, and instead requires balancing a number of competing factors.

➤ Individual Trustees

In those instances where serving as your own trustee does not impair the intent or function of the trust, you may be your own best choice. This assumes, of course, that you consider yourself to be up to the task of handling all the trustee's duties described above. At the very least, you have the best knowledge of what your assets are, what your goals in the trust are, and how you, as grantor, intended the trust to operate, both in foreseen and unforeseen situations. If, however, you don't have the ability, interest or time to be your own trustee, then it may be best to pass this position to someone else.

Family members can be adequate trustees in some situations. Assuming you pick the right person, your trustee should then be someone with enough connection to your family to understand your needs, how your assets have been handled historically, and how you would like to see the beneficiaries treated as individuals.

Unfortunately, the wrong family member can result in a trustee who isn't readily able to comprehend how to handle the duties, select investments, and take the necessary steps. Family members may also have personal, emotional involvement with the other parties to the trust which can confuse or cloud the exercise of their judgment. Time constraints may impair their ability to attend properly and promptly to the needs of the trust and its beneficiaries. They often have no experience in the hard business required to run the trust, and may have difficulty managing the competing interests which develop between beneficiaries. For example, if your trust provides for income from the trust to your child for life, and then the rest to charity when the son eventually dies, the child is going to want the trust to invest in high income instruments (such as junk bonds, etc) without concern for the stability or growth of the principal, while the charity is going to want to sacrifice reaching for higher return now in order to assure that the trust assets remaining at the time of your child's death are the greatest possible. You clearly intended to benefit both, and your trustee has to determine how to balance these. That, and the trustee may have to sit across the table from the beneficiary at a holiday dinner some day. So family members, while trustworthy, are not necessarily your best choice.

What about a savvy friend or business acquaintance? Such people may have a working knowledge of how you have run your life which will inform how they handle the assets, and bring more ability to manage the assets than many family members might. With common sense and tenacity, they may be able to handle the trust duties for you. Frequently, however, they either don't get paid by the trust, or decline to get paid because of their relationship to you. The unfortunate side effect is that your trust and its needs may be put on the back burner when their own personal or business life calls for their attention. Also, like a family member, they may treat beneficiaries differently due not to objective needs or activities, but because of a personal relationship or affinity they have or develop with them.

In selecting either family or friends as trustee, an important factor to consider is what will happen if they misbehave as trustee. Trustees have title to the assets in the trust, but not for their use. Nevertheless, trustees do on occasion convert the trust assets into their own piggybank, whether by inflating expenses, paying non-trust expenses or benefits, or simply stealing from the trust. The law may say that the trustee is responsible to make the trust whole again, by repaying the money lost. There is a big gap, however, between a court saying that the trustee owes the money and your ability to actually get the trust paid. Most people don't have insurance or asset levels which can reliably give you peace of mind that the trust won't suffer for mistake the trustee makes.

➤ Institutional Trustees

Some people select institutional trustees. Usually, a trust company or the trust department of a bank oversees the trusts they manage via several people or a committee. These people have a greater understanding of trust operation and principals than family or friends ever will. They have the professionalism to balance the competing needs of income beneficiaries and residuary beneficiaries, and they know ways to balance risks and diversify investments. Such benefits, however, are not without downsides, nor without cost. Professional trustees do, and deserve to, get paid. Whether they charge hourly, based on a percentage of the return gained or, more commonly, based upon the size of the trust, their efforts will be compensated. What you gain in professionalism with an institutional trustee, you may lose in humanity. Most institutional trustees will have no true knowledge of you, your life, your goals, your family, or anything beyond the terms of the trust as written. Even if you take the time to get to know a trust employee at the institution, such places can have significantly high turnover rates, so that you don't know if the same person will be available next year, let alone in 10 years when they might be needed. Trust officers can be hard to reach, as customer service isn't necessarily their strength, and they similarly may be too dispassionate about the needs of your beneficiaries.

Perhaps the biggest complaint about institutional trustees is that they are too conservative. In an effort to avoid liability for losing assets of the trust, many institutional trust officers go too far the other way, and invest assets in conservative instruments which are great at preserving the principal of the trust, but don't generate much income beyond the rate of inflation. Further, many such organizations tend to invest trust money in their own institutional funds. For example, the trust department of the Bank of Nod will take the assets given into the trust, say a collection of mutual funds, stocks and bonds, sell them, and then invest the proceeds in mutual funds run by the Bank of Nod which in turn invest in, yes, stocks and bonds. Such a passive approach concerns many potential trust creators. Further, it may let the bank 'double dip', collecting fees to manage the trust, and then collecting mutual fund fees for managing the mutual funds. You certainly should question an institutional trustee regarding the matters important to you. Such areas might include:

1) What training do you require before someone new starts handling a trust?

2) How long on average do trust officers stay, and what is the shortest time someone has been a trust officer here in the last 5 years?

3) How many accounts do each officer handle, or how many assets? You don't want your trustee to be so busy that your account is just another thing to be 'dealt with'.

4) How are trust accounts reviewed to determine if they are being handled in the best fashion? Things like asset allocation, performance and tax efficiency are all fair game to discuss.

5) What assets would a trust like the one I'm considering typically be invested in?

6) What are the fees?

Now don't get me wrong - institutional trustees have been around a long time, are insured usually, and the right ones provide value for the money. They are not, however, the best answer for everyone.

➤ Attorney Trustees

Finally, you may turn to your attorney or other financial planning professional. For obvious reasons, I think an attorney can be a good choice, but not just any attorney. There is no reason to think that your divorce or personal injury attorney is going to be a good trustee simply because they are an attorney. Instead, you need to select someone with whom you have a relationship of trust, who also has a demonstrated education, experience and/or interest in serving as your trustee. Some people find that the personal-yet-professional relationship with your attorney can make him or her the best trustee candidate, situated between the uninformed-but-caring family/friend group, and the informed-but-dispassionate institutional trustee, effectively balancing the relative risks and benefits of both groups. No one trustee type can be said to be the best, but instead, working with your planner, you have to find the trustee that represents the best fit for you and your planning needs.

SUCCESSOR TRUSTEES

Great. You found a trustee. Done? Sorry, but no. While finding a first trustee is a great start, you should provide in your trust for successor trustees. Sometimes a proposed trustee cannot, or will not, serve as trustee when it is time (say, when a will is probated), or decides to terminate their involvement as trustee sometime after they have started. Trustees die and move and go to dependency rehabilitation clinics just like the rest of the world, so you can't count on them always to be there for your trust. In addition, you may want to have a trustee step down, or be pushed aside, if the trustee isn't adequately performing their duties. Your trust should describe who has the right to remove a trustee, whether it's you, a beneficiary, or even just a 'friend of the trust' who decides if the trustee is not performing adequately. If you don't make provisions for a trustees removal and succession, then the court in your state will have to make the decision whether the trustee is acting in a manner which makes him unfit to continue (often tough to prove), and who to replace them with as trustee (which may be a friend or associate known to the Judge) . Instead of subjecting your trust and beneficiaries to this uncertainty, trouble and expense, you should identify successor trustees for any trustee you name. It doesn't hurt to even name successors to successors. Finally, you can identify in your trust someone who you permit to make the decision about it the trustee should be terminated, and to pick their replacement. This provision will keep the issue out of the courts, and in the hands of someone you know and trust.

You can even name multiple trustees to serve at the same time. For example, you can name your two adult children as trustees, and permit them to make joint decisions about the trust. This can be useful if you want to appoint someone close to you as trustee, such as a spouse, but you also want a more experienced person like your attorney to help her make decisions and take the necessary action as a co-trustee.

FUNDING A TRUST

A Trust Agreement is just a piece of paper unless assets are actually placed into a trust. The trustee of an empty trust is the King of a paper kingdom. Unfortunately, many people spend considerable time and money to evaluate and execute trust documents, and then fail to finish the process by arranging for funding of the trust. This is one reason why working with an attorney, rather than attempting to do it yourself, can be so much more beneficial. An attorney can work with you, either to guide you along or do the work themselves, to make sure that your plan turns into a reality. Whether from fear, uncertainty, time constraints or otherwise, however, the process of placing assets into the trust, called funding the trust, will continue to be a weak spot in many estate plans.

➤ Funded And Unfunded Trusts

There is no legal requirement that you place money into a trust when you execute the trust agreement, though it may be necessary to implement your plan effectively. Sometimes, a trust is purposely left unfunded. For example, if your purpose in preparing a trust for yourself, a living trust, is to have a vehicle to manage your assets if you become mentally or physically incapacitated, then you might not fund your living trust right now. Instead, you might accompany your living trust with a financial durable power of attorney, which provides that when you become incapacitated, your agent designated by the power has authority to transfer your assets into your living trust so that your trustee can then mange them consistent with your living trust instructions. Until such time, however, using an unfunded trust lets you retain full ownership and control of the assets, without the administrative inconvenience of them being in a trust.

If, however, your goal with a trust is to avoid the delay and expense of the Probate process for your assets, then you need to get all the assets you've planned for into your living trust before you die. Since none of us know when that time is going to be, it is often recommended that you move forward with the funding of the trust earlier rather than later. Anything left in your own name, rather than in the trust, will have to be handled in the probate proceeding in some fashion.

Funding the trust is essentially the process of taking the assets you now hold in your own name, solely or jointly with others, and arranging to retitle them into the name of the trustee of your trust. Further, for assets which will come into the trust via beneficiary designations at your death (such as the balance in a retirement account or a life insurance policy), you will change the beneficiary from a person's name to the trustee of the living trust. This is how the assets actually get into the hands of the trust, by title being placed with the trustee.

For some, the main reason for using a living trust is to keep their decisions about who to leave their property to at death private, and to maintain flexibility to make changes to that scheme easily. An unfunded living trust can be adequate for these purposes, as your will can merely pour all of your assets into the living trust, where they will then be transferred according to the terms of your living trust as of the time of your death. No public record of the trust terms is usually required, and it can be amended by you at any time prior to your death with relative ease.

For many trusts, however, the purpose of the trust is such that it should be funded when it is created or soon thereafter. It then is necessary to actually move forward with placing assets into the trust. For example, if you are trying to protect assets from someone's creditors, or make gifts for your children to reduce your taxable estate, or benefit from a life insurance trust or charitable trust, the funds must be there.

What happens if you don't fund a trust? First, any assets titled to you at the time of your death will have to go through probate. Any assets in a separate state may need to go through an ancillary probate proceeding in that state too. If you planned on using a Trust to preserve your valuable Unified Credit for estate taxes, but left your property titled in joint tenancy rather than moving it to the trust, then you've wasted that opportunity. Many other goals of your planned trust can be thwarted as well. Thus, if your trust is to be a funded trust, then you really should go ahead and fund it.

Now let's take a look at how various types of assets actually get into a trust.

Funding A Trust With Money

A frequent component of a trust is cash accounts, like your checking and savings accounts at the bank. Your bank will help you follow their procedures for placing assets they hold into a trust. Usually they have a specific form that they require you, as owner of the assets, to fill out. They also will want to see the trust agreement, and you will need to apply for a federal taxpayers ID number for the trust if it is not a grantor trust (i.e. a revocable trust from the grantor, for the grantor, by the grantor). A grantor trust usually will use the grantor's social security number, as all income from the trust is chargeable to the grantor. The trustee will need to sign signature cards for the bank to confirm their identity, and checks ordered to reflect the trust account. The new account should be titled something like "William Smith, Trustee of the Smith Family Living Trust, under a Trust Agreement dated January 1, 2009 and amendments thereto." Checks should thereafter be signed from the account by "William Smith, Trustee". It is not usually necessary to state on the checks that this is a trust account, though you can if that tickles your fancy.

It is worth noting that with the banking meltdown which occurred in 2008, the FDIC modified the way it insured bank accounts, and increased coverage for living trust accounts. According to the FDIC, "Deposit insurance coverage for revocable trust accounts is based on each owner's trust relationship with each beneficiary. While the trust owner is the insured party, coverage is provided for the interests of each beneficiary in the account. The FDIC insures the interests of each beneficiary up to $250,000 for each owner if all of the following requirements are met:

- A beneficiary must be a person, charity or another non-profit organization (as recognized by the Internal Revenue Service). All other beneficiaries are not eligible for separate coverage as revocable trust deposits.
- The account title must indicate the existence of the trust relationship by including a term such as payable on death, in trust for, trust, living trust, family trust, or an acronym such as POD or ITF.
- For POD accounts, each beneficiary must be identified by name in the bank's account records.

Thus, your living trust can have FDIC insurance up to 250,000 for each beneficiary, if done correctly, even under one trust account. The requirements here are a little trickier than the FDIC provides on its site, but your attorney can work with you to make sure this provision is satisfied if that becomes relevant for you.

Note that retitling some bank assets can be tricky. Many Certificates of Deposit provide for penalties for early redemption, and may consider the retitling of the CD to be a penalty event. In such circumstances, it may be better to wait for the CD to mature before placing the asset into the trust.

➢ Funding A Trust With T-Bills And Bonds

Treasury Bills are most often purchased by individuals in a Treasury Direct account. This account can be held in a living trust, and if you need to move it from you to the trust, you have to ask the Department of the Treasury for a form to retitle the account.

Savings bonds can also be retitled into your living trust. You need to arrange for the Department of the Treasury to reissue the bonds in the name of your trustee, using a Request to Reissue form. This process requires you to get a certified signature on the form, usually at your bank or credit union. A mere notary public seal on the form will not do. Make sure to use a certified or registered mail process to track these bonds as they go back to the treasury for security. Municipal and Corporate Bonds are transferred more like stock certificates than savings bonds, so you can generally follow the instructions for stock certificates below.

➢ Funding A Trust With Stock Accounts

Brokerage accounts for stocks, mutual funds and the like can almost always be placed into a living trust by merely retitling them on the proper form obtained from the investment firm. There are some, however, where your holdings may need to be sold and a new account opened for the Trust. A simple call to customer service can quickly get you the answer for your specific account.

Some people take possession of the stock certificates in a company, rather than holding them through a brokerage. You will need to return the stock certificates to the issuer, along with a letter of instruction complying with the transfer requirement for that company. Check with any company for which you hold the stock certificates for their procedures, though they will likely refer you on to their Transfer Agent for handling such matters. You could ask a brokerage firm to handle this for you, which they will do provided that you thereafter hold your trust account with them, at least for those securities. Holding onto individual securities can be risky and an inconvenience, however, so most people simply permit the brokerage to hold their trading assets via a brokerage account or mutual fund.

➢ Funding A Trust With Real Estate

When you speak of 'title' to assets, the first though for most people is the deed to their house, since that is what they imagine a title document to look like. Real estate is a common component of trust planning, and it must be formally retitled into your trust. This requires preparation of a new deed from the titled owner to the trustee. Sometime a Warranty Deed is used, essentially passing a guarantee of title from you to the Trustee, and sometimes a Quitclaim Deed is used.

The relative benefits of each are for your attorney to address in your situation. Notably, most 'do it yourself' books and websites fail to make any distinction here.

Transferring real estate into a trust has several unique considerations attached to it. You will need the consent of your mortgage company to place the property into the trust, as they have a lien on the property and a loan obligation which attaches to you, not the trustee. Transferring without their consent can make the loan be in default, and then due in full. There is an exception to this typical loan provision, known as the Garn St. Germain Depository Institutions Act of 1982, which provides that for property with less than five 'dwelling units', the lender can't exercise a due-on-sale clause because of a transfer into a living trust, so long as the borrower is the beneficiary of the trust. Nevertheless, this is better to do with the knowledge and consent of the lender, rather than risking a battle of legal nuances with a perturbed lender.

If you own a condominium, timeshare, or live in a community where a homeowner's association exists, you may need their consent to transfer the title. Your title insurance company should also be consulted, as their policy of insurance is issued to you, and not the Trustee. Some may consider the trustee as a successor in interest to you, and others will accept a substitute trustee. Others, though, may require a new policy. If you need a new policy, ask if there is a discount for a living trust transfer, since they only have to check the chain of title from the time you purchased the property up to the present.

Also, remember to contact your homeowner's insurance company. They will need to make sure that your policy works within a living trust, and may re-name the interests insured under the policy.

You should also consider how the transfer may affect the taxation of your property. Some localities will reassess a home whenever a transfer takes place, even to a trust for the same owners, which could affect your property taxes. A living trust may or may not qualify for a Homestead Exemption to real estate taxes in your state. If you want to refinance property held in a trust, you may find difficulty getting a lender to do so, though this may be remedied by transferring the property out of the trust, getting a refinance, and then re-funding the trust with the property. Finally, there may be taxes, recording fees and other costs associated with the transfer.

➤ Funding A Trust Through Contract Beneficiaries

You may arrange for assets from 'self planned' contracts to be paid directly to your trust. Examples include IRA's, 401(k)'s and Life Insurance policies. For these contracts, you need to contact the administrator for a Change of Beneficiary form, so that you can designate your Trust as the beneficiary.

Not all living trusts are appropriate to be the beneficiary of contract benefits. The trust agreement has to provide the trustee with the power and discretion to make appropriate decisions about the receipt and management of these assets. Retirement accounts are typically subject to required minimum distributions, which can be calculated in various ways which your trustee will need to be able to select. Otherwise, your retirement benefits may have to be quickly passed through to your beneficiaries, rather than enjoying years of tax free accumulation of growth permitted by the law. If your old 401(k) doesn't permit a trust to elect to keep the property in the account more than 5 years after your death, then you might consider rolling the 401K over into an IRA to gain greater flexibility. An IRA is controlled more by you, and you can permit your beneficiaries to take distributions over the course of their lifetime, rather than in only 5 years, extending the time for tax-deferred compounding.

➤ Funding A Trust With Tangible Personal Property

The vast expanse of the physical stuff we own, except as described above, is generally lumped under the category of tangible personal property. It's the stuff we can see and hold. This distinguishes it from intangible property (such as debts to us, patent rights, litigation claims, etc). Within this group, your trust will have to deal with two main categories; those items with their own certificates of title, and those without.

Most vehicles have certificate of title issues by some governmental body. Transferring vehicles into a trust requires this body to issue a new title to the trustee. If it's a car, the department of motor vehicles will have a form for this. Boats may be registered with a state department of environmental resources or some such body. Very large boats may be registered with the Coast Guard. Trailers for boats may be with the DMV or, more likely, the same body licensing the boat. As with a home, loan documents for vehicles should be consulted, and lenders contacted, before title is transferred. Similarly, contact the insurance companies you use for any such assets, to advise them of the pending transfer of title and see if they require any further information.

In some cases, you don't have to transfer title to the trust at all. If avoidance of probate inconvenience is a driving force behind your trust, your state may have streamlined procedures for handling title transfers at death. Your attorney can get this information to you readily.

The rest of the stuff we own, our personal effects, don't have certificates of title. Usually, ownership is presumed from possession (ergo the 'finders keepers' rule of old). This includes everything from your art collection, antiques and jewelry down to your clothes, furniture and the pens on your desk. Your 'stuff'. Rather than attempt to list all of these personal effects, you can create evidence of your intent to place them into the trust by a document variously called a Deed of Gift, Quitclaim Bill of Sale, or Assignment of Property. These all amount to a document signed by you saying that all the various categories of personal property you own is given to the trustee. As a practical matter, this has no impact on how you handle these items from day to day, but they are as much trust assets as your re-titled home and bank accounts. Moreover, you can include language in your document to provide that all the personal property you acquire thereafter belongs to the trustee too, or even execute a 'catch all' agreement every year or two.

As with your home, make sure to update any insurers of the property, so that they can update their records about who is insured under the policy.

SCHEDULE OF PROPERTY HELD IN TRUST

Typically, when a trust is to be a funded trust, the trust agreement will incorporate and include a Schedule of Property, listing the assets to be held in the trust at first. In days of old, merely doing this was legally sufficient to designate much of the property as being property of the trust. As modern methods of holding assets have developed, however, along with trust law and computerized records, many more jurisdictions now require a formal document to transfer the title beyond this mere schedule. Nevertheless it serves as a useful tool to identify for the trust grantor which property needs to be addressed in some fashion to get it into the trust, and tells the trustee what property they are responsible to manage. As changes to the trust assets are made, the Schedule should be amended as well.

Make sure that the documentation regarding all of the property transfers and beneficiary redesignations which you have made are kept with your trust agreement, so that the trustee, or any successor, has easy access to the records of what is in the trust.

SPECIAL CAUTION FOR BUSINESS INTERESTS

Care must be taken in the transfer of business interests. Frequently, people organize their business concerns for tax and liability reasons, and you must not impair that purpose if you decide to transfer your interest into a trust. Stock in a closely held corporation may require a shareholders' agreement, by-laws amendment, or even a change to the articles of incorporation. The board of directors or shareholders may have to approve the transfer, and document this approval. Failure to follow strict regulatory guidelines in this area can affect your tax and/or liability structure.

Similarly, for those organized as a partnership, limited liability partnership or limited liability corporation (LLP or LLC), you must review the applicable agreement governing your business to determine what transfers are allowed, and follow the necessary documentary niceties. This is no time to attempt to go it alone; use the experience and education of your attorney to get this done right the first time.

MOVING ON...

A trust can provide a powerful method to place measures of protection and control over assets which you want to manage for yourself or for others. With careful planning, you can maximize the benefits of the assets which you choose to give or leave to your family, friends, charity or others. You can use a trust to substantially cut down the length, expense and inconvenience of probate too. Even with careful planning, however, some probate of your assets may be required in order to legally finalize your affairs after you pass on. Let's now examine what exactly that probate process can entail.

CHAPTER 12

UNDERSTANDING PROBATE

A Step-by-Step Walk Through The Probate Process

All of the discussion about Estate Planning can be rather abstract, if one doesn't consider the actual process of estate administration. People spend significant time and energy to simplify or avoid Probate, despite the fact that most don't understand what probate entails. The purpose of this section is to remove the clouds around probate, and introduce you to the steps that have to take place during probate.

Probate is the process by which legal force and effect is given to the directions contained in a person's will. If no will exists, or an incomplete will is found, then the probate process relies on the rules for Intestate Succession described in your state's probate statutes. This section might be read by someone planning their estate, or by someone who has, or may be, named as an executor. Keeping both groups in mind, I will attempt to give a discussion of the probate considerations relevant to all those concerned.

Asking someone to be your executor, or accepting the position, concerns a position of honor, to which a substantial burden attaches. The person selected for a position as executor is someone the testator considered to have the intelligence, perseverance, and integrity necessary to put the dispositive scheme carefully drafted in a will into effect. These qualities are particularly important because the testator will no longer be around to see that the will is properly implemented. With the honor of this selection, however, comes responsibilities which in some cases put your intelligence, perseverance and integrity to the test. Depending upon the estate, the tasks undertaken, and decisions to be made, can be numerous, varied, daunting and complex, balanced against a backdrop of grieving family members, expectant beneficiaries, creditors, bankers, and state and federal governments. As you will see, the guidance of an attorney or other professional in whom you have confidence can be immeasurable help, and worth the fees involved.

So, what does an executor have to do? The easy version is to say that they have to submit the will for probate, organize and adjust the asset and liabilities of the estate, pay the necessary taxes, and distribute the estate to the beneficiaries. Easy, right? In fact, many people just give an executor a checklist of items to handle, without any further discussion of what needs done. Let's take a closer look at the numerous steps involved in implementing this summary description. I've attempted to make it chronological, flowing forwards as an estate would proceed through time, but any effort to do so is illusory. Every estate will involve some, all, or more than these steps, and the order in which they occur will be influenced by numerous factors, including the nature of the surviving family, the will scheme, the assets involved, pre-death planning undertaken, and more. Nevertheless, let's take a look.

IN THE BEGINNING, WAS THE PLAN...

The best way to simplify any probate which must take place is by making arrangements before an estate is ever necessary, i.e. before your death. Many of the planning tools are discussed throughout this book. Additional steps include:

Ask your proposed executor if they are willing to serve, and under what terms. There is no sense nominating an executor in your will if they don't wish to accept the appointment, unless you hope to guilt or pressure them into it later (which is not advisable). The executor will have a lot to deal with, as described below, so they must be willing to take on the task.

Let your family, executor, and/or attorney know where your will is, and how to get to it when you are gone. If it's in a safe, who will access the combination? If it's in a safety deposit box, does your state allow post-death Will inspections of safety deposit boxes. If your attorney has it, secured in his Will repository, make sure that someone knows the attorney's name so they can be contacted.

Many wills include reference to Letters of Instruction or a similarly entitled document to dispose of minor personal items. If you want your son to have your autographed baseball bat, or your daughter to take your mother's cameo necklace, many states let you make such disposition in a separate letter if it is referenced in your will. Often, however, the will references such a document, but the document itself is either never made, or never found. Let your family know how to find these types of documents.

Similarly, if you have prepared Letters of Instruction, let people know their location and means of access. This document is frequently used for your instructions and guidance immediately after death, and may advise your survivors about your wishes on topics like organ/tissue donation, funeral and burial arrangements, etc. Some people like to include their parting messages to family here as well, hoping to provide words of strength and solace at a difficult time. This might also remind people where your will is located for when they soon will need it. A simple version is included in Appendix One.

Include successor executors in your will. If your nominated executor cannot, or will not, accept the position, or cannot continue for any reason (health, frustration, other time commitments), then it is better that you have someone 'on deck' in your will rather than your family and friends having to find one later. Some people prefer to appoint an attorney as an executor for this reason alone; they will accept the appointment for their client.

Prepare a full inventory of your Assets and Liabilities. As the following discussions will demonstrate, a substantial portion of the executors time in probate is spent simply locating assets and determining liabilities. While you may have a records system which is very detailed and complex, or just carry the information around in your head as many of us do, it is far easier for an executor who hasn't lived with your assets as you have to simply look at lists. Write down everything you own, including what it is, where it is, who it is titled to or owned by if it isn't solely owned by you, account descriptions, contact persons at banks or brokerages, and even phone numbers and mailing addresses. Remember taxable and nontaxable assets, regular and retirement accounts, 'bricks and mortar' and internet accounts too. I make a planning document available for my clients to attempt to compile all of this. Hopefully yours does too. Don't forget your liabilities and debts. Who do you owe anything to? Mortgage banks, personal loans, credit cards, monthly utilities, subscriptions on automatic renewals, etc. What about that old loan from Uncle Frankie; do you have anything to show how much was paid back? The discussion below may highlight more items which are relevant to you. Put it all in your inventory, and you greatly simplify the Executor's role, saving your estate substantial expense and delay.

Sometimes in a separate document not as widely available, people prefer to put their Asset security information, such as detailed account numbers and passwords, safe combinations, alarm codes, key locations and the like. You might wish to have the security list maintained by someone other than the person holding your Inventory, if you feel the need for enhanced security. While your spouse or attorney may be trusted easily, perhaps you have greater qualms about giving someone else the keys to your castle. If it is in two persons hands, they would need to conspire together to access your assets, which is far less likely than one person. I don't want to alarm you; if you keep these lists within your tightest 'circle of trust' (Robert De Niro's term, not mine), then you are likely to have enough peace of mind here. Just have a contingency plan in the event your 'circle of trust' is not available when this information needs to be put into action.

Prepare a list with full contact information (names, relation to you, addresses, phone numbers, even email can be useful) for the people identified as beneficiaries under your will, and under any non-probate beneficiary designations your planning may have provided for. Include the contingent beneficiaries as well. This saves your executor from having to bother a bunch of people for family information, or spend time and money finding them.

Assemble, or at least say where the location is of, important documents regarding your future estate, including bank records, checkbook registers, deeds, titles, birth certificates, marriage and divorce papers, prenuptial agreements, social security card, military papers, filed tax returns and the like. Some of these will be necessary to pass assets to your beneficiaries, and others are used for information required for other purposes, while some may just be useful depending upon the circumstances. For a minor example which could easily be overlooked, if you want to pass your Frequent Flyer miles to your spouse after your death, the airline usually requires a death certificate and a marriage license or certificate.

Take the steps necessary to finish planning you conducted in your lifetime for various trusts. If you planned on funding a trust during your lifetime, then you should finish the funding process. Otherwise, assets intended to go into the trust may end up in your estate, and either be used for debts and taxes, or they may go to beneficiaries you didn't necessarily intend.

Now, let's turn to a fuller discussion of the actual process of probate.

PROBATE EXPLORED: STEP BY STEP

Despite the best laid plans to escape probate, often it is still necessary to move forwards with some type of probate following a person's death. Assets which are not conveyed outside of probate must move through probate in order to permit their title to legally pass from the deceased to the ultimate beneficiary, through operation of the proper legal documents signed by the executor. If the estate is small, an accelerated and simplified process for small estates may be used. For medium and large estates, the full complement of probate proceedings may need to occur.

Probate is the formal process where the court sees that a deceased person's estate is properly handled. The court determines if a person died with a valid will, appoints an executor or administrator to act as the personal representative of the estate for the duration of the proceedings, and empowers the representative to move forwards with collecting the deceased's assets and liabilities, managing them, preparing the necessary paperwork and tax returns, and ultimately paying the taxes and debts before distributing the remaining estate assets to the beneficiaries of the decedents estate. This is all done under the authority and guidance of applicable federal and state laws, local court procedures, and the will (or sometimes wills) of the deceased person.

To clarify our discussion, we need to agree on what several key terms mean. The person who has died is the deceased. The assets of the deceased are their estate. The estate assets which must pass through probate are called probate assets, or the probate estate. A deceased who has made a will is called the testator. If a testator appoints someone to execute the provisions of the will (collecting assets, distributing them to beneficiaries, etc), the person is the executor. A female executor may be called an executrix. If a person dies without a will, the court will select and appoint an administrator to perform duties much like an executor. Either an executor or an administrator is considered the personal representative of the deceased's estate. Someone receiving an asset from the estate may be called a beneficiary, a legatee, a donee, or sometime an heir. Technically, an heir is someone who would be entitled to property of the estate if there wasn't a will, but it is often used more loosely as a synonym for a beneficiary.

STEP ZERO: FIRST THINGS FIRST

This is called Step Zero, because it includes item which need done at the very beginning, right after the death of the deceased. First and foremost, the family of the deceased needs tended to. In addition to emotional support, it should be determined if their immediate physical and financial needs are being met. Are minor children safe and secure? Have assurances been made that the family has a safe place to stay, with adequate food and money to handle the day-to-day expenses of the next several weeks? Frequently, when a primary breadwinner/money-manager spouse passes, the surviving family is ill equipped to figure out what to do next.

The funeral and burial desires of the deceased need to be determined. Perhaps they were discussed with a spouse or family member, or instead there may be a Letter of Instruction from the deceased in their papers, describing items like funeral arrangements, burial preferences, organ donations, and the like. A well prepared person might even go into detail in their letters of instruction regarding the location of financial resources for the family, how income and debt issues need to be structured in the coming weeks, and more.

Determine whether the deceased was eligible and/or interested in military death services if they were a veteran. Benefits for burial, plot, honor guard, and even headstones may be available.

During this time, someone will likely be dealing with a funeral director. This is a simple opportunity for the family or proposed executor to get several copies of the formal death certificate, which will be needed in the days to come.

After the burial services have been put behind you, you should contact an attorney to guide your steps in the coming days and months, as you move forwards promptly with probate.

STEP ONE: FIND THE WILL

The first step in probating a person's will is to find the document in the first place. Hopefully, proper planning has provided for it to be easily found and retrieved by a trusted family member, attorney or your executor. Otherwise, such people will need to examine your filing system at home, contact your attorney, arrange to gain supervised access to your safety deposit box, or attempt to get into your home safe in an attempt to obtain your will. If a person dies without a valid will, or with a will that no one knows where it is or what it said, then their estate will instead be handled under the applicable state laws of Intestate Succession.

Intestate succession laws in each state set out a plan for disposing of the estate assets for anyone who dies without a will. Non-probate assets, like life insurance payable to a beneficiary, or jointly owned property, will still be governed by the contracts which support them, but the state provides for what happens to the rest. Frequently, this state plan is far different than a person would plan for themselves. For example, in Pennsylvania, a person who dies intestate, with a spouse, but no other living family, gives it all to the spouse. If, however, there are other family members of the deceased alive, then the spouse only gets about one-half of the estate assets. The other one-half goes to the first line of surviving family in this list: children of the deceased, parents of the deceased, siblings of the deceased and their children, grandparents of the deceased and their families. If there is no family or spouse, then it goes to the state government to use as they see fit. This isn't much of a system, but it's what we have, and it is easily avoided by simply preparing a will, and letting the people close to you know where it is located.

STEP TWO: DETERMINE IF PROBATE IS REQUIRED

Many relatively wealthy people don't need much in the way of probate, while others need a lot. The trick is to take the time to determine which you are dealing with. As described earlier, remember that the following assets won't need to pass through a formal probate proceeding:

> ➤ Jointly owned assets
> ➤ Pay-on-death accounts
> ➤ Transfer on death securities
> ➤ Assets passing via a trust
> ➤ Life insurance with a beneficiary
> ➤ Retirement accounts with a beneficiary
> ➤ Family vehicles may pass to a spouse
> ➤ Final wages due are paid to family

When these types of assets are excluded from consideration of the size of the estate, it may be that the remaining assets can be handled through an auxiliary process, such as small estate administration. Most states have a procedure for describing and resolving relatively smaller estates. Some states require the amount of the remaining estate to be less than 10,000, while others permit an estate as large as 150,000 to be handled in a simpler fashion. In any event, it needs to be considered for the state in which the decedent was living, and the states in which they might have otherwise owned property. If, however, small estate administration is not the answer, then you move forwards with the probate process.

STEP THREE: OFFER THE WILL FOR PROBATE

Every journey begins with a single step. Probate formally begins when you file the will of the deceased at the courthouse, and request that the executor named in the will be formally appointed in that role by the court. If you haven't met with an attorney yet, now would be a good time. Properly drafted wills usually will not require you to see a judge at this stage, and instead the court clerk will process your completed paperwork. The court will determine if the will does indeed appear to be valid, and if so, admit it for probate. At the same time, the executor is usually appointed to represent the estate. Certificates are provided to evidence this authority, and steps then taken by the executor to properly publish, or advertise, the existence of the estate and the name of the executor. This is usually the beginning of the assessment of various fees for the use of the probate court process. As an example, here are some typical fees imposed where I work:

Initial probate fee	$105 to $355
Excess probate fee on estates over $400,000	$150 per $100,000
Letters of Administration	$55
Affidavit or Oath	$5
Filing Account	$60 to $650
Excess Account Fee on estates over $1,000,00	$325 per $100,000
Filing a bond	$10
Certified copies	$25
Inventory filing	$20

Courts require the publication of information regarding newly probated wills, in order to provide notice to creditors that they should come forwards with claims. Many creditors will be contacted individually by the executor, but this publication serves as legal notice to all of the other potential creditors who cannot reasonably be identified for individual notice of the decedent's death. If there is anyone who chooses to contest the validity of some or all of the will, offering the will for probate will bring them out of the woodwork. Notice must be given to the family members and beneficiaries under the will, and any objections must be promptly filed.

Depending upon the terms of the will, the executor may need to purchase a security bond, which protects the estate in the event that the executor decides to walk away with estate assets. Most wills, however, select an executor which the testator trusts sufficiently to avoid this expense.

STEP FOUR : COLLECTION OF ESTATE ASSETS

Now, probate starts to bog down for many people, as the detail work begins.

The next step is for the executor to begin to collect, organize and manage the probate assets. An estate checking account is likely to be required for depositing money and paying expenses and bills. Any bank will open a free account for "Your Name, Executor of the Estate of (name of deceased), Deceased". It may be easiest to do this at the bank where the decedent kept his own accounts, as the bank may be more willing to transfer the assets of the deceased directly into the authorized Estate account. The executor, however, can choose any qualified bank or credit union for this account.

The executor then has to locate and collect the estate assets. Locating the assets may be as simple as review of a well prepared inventory or letter of instruction left by the deceased. Unfortunately, this is not the case often enough. Instead, the executor will have to interview the spouse, close family members, and others familiar with the decedent's assets and financial dealings to identify both assets and liabilities. Usually, a close review of the checking and credit card accounts of the deceased for the last 13 months before death (and any time thereafter) will uncover most transactions. For example, life insurance payments will be made, payments to creditors, deposits into investment or savings accounts, checks from mutual funds, securities and the like will be seen coming into the account, subscription payments made, etc. Note also any items which may be deductible on the decedent's final income tax returns, such as property taxes, medical expenses or charitable contributions. In addition to the checking account, the executor should review the decedent's tax returns for the last couple of years, and the contents of their desk, safety deposit box, and any home safe, strongbox or other paperwork storage vessel they may be known to have used.

Safe deposit boxes can be uniquely problematical, depending upon the state you are in. Some states permit the executor to inventory the assets freely, while others will only permit you to have access with a representative of the state treasury present to assure that you don't take valuables out of the box before the state can confirm their existence (and tax the estate thereon). Check with the bank early regarding their procedures. In any event, take your own witness any time you access the box, or ask the bank to provide one, so as to avoid any dispute with beneficiaries about whether you have accounted for everything which was in the box.

The executor should ask the post office to direct any mail addressed to the deceased forwards to the executor. This will identify further assets, as well as creditors of the deceased, and items like subscriptions which may need to be cancelled.

Detailed lists should be kept of all of the information regarding assets of the deceased, with the goal of ultimately preparing a full Inventory of Assets, which will all need to ultimately be accounted for in some fashion during the probate process.

Consideration should be given to whether any litigation claims need to be brought or continued as a result of the decedent's death. Wrongful Death claims need to be filed promptly, so your attorney should be consulted soon if the circumstances raise suspicion that a claim might exist. Moreover, any litigation maintained by or against the decedent during their life will need to be handled now by the Executor, and legal defense fees paid from estate assets.

If surviving family members haven't done so, the executor should initiate claims for benefits due, such as social security, Veteran's Administration benefits, and others.

Retirement benefits will need to be identified and collected. For example, a pension may remain payable to a surviving spouse, or a balance in the account be due for distribution to a listed beneficiary or payable into the estate.

Real estate owned by the decedent, solely, as a tenant-in-common, or jointly, needs to be identified. If any portion of it may pass under the Estate, then the executor may need to inspect the property personally, or by an agent, to ascertain its condition and any need for care and maintenance it may have during the pendency of the estate in probate. If rents need to be collected, mortgages, taxes or bills paid to preserve the property, or other management duties completed, it is the executor's duty to do them or hire someone to do so.

If real estate is located out-of-state from the decedent's home, then auxiliary probate proceedings may need to be initiated there to empower that court to let the executor manage and transfer the property in accord with the will provisions.

Any debts owed to the deceased need to be identified, and collected.

Identify if any wages, vacation, sick or worker's compensation benefits are due to the deceased or the family.

Retitle any securities, investment accounts, bonds and the like into the name of the executor on behalf of the estate, unless the probate process will be sufficiently quick that no real management of those assets is likely to be required. The executor can be liable for losses incurred by the estate due to a failure to control and manage estate assets.

If life insurance is payable to the estate, then the executor should make the claim. If payable to a beneficiary, then the executor should contact the insurance company to notify them of the death, and remind the beneficiary of the need to file the claim.

Subscriptions by the deceased should be cancelled to preserve estate assets, unless the remaining family desires them to continue. For example, magazines, data service subscriptions, recurring charge agreements like record clubs and health spas, and other ongoing expenses need to be individually managed.

Insurance premiums paid by the decedent may be partially refundable. For example, if the decedent paid for a year of car insurance, but only lives for 3 months of the term, then a 9 month refund is due. If you don't ask for it, however, you may find it is not automatically refunded.

Cars should be located and securely stored. The same is true for motorcycles, boats, planes, trailers, and other movable assets. Insurers for these should all be contacted to assure that proper coverage continues, such as comprehensive damage protection, but cancel unnecessary insurance, such as auto liability coverage on a vehicle which will remain in the garage until it is passed to its beneficiary under the will.

Credit cards in the name of the decedent should be cancelled, and final account balances determined for payment.

Some income received by the decedent after death may need to be returned. For example, usually Social Security checks arrive after death. Do not cash or deposit them. Instead, contact the Social Security Administration to make arrangements to return these, and further begin the process of obtaining survivor's benefits. If the deceased had a direct deposit arrangement, the payor may make an automatic adjustment to reclaim the money if it receives notice before the account is transferred to an estate account.

Utility and service providers will need to be notified of the death, and arrangement made to cancel or continue service as is found to be appropriate. For example, the plant watering service might be cancelled, but gas service to a home in the northeast in the winter continued, even if it is vacant, in order to avoid damage from frozen water pipes. Obviously, if the spouse or family of the deceased will continue to live in the house, then most of those services will continue, but the financial liability for the services will have to be shifted to them.

Medical expenses paid by or for the decedent, and any unpaid charges, need to be considered for submission to the applicable insurance companies.

Don't overlook any non-traditional assets of the estate. Examples might include royalties for artistic works, rents or payments by utilities for mineral or fuel mining, patents, pending litigation, or others.

Notify lien holders, mortgage holders, and other creditors of the decedent that you are now the executor, and determine final amounts due, and whether the debt might be transferred with the underlying property to a responsible beneficiary, if that is appropriate under the will.

STEP FIVE: FILE INVENTORIES WITH THE COURT

After you have identified and/or collected the assets of the estate, you usually have to file an inventory with the court which identifies these assets and their value. Appraisals may be required for this purpose, and many courts require this document to be filed in as little as 30 days after the executor is appointed. As a result, prompt attention to the details of identification and collection of the assets is critical in order to avoid missing this deadline.

STEP SIX : MANAGEMENT OF THE ESTATE

During the period of time between the beginning of the probate process and the ultimate distribution of the estate to creditors and beneficiaries, the executor is responsible to secure and manage the estate assets. Depending upon the nature of the assets themselves, this responsibility may involve next to no work, or may be complex enough to require not only the executor's time and experience, but also the input of attorneys, consultants, accountants or other professionals. Some examples of these types of responsibilities include:

> Assessing whether assets are productive, non-productive or wasting. Productive assets will generate income and/or growth which will need to be managed during probate. Non-productive assets will neither improve or degrade during the process, and generate no income. Wasting assets will deteriorate or lose value if untended during probate, and thus care must be taken to dispose of such assets in a reasonable manner as soon as appropriate. As examples, a rental apartment building is productive, a classic car collection is non-productive, and a silo loaded with corn is wasting.

➤ If the executor is in control of wasting assets, they can typically be sold or disposed of in a reasonable fashion without prior approval of the court. In the event, however, that such assets are specifically left to someone in the will, the executor should promptly check with them first in order to avoid a dispute.

➤ Securing the safety of real property, making sure structures are locked (if appropriate), insured and adequately maintained. The probate estate is responsible for paying these expenses. Similarly, taxes, assessments and utilities may need to be taken care of.

➤ Maintaining or replacing management of business interests owned by the decedent may be required. Sometimes the will specifies whether the decedent wanted his business to continue or not. If the will is silent on the issue, most times it is best to wind up the affairs of the business through a timely liquidation, in order to maximize the return to the estate. If, however, no creditors are harmed and the beneficiaries are in adequate agreement, then they may ask that the business be continued, not liquidated. During the time that the business is part of the probate, the executor will have duties of due diligence to maintain the business, so it is often best to move with all due haste in such situations. Depending upon the nature and form of the decedents business, provisions for continuing the business after death may already exist. For example, a partnership may have addressed what happens to a partner's interest when they die. A corporation may have a buy/sell provision in the shareholder agreement by which the corporation buys back the decedent's shares, sometimes using life insurance proceeds.

➤ Make investment decisions regarding the securities and like assets held by the decedent, as well as for the assets collected by the executor. You have an obligation not to 'waste' assets during probate by failing to put them to work through prudent investment, but you also can be held personally liable for losses incurred by the estate as a result of imprudent investment decisions. Most states provide for a limited list of approved conservative investment options to which the executor should adhere, such as insured bonds, U.S. bonds, or money market accounts. If the will authorizes the executor to invest in securities and/or mutual funds, then the executor can exercise such authority, though absent an exculpatory clause in the will which absolves the executor of liability for losses thereby, such investments are not likely a wise choice.

➤ Obtain appraisals of property as may be required for tax purposes and/or for determining distributions.

➤ Determine if property is not worth managing. For example, it can cost hundreds of dollars to have a boat taken out of the water and prepped for storage. The boat may then cost hundreds of dollars more to store over winter, or during probate. If the boat is only worth a thousand dollars in the first place, then this process is rather wasteful. Instead, you can usually petition the court to permit an early distribution to the ultimate beneficiary, provided that you can reasonably assure the court that assets necessary for creditors and taxes will remain. Alternatively, you can seek authority to sell the asset, keeping the proceeds in the estate.

STEP SEVEN : RESOLVING TAX LIABILITIES

As bad as taxes are when you are alive, they are that much worse after a death. There are multiple types of taxes to be considered, and many of them are unfamiliar to an inexperienced executor. The executor also doesn't have the ready access to the micro- and macro-understanding of assets which many of us have about our own affairs. Add to this is the stress of the executor's liability for late fees, improperly calculated taxes, and unpaid taxes, and you can see why the tax process is one which makes many executors regret their agreement to take on the job in the first place.

Federal taxes (income and estate tax) take priority in payment over the claims of most creditors. Thus, you need to determine the tax liabilities (and availability of funds to pay them) before you take care of paying creditors, let alone beneficiaries. Typical taxes to be evaluated include:

> ➢ Final Federal Income Tax return for the deceased : April 15 rolls around for everyone, even after their death. Depending upon the date of a decedent's death, and the extent to which they were up to date with tax filings, one or even two income tax returns for income during the decedent's lifetime may be due. For example, if a person dies in February of 2010, then the executor is going to need to prepare a return for income from January to February 2010, and a return for income from 2009, if the decedent didn't get it filed before death. Depending upon the wishes of any surviving spouse, the executor can file jointly with the surviving spouse, or file a separate return. Often, the joint return yields the greater benefit for the survivor spouse.

> ➢ State/Local Income Tax return for the deceased : At the state level, the same income tax requirements typically exist, such the returns will need to be filed for any year in which the decedent did not file.

> ➢ Federal Income Tax for the estate: If the probate assets earn more than $600.00 during probate administration, then the executor must file a federal income tax return for the estate. The estate will need to be issued its own EIN by the federal government, much like a business does. The tax rates essentially treat the estate as though it was an individual, but with fewer deductions.

> ➢ State/Local Income Tax for the estate: State and/or local governments may impose taxes on income earned by the estate during probate. Make sure to check your local laws in this regard.

> ➢ Federal Estate Tax Return for the estate : Depending upon the size of the estate, federal estate taxes may be due. This topic is dealt with separately in this book, so suffice it for now to say that if this liability exists, it can quickly diminish the size of the remaining estate. If not paid, however, then personal liability

for the unpaid tax can attach to the executor and/or beneficiaries. Remember that a small probate estate doesn't necessarily mean a small estate for federal estate tax purposes. Included in the taxable federal estate are jointly owned assets, life insurance proceeds, many trust assets, POD/TOD accounts, recent gifts, and other "non-probate" property. This estate tax return must be filed within 9 months of the date of death, with a 5% per month penalty for late filing.

➤ State Estate or Inheritance Tax: Many states still impose one or the other of these death taxes. State Estate Tax, much like the federal counterpart, is based upon the size of the estate, and payable by the estate. State Inheritance Tax is based upon the size of the assets each beneficiary inherits, and is usually the obligation of the beneficiary receiving the assets, though the estate may pay these sums if the will so provides.

STEP EIGHT : DEALING WITH CREDITORS

One of the day to day headaches of being an executor can be coordinating the identification, validation and payment of expenses and debts of the estate. Some payments will need to be made on an ongoing basis in order to preserve estate assets, such as insurance on properties, necessary utilities, or taxes. Failing to make such payments may jeopardize the assets, leading to liability of the executor to the estate. Other debts can, and should, be put in a delayed status while the comprehensive assets and liabilities of the estate are assembled. If the executor pays 'routine' bills early, and comes to find that the estate assets, after payment of taxes, are insufficient to pay all of the creditors, then the executor may be liable for the misallocated payments, even if they were otherwise valid. Instead, the executor must take the time to determine what debts are alleged, whether they are valid and/or enforceable, which debts are by law entitled to payment before others, and how much money is ultimately available to pay the entitled creditors.

Unlike taxes, creditor's unsecured claims are paid from the probate estate assets. Joint tenancy property and life insurance paid to beneficiaries are examples of assets not required to be used for payment of the debts of the decedent and estate. Some creditors may find that there isn't enough money in the estate to pay them. When that happens, it is not the executor's obligation to pay the bills from their own assets, provided that probate was otherwise handled properly.

In order to permit the probate to move forwards promptly, the states have laws which provide for the executor to give notice of the decedent's death and the estate to known creditors, usually accompanied by a publication of the information in a newspaper to give unknown creditors a chance to make a claim. The laws typically provide that any creditors must notify the executor of their claim within a certain period of months, (usually around 6 to 12 months), or their claim will be barred.

While waiting for creditor's claims to come in, the executor should look to see what arrangements the decedent may have make for payment of those debts. The will may provide a framework to describe what assets are to be used to pay debts if possible, such as a will directing the executor to use money from an investment account before selling any real estate left to beneficiaries. Sometime there are credit payment policies (life insurance, credit life insurance, or similar arrangements which specifically provide that debts are paid in the event of death. Health expenses should be submitted to health insurers for payment too.

You may also need to notify public assistance agencies, such as Medicaid, to see if there are any liens for benefits the decedent received during their lifetime.

After claims are filed by the creditors, you and the other people interested financially in the outcome of the probate process can file objections to the claims. If, for example, a beneficiary believes that the debt for some service was already paid off, or you find that the furnace installed shortly before the decedent's death needed early repair, the claim can be objected to. As executor, you should look at each individual claim, and see that the amount is reasonable determined, the decedent actually contracted with the creditor, and that there is no bar to the claim (such as expiration of the statute of limitations). After objections are filed, the creditor must respond to the objection, and the court will resolve the objection at a hearing. In many jurisdictions, if the creditor does not respond to the objection, then the executor won't have to pay the bill. An executor should be careful about paying bills which the executor considers 'proper', but for which claims haven't been filed or allowed. If the beneficiaries object, the court could find that the executor paid a debt which hadn't matured to an obligation of the estate, and thus hold the executor liable therefore.

After the end of the creditor claims period, the executor is equipped to assemble an inventory of the claims against the estate, and arrange for payment. The payment of claims comes from the probate estate assets, however the decision of which assets to use can be vexing. Suppose a $2 million dollar estate includes $1.5 million in real estate, $200,000 in securities, $100,000 in cash, and $200,000 in jewelry. The will gives the real estate to Son 1, securities to Son 2, Jewelry to Son 3, and the cash to charity. Who pays the bills?

If the will contains provisions regarding which assets are to be used for payment of debts, then the will controls the issue. If not, most state statutes provide for a payment scheme. For example, the law may provide that property passing to the residuary beneficiary (the one who gets 'all the rest and residue of the estate') gets used first, then property passing to people other than children or spouses, or property described generally rather than specifically, and so on. The law guides the executor in determining which items to liquidate to pay claims and taxes if the will wasn't planned to provide such guidance. Alternatively, if the beneficiaries of the will can reach an agreement on the issue, the executor can be protected, the beneficiaries satisfied, and the creditors paid.

What if there isn't enough money to pay all of the bills? My mother in law used to joke that all she was leaving me in her will was her debts. Fortunately, however, neither the executor nor the heirs of a decedent are responsible for the decedent's debts beyond the probate assets. What money is available to pay creditors, however, must be carefully applied in such situations in order to avoid a claim against the executor for improper payment of a non-priority creditor. For example, in Pennsylvania, the order of priority for payment of claims by an insufficiently funded estate is:

> ➤ The costs of administration (including attorneys fees)
> ➤ The family exemption
> ➤ The costs of the funeral, burial, and final medical care
> ➤ Federal Taxes
> ➤ Rent due
> ➤ Claims by the State
> ➤ All other claims.

Within the final category of claims for which assets are available, the pool of creditors therein will usually split on an equitable basis the remaining assets. After deciding if court approval is required before payments are made, the executor then pays the approved debts using the estate checking account.

STEP NINE: PROBLEMS ENCOUNTED IN DISTRIBUTION OF THE ESTATE

After the estate debts have been settled, including taxes, the executor can finish the process of distributing the remaining estate assets. Hopefully the will has been clearly drawn, and a relatively straightforward process then ensues as the executor prepares the necessary paperwork to transfer title for assets from the decedent or executor into the name of the beneficiary. In some states, the executor is required to file an accounting with the probate court before distributions are made, and obtain approval of the distribution plan.

Potential problems arise when there are insufficient assets to distribute to the beneficiaries. With the reduction in the estate brought on by taxes and expenses, as well as payment of estate debts, some or all of the beneficiaries may receive less than they anticipated, and less than may be described in the will. The law will provide a method of "abatement", describing which gifts in a will are cut or reduced first, and which receive higher priority in satisfaction. In Pennsylvania, for example, specific gifts to the spouse, children, and then other beneficiaries are given priority in that order, followed by general gifts of cash/securities, other general gifts, the residuary clause, and any property which escaped inclusion in the Will. The closer you are to the top of the list, the more likely you are to receive your gift. Thus, a gift of "my vacation cabin to my son" will receive higher payment priority than "$200,000 to my brother", which in turn is higher in priority than leaving "all the rest and residue of my estate to the Heart Association...". If necessary, the executor can sell assets with a lower priority to satisfy those with a higher priority. In many cases, however, it is possible to get the beneficiaries to come to an agreement regarding the distribution method which avoids hard feelings which can affect families for a lifetime if handled poorly.

Another issue is how to distribute the income generated by the executor's management of the estate during probate. Mere appreciation of a specific piece of property, such as a house, will just inure to the benefit of the specified recipient of the gift, but what about income and/or growth on sums the executor has invested while collecting and maintaining the estate? In most areas, the law provides for the executor to share it among those taking under the will in a fair and equitable manner, while others may assign it to the beneficiary of any residuary clause. This is another area which is ripe for court approval and/or a signed agreement from the beneficiaries.

The first distributee is often the spouse of the deceased, if any. Most states provide special rights to the spouse, to make sure that he or she is treated with some equity in the will. The first of these rights may be called a Family Allowance, or Spousal Exemption, or other term. This right typically provided that the surviving spouse and/or children of a deceased are entitled to certain estate assets as a top priority claim. In Pennsylvania, this sum is currently $3,500.

A separate claim for the spouse exists, called the Elective Share in many states. In order to avoid a surviving spouse from being disinherited by the decedent (such as a man who leaves all his property to charity, or a girlfriend, while impoverishing his spouse), a spouse may 'elect against the will', and receive a statutory share of certain property. When this is invoked, the math can get complicated, because the estate against which the elective share is calculated is not the same as the probate estate. For example, in Pennsylvania, the spouse can take her elective share of one-third of the probate estate passing by will (or by intestacy), plus income from or use of property owned by the decedent (including the home they lived in), trusts which the decedent controlled for the decedent's benefit, annuity benefits payable to others than the spouse, and the value of gifts made by the decedent alone (i.e. not joined in by the spouse) less than one year before the decedent's date of death. The elective share cannot be taken against insurance proceeds, pensions, and certain other property. Finally, there is usually a time limit within which the spouse must exercise the elective share. As you can see, this process can get messy, and the input of an attorney is absolutely essential if this claim may arise.

Another common problem in distribution is known as ademption. If the will leaves his BMW to his son, his diamond ring to his daughter, and $10,000 in stock to his friend, then all may happily receive their gift. But, what if at the time of death, the decedent had traded his BMW in for a new Honda, lost the diamond ring, and had already given $5,000 in stock to his friend before he died? Gifts may be considered as being subject to ademption if they either don't exist at the time of death (known as ademption by extinction), or if they have previously been given to the beneficiary (ademption by satisfaction). Partial ademption by satisfaction may be found where a lifetime gift was meant to be in partial satisfaction of a gift to be found in the will. Most states have statutes which must be consulted to resolve such situations. For example, in Pennsylvania, if the testator intended to gift certain stocks to a beneficiary, but sold them, then the gift is adeemed, i.e. void. If, however, the company was bought by another company and new shares issued in the parent company, then the gift may survive. If the diamond ring was lost but insured, then the daughter is entitled to the insurance proceeds. The car to the son will depend upon the language in the will; if it is clear that the testator intended to give what car he had to his son, then the Honda will pass to the son. If the language is read to mean that the BMW was the specific gift, then the gift is subject to ademption by extinction, i.e. it doesn't exist to give anymore. Finally, as for the lifetime gift made to the decedent's friend, most state statutes now provide that the lifetime gift is not interpreted as a partial satisfaction of the gift in the will, unless there is written evidence to the contrary. Fortunately, with careful estate planning, these types of issues can be avoided.

Believe it or not, some people don't want to receive an inheritance. Yes, that's right, they turn down the money. The most common reason for this is to avoid having the inheritance seized by creditors of the intended beneficiary. If the decedent's son is to receive 50,000 under the will, but is currently subject to a claim from a creditor to whom he owes 40,000, then the son's gift will mostly just end up in the hands of the creditor, which was likely not the decedent's goal under the will. Instead, the law permits the beneficiary son to 'disclaim', or reject, the inheritance. If the will provides for how to handle such a situation, for example by naming alternate beneficiaries, then the property will avoid the son (and his creditors), and go to the alternate beneficiaries. If no provision in the will is made, then it will typically pass through to the residuary clause, and be distributed to whoever gets 'what's left'. Other times, the property may simply pass over the disclaiming beneficiary, and go to their own children.

A final problem which arises is what to do when a beneficiary under the will doesn't survive longer than the decedent. What does an executor do with a gift in the will to someone already dead? In most states, that gift then 'lapses', or becomes void. If, however, the gift is to a family member, then state 'anti-lapse' statutes can cure this defect, and instead substitute the surviving descendants of the deceased beneficiary to receive the gift. This situation can also present problems when a testator and a beneficiary under a will die at the same time, very close in time, or in an undermined order. If they both die in a car crash, or don't return from a fishing trip in the Atlantic, how is the will to be interpreted? Many states have addressed this by passing a version of the Uniform Simultaneous Death Act. This provides that if you can't determine if two such people died other than simultaneously, then the will of each is administered as through the testator survived. This statute, however, can create further problem, because if one person survives by just a day, or even hours, then they haven't died simultaneously, and unanticipated distribution of assets can occur. As a result, many attorney's drafting wills, and even some state statutes, require a beneficiary to survive a deceased testator by at least a specified period of days, weeks or months in order to be considered a surviving beneficiary who would take property (into the second-to-die person's estate) under the will.

STEP TEN: DISTRIBUTION OF THE ESTATE

At last, the long awaited distribution of the estate assets can move forwards. The executor must transfer title in all of the remaining assets to the appropriate beneficiary. While some assets may have been converted into cash during the probate process, most of the assets are likely still in the format in which they previously existed, and they can be distributed in such form (known as a distribution in kind). Different types of property will need to be handled in differing manners, for example:

> ➢ Money gifts can be paid by estate check.
> ➢ Real estate will likely need a deed from the executor
> ➢ Personal property can be delivered, though you may need to create an Assignment of Title document for the court and/or insurance purposes
> ➢ Property with title documents (cars, boats, etc) will require new titles issued
> ➢ Securities and investment accounts will need to be retitled at least.
> ➢ Savings bonds may be redeemed for cash, or reissued in the name of the beneficiary
> ➢ Minor's property may need to go into a custodial account (UTMA/UGMA), or a trust, or may be paid in some cases directly to the child's parent or guardian if permitted under state law.
> ➢ Trusts may need to be created or funded, with trust accounts opened.

For all distributions made, you should have detailed records, and keep a receipt from each recipient. Some courts require you to file an accounting of the distributions, and attach the receipts. Moreover, it protects the executor from claims of unaccounted for property or undelivered inheritances.

STEP ELEVEN: CLOSING THE ESTATE, AND LOOKING FORWARDS

The executor, having completed the above steps, should now be ready to close the estate and obtain discharge from the duties of executor. Some jurisdictions permit an affidavit to be filed by the executor which simply describes the actions taken, and the estate is administratively closed. Others require, or permit, the court to issue an order which closes the estate and releases the executor from his or her obligations and bond. Far too many people, exhausted from the probate process, neglect to take this final step, but the court will someday make you do it, and may express its displeasure that this task wasn't handled in a timely fashion, so you are best served by just finishing the probate process off in the correct manner.

I suggest to most people that they take the opportunity after probate is completed to consider how this has affected their own estate planning. All of our estate planning steps are undertaken based upon the state of affairs which existed at the time. Your plan should take into account your assets, your intended beneficiaries, your business interests, your goals, and the current state of the law. While good planning documents do provide for flexibility or anticipation as future events unfold, the passage of a significant event like the death of a loved one is a milestone at which such documents should be reviewed. Some examples of planning considerations at this time include:

> ➤ Wills may describe a dispositive scheme which includes gifts to the person now deceased. Such wills may be redrafted in light of the current situation.
> ➤ Living Trusts may be appropriate for beneficiaries seeking to shelter assets from future spouses, or current ones.
> ➤ Various forms of Pay On Death accounts, retirement accounts, and securities may still include the deceased as the POD beneficiary.
> ➤ Life Insurance policies listing the deceased as a beneficiary should be revised.
> ➤ Joint Tenancies may now be sole tenancies in the survivor; new planning can benefit the tax and/or probate treatment of this property when the sole owner dies.

➤ Consider whether a charitable annuity, immediate annuity, or reverse mortgage may be an appropriate financial and estate planning tool for a surviving spouse.

Remember that if you are called upon to serve as an executor, you don't have to do it alone. The duties of an executor can be handled with the assistance of attorneys, accountants, bankers, and other professionals who are experienced in this field, and their professional services greatly reduce the stress and anxiety of fulfilling the role of an executor.

CHAPTER 13

MOVING ON

Continuing Your Adventures In Estate Planning

If every journey starts with a single step, you can safely say that you now have a running start on your road to understanding what an effective estate plan can do for you. The goal in this book was to enable you to be able to understand the issues and language of estate planning in order to empower you to be an active participant in the estate planning process with your attorney. Knowing what information you will need to assemble and consider, as well as what questions you have when you meet with your attorney will give you the advantage of being an informed client. In that position, you will also be far better able to evaluate whatever plan elements are being suggested, and understand the directions provided by your attorney regarding how to complete any necessary steps to establish and maintain your estate plan.

If you haven't yet taken action to discuss your estate planning needs with a qualified attorney, then I encourage you to make that the next step of your journey. Most attorneys will meet with you for little or no cost during an initial consultation. You can then start to get your arms around the idea of just how much work is required to take the general information in this book and weave it into a comprehensive plan which accommodates the details of your life. Please don't be intimated by the concept of hiring an attorney to customize an estate plan for you. Your life, every life, is its own unique and wondrous thing. There is no reason for you to expect an estate plan for such a life to fit in some generic form from a book or website.

If you have moved forwards with your estate planning efforts, then I congratulate you on your preparedness and foresight. Your family, beneficiaries, physicians, executors and many others will all benefit from the fact that you took the time to take care of your personal affairs. Remember, however, that as life continues and changes, so too may your estate planning needs. You should continue to periodically reevaluate your planning status, whether by yourself or hopefully in brief consultation with your attorney. Continued vigilance over your plan is one of the best ways to see that what once was a tailored estate plan does not become inaccurate, misdirected or irrelevant with the passage of time.

I hope this book has been of value to you. Please feel free to contact me with any questions you have about the book, or to share stories about the highs and lows of your estate planning journey. My information is available on the copyright page immediately following the title page in this book, and on the Personal Information Inventory and Letters of Instruction which follows in Appendix One.

Best of luck,

MTC

APPENDIX ONE – FORM BONUS

As a bonus for those of your who purchased this book, I have included in the following pages a form which I developed to help my clients organize their affairs, develop an understanding of the nature of their estate, and to provide a convenient method for them to provide information to their family, friends and other important people in the event of their death or incapacity. I hope you will find it useful.

Please remember that this form is the property of Mark T. Coulter, and is protected by U.S. Copyright laws. Except for personal use by the purchaser of this book and family thereof, this form should not be copied or reproduced in any way without the written permission of Mark T. Coulter. Copyright 2009 Mark T. Coulter. All rights reserved.

If you need more information regarding this form, please contact me at <u>MCoulter@EstatePlanningCenters.com</u>.

THE ESTATE PLANNING CENTERS

EPC

www.EstatePlanningCenters.com

CONFIDENTIAL
PERSONAL INFORMATION INVENTORY
AND LETTERS OF INSTRUCTION

PREPARED FOR:	

Date revised:	

The following information will assist in accurately understanding your current estate planning position, and assist your family, friends and/or associates in handling your personal affairs in the event of your illness or death. My attorney, Mark T. Coulter, Esquire can be reached at 412-225-2018, or by email to MCoulter@EstatePlanningCenters.com. In the event you cannot contact him there, please contact the Supreme Court of Pennsylvania at (717) 731-7073, or online at http://www.padisciplinaryboard.org to obtain current contact information. ©2009 Mark T. Coulter

This document contains the following sections:

1. **PERSONAL INFORMATION (ASSUMES A MARRIED COUPLE)**
2. **FAMILY INFORMATION**
3. **LETTERS OF INSTRUCTION UPON MY DEATH TO MY FAMILY, FRIENDS AND ASSOCIATES**
4. **ASSET AND LIABILITY SUMMARY**
5. **INVENTORY OF ASSETS**
6. **INVENTORY OF LIABILITIES AND OBLIGATIONS**
7. **ESTATE PLANNING INFORMATION**
8. **CONFIDENTIAL INFORMATION**

1. **PERSONAL INFORMATION (ASSUMES A MARRIED COUPLE)**

	HUSBAND'S INFORMATION	WIFE'S INFORMATION
Legal name for signatures		
Other names used		
Address		
Home Phone		
Cell Phone		
Work Phone		

Email address		
Employer		
Employer address/phone		
Job title		
Social Security #		
U.S. Citizen?		
Date of Birth		
Military Service ID		
Branch		
Dates of Service		
Discharge location		
Current marital status		
Date married		
Location married		
Prior Marriage		
Prior spouse		
Divorced/Widow/Annul		
Prenuptial Contract		
Mother's full maiden name		
Fathers full name		
Income Sources/amounts		
Payroll		
Social Security		
Workers Compensation		
IRA's/401k's		
Pensions		
Disability		
Other		
Comments		

2. **FAMILY INFORMATION**

Children's Names (current marriage)	Address	Age	Phone Number/email
Proposed guardian for minor children if necessary:			

Children's Names (from prior marriage)	Address	Age	Phone #/email	Parents Names
Proposed guardian for minor children if necessary:				

Are any of your children adopted? If so, please list names:_____
Are any children deceased? If so, please list names: _____

Parent's Names	Address	Living or Dec'd.	Phone Number
H			
H			
W			
W			

Siblings Names	Address	Age	Living or Dec'd.	Phone Number
H				
H				
H				
W				
W				
W				

Siblings Names	Address	Age	Living or Dec'd.	Phone Number
H				
H				
H				
W				
W				
W				

Grandchildren names	Grandchildren parents	Address/Phone	Age

Any other dependents, either now or planned in the future?

Do any of your children, grandchildren or parents have special needs which should be taken into account in your planning? Examples include autism, mental/physical disabilities, Alzheimer's disease, dementia…). If so, please explain below.

3. **LETTERS OF INSTRUCTION UPON MY DEATH TO MY FAMILY, FRIENDS AND ASSOCIATES**

DISPOSITIVE LETTER OF ADMINISTRATION – TO DIRECT TANGIBLE PERSONAL ASSETS IF INCORPORATED INTO YOUR WILL	
-I give the property listed below in the left column to the beneficiary(s) listed in the right column, as follows:	
Description of property which I leave to the named beneficiary	*Beneficiary*
List the personal items you wish to give in the left column, the person they go to in the right, and then sign and date this page below.	
Print your name:	Signed by: Date:
Comments for my family and friends:	

DESCRIPTION OF BURIAL AND FUNERAL ARRANGEMENTS	
-To ease decision making following my death, I have made the following arrangements, and/or have the following preferences for my funeral arrangements	
Organ/Body/Tissue donation:	Preferences for funeral service:
Autopsy preference if recommended:	Grave plot location/information:
Embalming preference (yes/no):	Eulogy:

Open/closed casket:	Headstone/marker information:
Cremation/burial/other:	Charity for gifts in lieu of flowers:
Funeral Home:	Prepaid services:
Location/method of burial or disposition of remains:	Special comments for obituary:
Final Clothing:	Pallbearers:
Location of contact information for friends and family to notify:	Other comments about service or anything:

People to notify (with numbers/email)

(Employer, Employees, Daycare, Clergy, Family, Friends, Animal care, housekeeper, etc)

| Signed by: | Date: |

4. **ASSET AND LIABILITY SUMMARY**

Type of Asset	Value-Joint H/W	Value-Husband	Value-Wife	Other Title?
Cash (checking/savings)				
Certs. Of Deposit				
Bonds				
Investment Accts				
Bonds				
Loans/Notes				
Life Insurance (cash value amount)				
Life Insurance (death benefit)				
401K savings				
IRA/Roth IRA				

Primary Residence				
Farms/Ranches				
Other Real Estate				
Business interests				
Other stocks held				
Partnerships				
Royalties				
Anticipations (inheritance, gift, judgments…)				
Personal items of value (cars, jewelry, collections, art…)				
Other – (describe):				
TOTAL				

Type of Liability	Debt-Joint H/W	Debt-Husband	Debt-Wife	Debt - Other
Primary Residence Mortgage				
Credit Cards				
Installment Debt				
Secured Debt				
Life Insurance Loans				
Unpaid Taxes				
Government assistance				
Other – (describe):				
TOTAL				

5. **INVENTORY OF ASSETS**

-		- CASH AND FINANCIAL ACCOUNTS					
Account type CK/SAV/CD	Institution name	Institution City,State	Value	Cost Basis	Account Number	Titled To: Beneficiary?	

- INVESTMENT ACCOUNTS AND RETIREMENT PLANS – Stock accounts,401k's, IRA's, Pensions, Profit Sharing, Other						
Account Type 401K,IRA,Pens.	Institution name	Institution City,State	Value	Account Number	Titled To: Beneficiary?:	

- LIFE INSURANCE POLICIES – Whole life, Group, Term, Annuity…On or Owned by you or spouse								
Insurance Co.	Policy # + Document Location	Owner	Who is Insured	Type	Cash Value	Death Benefit	Loans taken	Primary Beneficiary? Secondary Beneficiary?

- REAL ESTATE HOLDINGS – Primary residence, vacation homes, condos, investment property, oil/mineral leases				
Type of Holding + Street Address City, State, Zip	Purch.Date Purch. $	Titled To:	Value $ Mortgage $	Lienholders

- RECEIVABLES: LOANS, DEBTS, JUDGEMENTS, SETTLEMENTS, CUSTOMER REWARDS, ETC.			
Debtor	Amount	Owed to:	Terms summary and Note location

- BONDS – Savings bonds, Municipal, Corporate, other			
Type/Description	Face Amount	Owners	ID# and Location of Bond

- EXPECTATIONS - Inheritances, personal injury judgments, other						
Description of Expectation	Recipient of Expectation	Payor of Expectation	Approx Value	When expected	Location of documents	Other info

PERSONAL ASSETS OF SIGNIFICANT VALUE – Stock certificated, vehicles, art, antiques, jewelry, collections, etc						
Description	Owners	Your interests held	$ Value $Pricepaid	Location of Item	Location of documents	Info (buyers, keys,liens)

REAL ESTATE INFORMATION – Primary residence (home, condo, apartment)

-Information regarding your other real estate holdings and tax issues

Nature of R.E.	Address	Title Insurer	Property Tax get paid to:	Mortgage holder	Mortgage payment$
Purchase price	When purchased:	Closing lawyer/agent	Approx total annual tax	Mortgage balance	Mortgage payments due:

Describe any capital improvements which might increase the taxable basis of this property, including the date and cost thereof, and if any records or receipts exist:

Other info (location of records, tenant arrangements, maintenance needs, special concerns, or other…)

REAL ESTATE INFORMATION – other real estate

-Information regarding your other real estate holdings and tax issues

Nature of R.E.	Address	Title Insurer	Property Tax get paid to:	Mortgage holder	Mortgage payment$
Purchase price	When purchased:	Closing lawyer/agent	Approx total annual tax	Mortgage balance	Mortgage payments due:

Describe any capital improvements which might increase the taxable basis of this property, including the date and cost thereof, and if any records or receipts exist:

Other info (location of records, tenant arrangements, maintenance needs, special concerns, or other…)

CHILDRENS OR MINORS ACCOUNTS

Please describe any accounts maintained for a child of yours, and/or any account involving a minor in which you have, or may have, a financial interest. This includes custodial accounts, UGMA/UTMA accounts, 529 College Savings accounts, tuition plans, trust funds, and anything else.

BUSINESS INTERESTS

If you hold any ownership interest or other involvement in a business organization, then you should separately prepare detailed information which may be required for your family or executor in order to continue, sell or liquidate your interests.

INTELLECTUAL PROPERTY

If you hold any ownership interest or other involvement which include patents, copyrights, trademarks, royalties or things of that nature, describe them below.

©2009 Mark T. Coulter

6.   **INVENTORY OF LIABILITIES AND OBLIGATIONS**

CREDIT ACCOUNTS AND LOANS

List your credit accounts, including major cards, local stores, and others

Issuer	Account #	Creditor	Names on account	Contact info, etc.
Mortgage1				
Mortgage2				
Auto loan				
Life Insurance loan				
Unpaid taxes				
Government Assistance				
Major Credit card 1				
Major Credit card 2				
Store credit card 1				
Store credit card 2				
Other loans				

FAMILY OBLIGATIONS

-Information regarding debts and obligations affecting family members

TYPE OF OBLIGATION	DESCRIPTION	Other Info
Alimony		
Child Support		
Educational Commitments		
Institutionalized Persons		
Other		
Pets Needing Care		
Charitable Commitments		

Describe any gifts over the annual exclusion amount ($13,000 as of 2009), including the recipient, what was given, value of the gift, the year, the Donor (giver) of the gift, and if any gift tax return was filed. If NONE, then write NONE please.

| |
| |
| |

- FIDUCIARY OBLIGATIONS

Please describe any current fiduciary duties you have, such as a positions as a trustee, guardian, custodian, executor, agent, and include the location of any relevant documents.

| |
| |
| |

- LITIGATION

Describe any litigation you are currently involved in, or any known possibility thereof.

| |
| |

7.   **ESTATE PLANNING INFORMATION**

- ESTATE PLANNING DOCUMENT STATUS						
Document ID	Does Husband have	Date	Location of Docs	Does Wife have	Date	Location of Docs
A Will						
A Codicil						
A Trust						
A Power of Attorney						
A Living Will						
Any other planning Docs						
Disability application						
Burial Arrangements						
Do you currently suffer any serious medical condition?						

- ESTATE SECURITY STATUS				
Is there a...		Include who or how to access		Include who or how to access
A Safe				
A Safe Deposit Box				
An Account Password list				

- PROFESSIONAL ADVISERS FAMILIAR WITH YOUR AFFAIRS				
Name	Occupation	Address	Phone	Nature of involvement
	Accountant			
	Health Care Proxy			

	Insurance Agent			
	Financial Planner			
	Attorney			
	Banker			
	Broker			
	Advisor			
	Agent -Pwr of Atty			
	Primary Care Dr			
	Clergy			
	Executor			
	Trustee			
	Other:			

SEMI-CONFIDENTIAL : LIST OF LESS- SECURE ACCOUNT PASSWORDS, UTILITY INFORMATION, ETC

-The following information may be required to access other information in the time following my death

ITEM	Phone #	ACCESS METHOD/PASSWORD/KEY LOCATION/OTHER
Gas service provider		
Electric provider		
Cable Television provider		
Online Service/Internet provider		
Online subscriptions or services		
Water/sewage service provider		
Phone service		
Cell phone service		
Signed by: Date:		

ESTATE DOCUMENTS – CROSS OUT ANY WHICH DON'T EXIST, AND ADD ANY OTHERS NECESSARY

-The following documents should be secured for my family and/or executor

DOCUMENT	DATED	LOCATION
Will titled:		
Codicil titled:		
Trust titled:		
Insurance Policy (Co./#)		
Insurance Policy (Co./#)		
Letters of Instruction		
Power of Attorney		
Living Will		
Health Care Proxy		
Beneficiary designation forms:		
Other estate planning documents:		

IMPORTANT DOCUMENTS – CROSS OUT ANY WHICH DON'T EXIST, AND ADD ANY OTHERS NECESSARY

-The following documents may be useful for my family and/or executor

DOCUMENT	DATED	LOCATION
Deeds: (describe any applicable)		
Mortages:		
Annuities:		
Tax returns filed:		
Current tax information:		
Receipts:		
Warranties/Guarantees:		
Owner's manuals:		
Financial records/files:		
Check register:		

Bank Statements:		
Marriage license		
Loan payment books/certificates:		
Birth certificate		
Passport		
Licenses (drivers, other)		
Military records:		
Car titles		
Other titles:		
Business records:		
Government benefits(SS,Medicare,Medicaid,VA,?)		
Adoption papers:		
Citizenship records:		
Social Security card		
Divorce papers		
Signed by: Date:		

MISCELLANEOUS INSURANCE COVERAGE		
-The following insurance coverage information may be useful		
TYPE OF COVERAGE	COMPANY	Other Info
Major Medical		
Medigap		
Medicare Part D		
Other medical:		
Car insurance		
Home insurer		
Credit insurances:		
Mortgage Insurance:		
Long term care		
Dental		

Vision		
Other:		

CONFIDENTIAL : LIST OF SECURE ACCOUNT PASSWORD, SECURITY COMBINATIONS, AND OTHER ACCESS INFORMATION

This list, if it exists, will be on the following page. If it is not, the following arrangements have been made to obtain this information:

-The following information may be required to access important information in the time following my death

SECURITY ITEM	ACCESS METHOD/PASSWORD/KEY LOCATION/OTHER
Online accounts: site/account name or number:	Password/security questions/PIN:
Bank	
Broker	
Retirement account	
Email	
Website Hosting	
Cellphone voicemail	
Home Computer passwords	
Safety Deposit box at:	Key location:
Home Security alarm	
Home safe location:	Combination: (or key location)
Offsite storage at:	Access method:
P.O.Box	Key/Combination:
Locked cabinets/storage:	Access method:
Bonds/valuables stored:	
Secret hiding places	

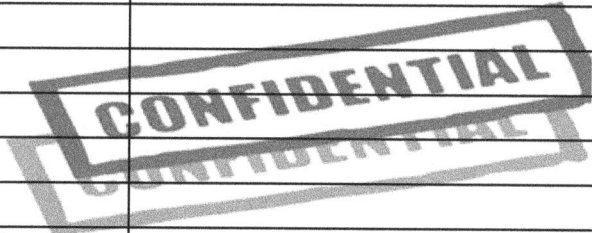

WARNING: CONFIDENTIAL: KEEP THIS SECURE, AND ADVISE TRUSTED FAMILY MEMBERS OR ADVISORS WHERE IT CAN BE LOCATED IF IT IS NEEDED

APPENDIX TWO – GLOSSARY of Estate Planning Terms

GLOSSARY OF COMMON ESTATE PLANNING TERMS

⇒ **2053 Trust** – see Section 2053 trust

⇒ **A/B Trust** - A revocable living trust often used by married couples, where two trusts are created (A Trust and B trust) to be funded by property protected by the Unified Credit (trust B) and the unlimited Marital deduction following the death of the first spouse. Following the death of the second spouse, another Unified Credit amount is available to further fund trust B. Trust A may be called a marital trust, and Trust B may be called a credit shelter trust.

⇒ **Accumulation Trust** – refers to any trust which accumulates some or all of its income, rather than distributing all of the income to the beneficiaries each year.

⇒ **Ademption** – occurs when property described in a Will is no longer owned by the decedent at death. Such a gift may be adeemed, or rendered void if the Will or state law so provides.

⇒ **Administration** – The steps required of an executor or administrator to resolve the estate, including appointment of the personal representative, collection and management of assets, resolution of taxes and debts, and distribution of the remaining property.

⇒ **Administrator** – the personal representative appointed to handle administration of the estate of someone who dies intestate (without a will).

⇒ **Adminstratrix** – a female administrator

⇒ **Advance medical directive** – also called a Living Will, this document can describe the type of life-saving care you would like to be administered if you are unconscious and either in a permanent vegetative state or suffering a terminal disease. Often coupled with a Health Care Proxy or Medical Power of Attorney.

⇒ **Affidavit** – a document which is sworn under oath, usually in front of a notary or other person authorized by the state to administer oaths.

⇒ **Agent** - a person authorized to act for someone else, frequently under a power of attorney.

⇒ **Ancillary probate** – separate probate proceeding which needs to be conducted in a state outside of the decedent's domicile in order to probate assets located in such nondomiciliary state.

⇒ **Annual Gift Tax Exclusion** – describes the value of property which any person can give to any number of other people in a given calendar year without having to file a gift tax return or account for any gift tax consequences. This amount is per-donor/per-donee, and there is no limit on how many people a donor gives such gifts to, so long as they remain under the annual exclusion amount.

⇒ **Applicable exemption amount** - correlated to the amount of assets which a tax credit (such as the Unified Credit) can shelter from tax consequences. Each person is entitled to a tax credit which is used to reduce the tax assessed on their property. The value of property which will generate tax which can be sheltered by the available credit is referred to as the Applicable Exemption Amount, or sometimes the Exemption Equivalent.

⇒ **Ascertainable standard** – often required to prevent trust property from being included in a beneficiary's estate when they die, an applicable standard provides discretion for the trustee to distribute assets for a beneficiary's health, education, support, or maintenance.

⇒ **Asset Protection** – The process of using estate planning tools to protect your assets from attack by legal judgments, creditors, or risks.

⇒ **Attorney in fact** - see Agent.

⇒ **Beneficiary** – someone who is or may be entitled to assets such as from a will, trust or contract benefit.

⇒ **Bequest** – describes a gift to someone from a will. May be a specific description of identified property, or a general bequest of assets which doesn't direct the use of specific property.

⇒ **Bond** – a type of insurance which provides payment if the bonded person (such as an executor or trustee) performs duties improperly and/or contrary to law and thereby causes loss or damage.

⇒ **By Right of Representation** – see per stirpes.

⇒ **Bypass Trust** - another name for a credit shelter trust or a B Trust in an A/B Trust plan. See these terms.

⇒ **Charitable Gift Annuity** – contract with a charity where in exchange for a sum given to the charity, the donor receives a calculated income back from the charity, usually for the donor's lifetime. The value of the donation, less the present value of the payment stream, is a charitable deduction. Annuity payments from the charity are based on IRS valuation tables.

⇒ **Charitable Lead Trust** – A trust which pays benefits to a charity for a period of time, after which the trust income and/or assets are typically paid to a non-charitable beneficiary of the donor. The gift to the non-charitable beneficiary is reduced in value by the IRS by the value of the income stream to the charity.

⇒ **Charitable Remainder Trust** – the opposite of a charitable lead trust, in that a non-charity beneficiary receives income from the trust for a period of time, and the balance is distributed to the charity. The donor or beneficiary receives the benefit of income, while the donor still receives a charitable deduction.

⇒ **Charitable Remainder Unitrust** - A charitable remainder trust wherein the income paid to the non-charitable beneficiary is based upon a percentage of the trust assets, rather than a set payment amount.

⇒ **Chattel** – see tangible personal property.

⇒ **Codicil** – A document which changes or adds to a will.

⇒ **Community property** – in some states, describes property acquired by either party to a marriage during the time they are married, excluding gifts, inheritances or court awards in favor of only one spouse to the extent the asset are thereafter maintained as separate property.

⇒ **Conservator** - the person appointed to act as the agent for someone who has become incapacitated or is otherwise legally incompetent, typically having jurisdiction over the incapacitated persons assets rather than their personal care and safety.

⇒ **Conservatorship** – proceedings under which a conservator is appointed for an incapacitated or legally incompetent person.

⇒ **Contract** – agreement between two or more parties describing their duties and/or rights regarding a topic. Depending upon the subject matter, it may be oral or written.

⇒ **Creditor** – People or organizations to which a debt is owed.

⇒ **Credit shelter trust** – a 'B Trust' under an A/B Trust plan, described above. Used to maximize the advantage of a married couple's Unified Credit and Marital deductions for estate and gift taxes.

⇒ **Crummey Trust** - A trust which does not give the beneficiary the general right to any assets, but instead provides a window of opportunity each year to access contributions made to the trust in a given year. Used frequently to gain the benefit of a gift exclusion or credit by the donor without giving the beneficiary substantial present access to the funds. Frequently used in an irrevocable life insurance trust.

⇒ **Custodianship** – used to permit a person to hold and manage property for another person who may be unable to do so, such as a minor or incapacitated person under the Uniform Gifts to Minors Act. The custodian must handle the funds for the benefit of the minor or incapacitated person, and the funds typically must be given to the beneficiary when a certain age in majority is reached or they otherwise attain legal capacity.

⇒ **Death taxes** - term used to quickly describe the numerous taxes which a decedent's estate may generate, including the federal estate tax, estate income tax, state inheritance/estate taxes, and the generation skipping tax.

⇒ **Declaration of Trust** – the document wherein a Settlor describes the salient terms of a trust, including the Settlor, Trustee, Beneficiaries, as well as such terms and conditions of the trust as the Settlor may include, such as the Assets of the trust, provisions for guiding the Trustee's management and distribution obligations, successor trustees, contingent beneficiaries, and more.

⇒ **Decedent** - a person who has died, as in "the decedent".

⇒ **Descendants** – Also referred to as a person's "issue", the blood relatives (or sometimes also legally adopted individuals) from a person's children on down, including grandchildren, great grandchildren, etc. Does not include parents, in-laws, siblings or other people who are either up or equal on the family tree or are related by marriage only.

⇒ **Deed** - document which is the evidence of title to real estate, and also its passage from past owner to new owner.

⇒ **Devise** – typically refers to a gift of real estate under a will.

⇒ **Direct Skip** – When calculating generation skipping tax issues, a gift or bequest to a person two or more generations below the donor or testator.

⇒ **Disclaim** – a beneficiary who refuses property left in a will or trust, usually for tax or creditor reasons. The property involved typically passes to the descendants of the disclaiming person, unless the document creating the interest provides otherwise.

⇒ **Devisee** - A person to whom a gift, typically real estate, is made in a will.

⇒ **Discretionary trust** – a trust wherein the trustee is given discretion to use their judgment to determine how to manage and/or distribute trust principal and/or income to the beneficiaries.

⇒ **Disinherit** – to exclude a person from a will when they otherwise would have had a right to a portion of the estate, such as under the state intestacy scheme. Usually applies to the spouse and/or issue of a testator, and some statutory protections may apply to such legal heirs.

⇒ **Do-Not-Resuscitate Order** – A physician-authorized order which permits the paramedics to respect a terminal patient's prior request that paramedics do not provide certain life-saving or life-prolonging procedures if they encounter a patient who is unconscious and otherwise would receive such procedures, such as cardiopulmonary resuscitation.

⇒ **Domicile** – legally where a person lives and intends to make their home. Usually, it is the same state as where a person resides, but the two can intentionally be different, such as a person living in a northern state who has purchased a home and car in the south, transferred their license and voting registrations, etc with the intent to make their vacation home into their retirement location. The location of a person's domicile can determine which state's laws, taxes and other rights and obligations attach to a person's property or estate.

⇒ **Donee** - A person to whom a gift is made.

⇒ **Donor** - A person who makes a gift.

⇒ **Durable power of attorney** – a power of attorney which remains legally effective even if the principal who executes the power suffers legal incapacity.

⇒ **Economic Growth and Tax Relief Reconciliation Act of 2001 (EGTRRA)** – 2001 tax act during the Bush administration which reduced federal gift taxes, including a repeal of the estate tax effective in 2010. By the terms of this Act, it will expire after 2010, and the law will revert to pre-2001 law unless Congress passes new legislation

⇒ **Electing against the will** – Action of a surviving spouse to claim a statutorily described share of a decedent's estate, usually when the will provided a lesser amount to an aggrieved spouse.

⇒ **Escheat** – property passing to the government due to a lack of heirs or others entitled to take title thereto. **Estate** – broadly, the property and interests owned by a person, of any type or nature.

⇒ **Estate plan** – A plan developed, based upon your personal assets, goals and family situation, which attempts to maximize your ability to achieve your goals, while minimizing costs, taxes, risks and burdens. Ideally, it functions well during periods when you are health, ill, and incapacitated, as well as at your death.

⇒ **Estate tax** – potentially the biggest of the taxes imposed following a person's death, payable to the federal government based upon the size of your taxable estate. May also refer to similar taxes collected by some state governments.

⇒ **Executor** – The person a testator names in their will to handle estate administration.

⇒ **Executrix** – a female executor.

⇒ **Exemption Equivalent** – see Applicable Exemption Amount.

⇒ **Family limited partnership** - A limited partnership which may used to decrease the value of family assets in order to reduce gift tax obligations, and also to provide for patriarchal control over assets while family members are educated in how to manage them, such as business or investment interests.

⇒ **Family Trust** – A Living Trust with family beneficiaries, and usually the donor as trustee.

⇒ **Fiduciary** – describes a person who is obligated to act for the benefit of someone else, such as an executor, trustee, custodian or guardian.

⇒ **Future Interest** – An interest in an asset which will not be enjoyed by the owner of the future interest until some event or time in the future.

⇒ **General Bequest** – A gift in a will which is not to be given in the form of a specifically identified asset, but instead from the estate assets generally. Distinguished from a Specific Bequest. See also General Devise.

⇒ **General Power of Attorney** - A Power of Attorney which gives broad legal authority to an Agent to do a number of actions on behalf of the Principal, as defined in the document itself.

⇒ **Generation Skipping Transfer** - A transfer of property to a beneficiary who is two or more generations younger than the generation of the grantor, such as from grandparent to grandchild.

⇒ **Generation Skipping Transfer Tax** - A transfer tax on Generation Skipping Transfers, to avoid wealth missing a round of estate taxes between each generation.

⇒ **Gift** – Any transfer of property without receipt of fair market value in return.

⇒ **Gift tax** - A tax imposed by the IRS on gifts exceeding certain amounts, which is owed by the person making the gift.

⇒ **Grantee** –The recipient of property under a deed, or sometimes under other documents such as a trust.

⇒ **Grantor** – The person transferring property to another under a deed, or sometime refers to a person transferring property into a trust. May also be called a Settlor, or even a Donor if a gift is involved.

⇒ **Grantor Retained Annuity Trust (GRAT)** - A trust which gives the Grantor fixed annual payments for a described term, after which the remaining assets pass on to other beneficiaries, which is used to exclude assets from a Grantor's estate at a decreased value for tax purposes, provided that the Grantor survives for the full term of the annuitized period.

⇒ **Grantor Trust** – A term used to describe a trust where the Grantor has retained enough rights or interest in the trust that its income is attributed to the Grantor for tax purposes.

⇒ **Gross estate** – The total assets of a decedent, prior to reduction for debts and permitted deductions for estate tax calculation.

⇒ **Guardian** – A person who is appointed by the court to serve in a fiduciary capacity for a minor or incapacitated person, with responsibility for either their personal care, their financial care, or sometimes both.

⇒ **Health Care Power Of Attorney** – See Health Care Proxy

⇒ **Health Care Proxy** - A document used to appoint another person to make medical decisions if the person signing the health care proxy is medically unable to make decisions about their medical care.

⇒ **Heir** – Technically refers to a person who might receive a portion of your estate if you were to die without a will (i.e. intestate), though more commonly today, this term may be used to refer to anyone who can take property from an estate, by will or intestacy.

⇒ **Heirloom** – Tangible personal property whose fair market value is likely smaller than its personal or sentimental value to the owner and/or their heirs.

⇒ **Holographic will** - a handwritten will, legal in most states, but not preferred.

⇒ **Homestead Law** – A law in many states which protects your family from losing certain assets crucial to the family's existence, such as the family home and clothing, to claims of creditors.

⇒ **Household Items** – refers to the contents of a house which are there for the use and convenience of people residing there, such as furniture, linens, and the like. Contents of the house which are not traditionally considered a part of a house are often excluded, even if stored there, such as clothing, weapons, books and others.

⇒ **Incapacitated** - A person who is unable to make reasonably responsible decisions and/or communicate such decisions to others, as a result of mental illness or deficit, physical disability, or any other reason.

⇒ **Income Beneficiary** – A trust beneficiary who is to receive income from a trust, though usually not distributions of principal as a matter of course. .

⇒ **Incompetent** – See Incapacitated.

⇒ **Independent Trustee** – A trustee who is not closely related to the trust Settlor or the Beneficiaries, which may be required in order for certain trusts to qualify for favorable tax treatment. Often an institutional trustee or an attorney is selected for this role.

⇒ **Inheritance tax** – A state death tax in some jurisdictions which is due from a beneficiary under an estate on the value of the amount received, as distinguished from an estate tax which is usually due from the estate.

⇒ **Intangible Property** – A legal term for property which has value but does not physically exist except for documentary evidence thereof, such as debts and loans, contract rights, patents and copyrights, etc.

⇒ **Intestate/Intestacy** – When a person died without a valid will, or with a will which does not address all of the decedent's estate.

⇒ **Intestate Succession** – The statutory plan for disposition of a decedent's estate in the absence of a will.

⇒ **Inter vivos** – Legal phrase in Latin, which means "during life" used to refer to transactions such as gifts or trusts made during a person's lifetime.

⇒ **Inventory** – typically refers to a list of estate assets which a personal representative of a decedent's estate must file with the probate court.

⇒ **Irrevocable Live Insurance Trust (ILIT)** – a trust created to hold an insurance policy outside of the insure person's estate in order to avoid estate taxes thereon, usually coupled with Crummey provisions to fund the insurance policy premiums with payments free of the gift tax.

⇒ **Irrevocable trust** – Any trust which by its terms cannot, for the most part, be modified by the Settlor or the Beneficiaries.

⇒ **Issue** – descendants related to you by blood, such s your children, your children's children, etc.

⇒ **Joint Ownership** – Generically used to refer to any title ownership by two or more people, including Joint Tenancy, Tenants In Common, and Joint Tenants by the Entireties.

⇒ **Joint Tenancy by the Entirety** – see Tenants by the Entirety.

⇒ **Joint Tenants With Rights Of Survivorship** – A Joint Ownership form where each of two or more owners holds title to the entire property, and the interest of any deceased owner automatically passes to the remaining owners upon death.

⇒ **Lack of Marketability Discount** – An accounting principal used to reduce the value of a restricted asset, such as a limited partnership share, to reflect the fact that it cannot be sold widely in any available market, unlike a publically traded stock

⇒ **Letters of Administration / Letters Testamentary** – Form issued by a probate court which empowers an executor or administrator to perform statutory duties under a will or intestate estate.

⇒ **Letters of instruction** – A document, which may be formally drawn or even only be in the form of a letter, which may direct the disposition of some personal property items of a decedent if incorporated by reference into a Will in some states, and may also provide direction or comfort to the surviving family following a person's death.

⇒ **Life beneficiary** – A person who is entitled to receive benefits for their lifetime, as from a trust.

⇒ **Life estate** – A legal interest which permits the owner of this interest to use the property for their lifetime.

⇒ **Living trust** – A trust created during a Settlor's lifetime, usually referring to a revocable living trust. See also inter vivos trust.

⇒ **Living Will** - A document authorized by many state's statutes which permits you to specify how certain medical decisions should be made if you cannot participate in the decision process due to unconsciousness or incapacity, and you are suffering a serious condition such as a persistent vegetative state or a terminal disease.

⇒ **Loving Trust** – A sales term used to describe a revocable living trust.

⇒ **Marital deduction** – tax provision which permits a surviving spouse to receive unlimited estate assets without the estate incurring estate taxes.

⇒ **Marital exemption** – See Marital Deduction.

⇒ **Marital Trust** – A trust which is funded by assets protected by the marital deduction to benefit the surviving spouse. Usually the "A Trust" in an A/B Trust plan.

⇒ **Medical power of attorney** – see health care power of attorney.

⇒ **Minor (child)** -A child who has not reached the age of majority in a given state, usually 18 years old.

⇒ **Minority Discount** - An accounting principal used to reduce the value of a restricted asset, such as a limited partnership share, to reflect the reality that someone with a minority interest has less ability to control the underlying assets or demand distributions of income or otherwise. Usually coupled with a Lack of Marketability Discount.

⇒ **Notice** – a legal concept for taking required steps to attempt to give information about a matter, even if the information isn't received. For example, publication of an estate is required to give creditors 'notice' of the need to file claims, which has effect even if the creditor doesn't actually read the notice.

⇒ **Notarized** – affixation of a seal of a state-authorized agent to demonstrate that a person's signature was confirmed as genuine by confirmation of the identity of the person signing.

⇒ **Partition** – A court action to separate the interests of joint property owners into individual shares.

⇒ **Pay on death (POD) account** - A financial account which provides for any balance remaining upon the primary owner's death to be transferred or paid to the POD beneficiary.

⇒ **Per Capita** – as distinguished from Per Stirpes, this method of splitting assets among a group of beneficiaries, wherein each member gets an equal share without regard to their lineal closeness to the decedent or settlor. Also referred to as Pro Rata.

⇒ **Per Stirpes** – Distribution as under an estate wherein any deceased members of a class of beneficiaries are represented by their issue, who thereafter similarly share as a class with any deceased members being represented by their issue, and so on. Provides for equality in apportioning assets within the same level of generational decendancy, while permitting assets to fall fairly to the representative children of any deceased members. Also know as By Right of Representation.

⇒ **Personal Letter** – See Letters of Instruction.

⇒ **Personal property** – See Tangible Personal Property and Intangible Personal Property.

⇒ **Personal Representative** – an inclusive term for executor or administrator, whether male or female.

⇒ **POD** – see Pay on Death account

⇒ **Pour-over will** -- A will which acts to 'pour' assets from an estate 'over' into a Living Trust, to finish funding said trust from the estate.

⇒ **Power of appointment** - power given to a person to make the decision about to whom property should pass to at a time provided at the creation of the power. May be limited (only certain people can be given the property) or unlimited (able to pass assets to anyone).

⇒ **Power of attorney** - A document by which a person (Principal) signs to empower another person (Agent) to act on their behalf in matters described within the document.

⇒ **Pretermitted Heir** - A child or spouse of a decedent who is not mentioned in the decedent's will, either intentionally or by oversight.

⇒ **Probate** – The process of validating a decedent's will and then carrying out the procedures for Administration of the estate.

⇒ **Probate court** – the court where probate proceedings take place, as well as other fiduciary proceedings such as trust proceedings, appointments of guardians or custodians, etc.

⇒ **Probate Estate** – the property of a decedent which has to pass through probate, as distinguished from property which otherwise passes to a new owner, such as by joint title, beneficiary designation in a contract or account, or otherwise.

⇒ **Probate Fees** – describes generally the expenses of probate, including court costs, attorney's fees, executor's fees, and fees for professional assistance to the estate.

⇒ **Property** – describes not only real estate (real property) but in broad fashion any thing which can be owned, including contract rights, financial assets, personal belongings, and even pets.

⇒ **Qualified personal residence trust (QPRT)** - A trust which permits a Grantor to transfer his residence out of his taxable estate by transferring it to a trust. The grantor can remain for a specified period of time, after which title to the house will pass to the named beneficiaries of the trust. If the grantor dies before the time stated in the trust, then the trust purpose will fail, and the value of the house is still included in the estate. If the grantor survives for the term of the trust, then the house is excluded from the taxable estate.

⇒ **Qualified Terminable Interest Property Trust (QTIP)** - A trust designed to permit the Grantor/Testator to give the surviving spouse reasonable control over estate assets which will be thus entitled to the Spousal exemption/deduction, while still permitting the Grantor/Testator to exercise some control over what happens to the assets after the surviving spouse dies.

⇒ **QTIP Election** – an executor must make an election on tax returns to qualify property passing to a QTIP trust as being subject to the marital deduction. This delays the tax on the property from the time of the death of the first spouse until the time of the death of the second spouse, who is until then a beneficiary of the QTIP trust.

⇒ **Real property** – real estate, and items affixed thereto, such as buildings and fences.

⇒ **Remainder interest** – following the expiration of some interest in property which isn't permanent, the remainder of the use or value of the property may pass to the remainder interest, i.e. it is an interest in the value of the property which remains upon the expiration of an intervening interest the property.

⇒ **Residue** – describes the property in a decedent's estate which remains after the expenses, taxes and debts have been paid, and the specific and general bequests have been satisfied. Also known as the residuary.

⇒ **Residuary estate** – See residue.

⇒ **Revocable trust** - A trust which the Grantor reserves the right to revoke or modify during the Grantor's lifetime.

⇒ **Right to Die** – Refers to the movement to recognize the right of a patient to decline extraordinary life saving measures, or even care which simply prolongs life when the patient's medical condition is such that they might reasonably not want to extend it artificially.

⇒ **Second-to-die insurance** – A joint-lives insurance policy which provides payment upon the death of the second of two people (usually spouses) which is often used as a tool to pay taxes which will be due on assets which previously escaped taxation under the marital exemption.

⇒ **Section 2053 Trust** – named after the IRS code section which permits them, this irrevocable trust is created to permit gifts up to the annual gift tax exclusion to be paid into a trust for minor children and still qualify for the annual gift tax exclusion, provided that the income and principal all vests absolutely in the child at or before the age of 21.

⇒ **Self-proving will** – A will which is executed following statutory formalities which permit it to be accepted as valid and admitted to probate without the testimony of any witnesses to the signature of the testator.

⇒ **Separate property** - property owned by one spouse which is not held or entitled to joint ownership, but instead is kept in the name of the one spouse. Such property typically is not subject to claim under an elected share distribution, nor considered a joint asset to be divided in a divorce action. Examples might include gifts and inheritances which the spouse retains in a self-titled account following receipt.

⇒ **Settlor** – a person who creates and funds a trust.

⇒ **Sound Mind** – describes the mental state which a testator may require to validly execute a will, and commonly involving the ability to know they are signing a will, they understand the general nature of the dispositions made in the will, they understand what property they have, and they know who the 'natural objects of their bounty' (i.e. close statutory heirs) are.

⇒ **Specific Bequest** - A bequest in a will of a specific item of property, or property from a specific source.

⇒ **Special needs trust** – A trust which is created for a person suffering mental or physical disability, and usually designed to permit the person to continue to receive government benefits which are of value but only available to persons of limited financial means. Also may be described as a Supplemental Needs Trust, because it is designed to supplement the government benefit, not substitute for it.

⇒ **Spendthrift** – a person who is perceived to have an inability to make prudent decisions about their assets, and is considered likely to waste and squander assets.

⇒ **Spendthrift provision** – language included in a trust to protect a perceived spendthrift from being able to waste their gift or inheritance, by limiting the beneficiary's access to it, and making it expressly unavailable and/or unattachable by creditors.

⇒ **Split Gift** – When both parties to a marriage combine their annual gift exclusion so as to increase the amount which they can give to any individual donee. A tax form must nevertheless be filed to demonstrate how the gift was split between the couple in order to avoid it being deemed a single taxable gift from one of them.

⇒ **Springing Power** - A power which 'springs to life' when a specified event occurs, such as a power of attorney which provides that it is only effective when the Principal is certified to be incapacitated by a physician.

⇒ **Sprinkle Power** – broad discretion given to a trustee to determine whether, when and how to distribute trust benefits to the beneficiaries, which does not require the beneficiaries to receive equal treatment. The power given a trustee to decide how, when and why to distribute trust income to the trust's different beneficiaries.

⇒ **Spouse** – husband or wife of a married person.

⇒ **State Death taxes** – general description of a state's ability to impose estate taxes on an estate, or inheritance taxes on the beneficiaries of an estate, or sometimes both.

⇒ **Step-up basis** – The increase in the taxable basis of property passing as a result of the owner's death, whereby the basis is increase from its owner's basis to the fair market value at the time of death (or six months thereafter if the executor so elects for the estate.)

⇒ **Survival Clause** - A clause in a will or trust which requires a beneficiary to outlive the testator/settlor, sometimes by a further specified period of time, in order to receive the benefit of the will or trust. Intended to avoid transfers to a deceased beneficiary's estate or heirs which may not have been the intent of the Testator/Settlor.

⇒ **Tangible personal property** – Personal property which has a physical existence in and of itself, and is not affixed to real property. Examples include jewelry, cars and furniture. Distinguished from intangible personal property or real property.

⇒ **Tax Clause** – descriptive clause in a will which informs the personal representative which property should be used first to pay estate taxes.

⇒ **Taxable estate** – term used to describe the property and interests which the IRS considers subject to estate tax.

⇒ **Tenants by the Entirety** – Joint tenancy with rights of survivorship between married people, which involves substantially greater protection of the joint rights, including limitations on the ability of either tenant to seek a partition of rights, and protection from creditors of either spouse (but not creditors of both).

⇒ **Tenants In Common** – A mutual ownership of property wherein the owners do not enjoy the rights of survivorship. Instead, each owner's interest in the property can be separately sold, attached and left by will.

⇒ **Testamentary Trust** – Any trust which is created by the provisions of a decedent's will, as compared to any inter vivos trust.

⇒ **Testate** - to die with a valid will.

⇒ **Testator** – a person who executes a will

⇒ **Totten Trust** - a revocable trust agreement easily created at many banks and financial institutions whereby the account creator states that title is held thereby "in trust for" a named beneficiary, and the beneficiary receives the balance in the account upon the creator's death.

⇒ **Transfer On Death (TOD) Designation** – same concept as Payable on Death above, though applicable to a broader range of asset classes in states which have adopted the necessary legislation.

⇒ **Trust** – An agreement whereby a Settlor transfers assets to a Trustee to hold and manage for the benefit of one or more beneficiaries.

⇒ **Trust Agreement, Declaration** or **Instrument**- see Declaration of Trust.

⇒ **Trust Certificate** – A document which summarizes the key terms of the trust as may be relevant for a financial institution or creditor dealing with the Trustee which does not typically disclose trust provisions beyond those necessary to consummate a given transaction in order to maintain privacy.

⇒ **Trust Corpus** – The body of the trust, i.e. the assets it contains.

⇒ **Trustee** – a person who holds legal title to property, not for their own benefit, but in order to consummate a fiduciary relationship with a defined beneficiary, as under a Trust Agreement.

⇒ **Unified Credit** - A tax credit authorized by federal statute which permits the IRS to allow everyone a credit against tax which otherwise would be imposed upon the transfer of wealth by gift or will; the gift and estate tax rates were unified by Congress in the 1970's, giving this credit its name.

⇒ **Uniform Gifts to Minors Act/ Uniform Transfers to Minors Act (UGMA/UTMA)** – state statute based upon a recommended model code which permits the transfer of assets to minors who otherwise could not legally hold title alone, and which instead provides for title to vest in the name of a Custodian who holds the property for the benefit of the minor.

⇒ **Will** - A document signed at the end wherein a Testator describes his or her intended disposition of their assets upon their death, and the manner in which distribution is to be managed. May also indicate the identity of the desired Executor to pursue the necessary Administration, etc.

INDEX OF TOPICS

ABOUT THE AUTHOR

Mark T. Coulter, J.D. is an attorney who has practiced law in Pittsburgh, Pennsylvania since 1993. An Honors graduate of the Duquesne University School of Law after graduating from the University of Pittsburgh, he was selected as a publishing member of the Duquesne University Law Review while still getting his law degree. He has been admitted to practice law before the highest state courts in Pennsylvania, New York, Florida, West Virginia and Indiana, though he currently only keeps his Pennsylvania and West Virginia privileges active. He also has been admitted to practice before the United States Supreme Court, the United States Courts of Appeals in many circuits, and the United States District Courts of multiple jurisdictions.

Mark has represented thousands of clients across the country, from all walks of life. His work securing financial security for his clients led to his induction into the Million Dollar Advocates Forum, reserved for those select attorneys who generate a recovery for a client in excess of $1,000,000. Mark has served as lead trial counsel in a variety of cases in both state and federal courts, and also achieved recognition through the publication of numerous important opinions by various courts of appeals.

Mark lives in the Monroeville, Pennsylvania area with his wife and 6 children.

And yes, he has a Will...